Businessmen

"The chief hypocrites of A.D. 30 were the businessmen and they are still tops. . . . Any procedure that was technically legal, or could be made so to seem, became the businessman's definition of ethics and, thus, the public definition of morality."

Congress

"It is a waste of words here to berate Congress . . . the men in our Senate and the men in our House of Representatives are, indeed, the representatives of the people. . . . The withered emasculation of our democratic statesmanship is the withered emasculation of America. The witch-hunting savagery of pompous male sluts in our national halls is that quality of all the people."

Education

"What the colleges need is, first, undergraduate bodies who are there for hard study only—all others being tweedy morons and a waste of human effort; second, courses not in economics, but in Sin. . . . Thus, a college earnestly seeking to abet mankind would have, along with its science, its arts, and history, such courses as: How to Tell Your Mother from a Wolf . . . Middletown—What's in Its Bureau Drawers? . . . Clean Cities and How to Have Fun in Them. . . ."

Mothers

"Today, while decent men struggle for seats in government with the hope of saving our Republic, mom makes a condition of their election the legalizing of Bingo. What will she want tomorrow when the world needs saving even more urgently?"

Books by Philip Wylie

FICTION

Heavy Laden
Babes and Sucklings
Gladiator
Blondy's Boy Friend
The Murderer Invisible
Footprint of Cinderella
The Savage Gentleman
Finnley Wren
As They Reveled
Too Much of Everything
An April Afternoon
The Big Ones Get Away
Salt Water Daffy
The Other Horseman
Corpses at Indian Stones
Fish and Tin Fish
Night unto Night
Crunch and Des
Opus 21
The Disappearance
Three to Be Read
Tomorrow!
Treasure Cruise
The Answer
Triumph
They Both Were Naked
The Spy Who Spoke Porpoise
Los Angeles: A.D. 2017
The End of the Dream

NONFICTION

Generation of Vipers
An Essay on Morals
Denizens of the Deep
The Innocent Ambassadors
The Magic Animal
Sons and Daughters of Mom

COLLABORATIONS

When Worlds Collide
After Worlds Collide
The Army Way

Generation of Vipers

PHILIP WYLIE

Preface by

CURTIS WHITE

Dalkey Archive Press
Champaign • Dublin • London

Library of Congress Cataloging-in-Publication Data
Wylie, Philip, 1902-1971.
Generation of Vipers / Philip Wylie. — 1st Dalkey Archive ed.

Previously published: Rev. ed. New York : Rinehart, 1955.

1. United States—Civilization—1945- 2. National characteristics,
American. I. Title
E169.12.W89   1996   973.92—dc20   96-15873
ISBN 1-56478-146-8

Partially funded by a grant from the Illinois Arts Council, a state agency

www.dalkeyarchive.com

Cover: design and composition by Nicolene Labuschagne

Contents

Preface

"There are more idols than realities in the world."—Nietzsche

Wylie's title comes, of course, from Jesus haranguing the Pharisees in Matthew 23:33.* It is not Jesus-the-Rabbi who speaks these words but Jesus-the-Old-Testament-Prophet, the heir of Isaiah. But Jesus' take on the role of the prophet is something new. Whereas Old Testament prophets argued in the name of the Truth of the Law, Jesus argues exactly against it. The confidence of the Pharisees in the sufficiency of the Law is what he blames them for—a point Paul will make repeatedly in the epistles. It is thus as if his prophetic acts were directed against the tradition of prophecy itself. He's the anti-prophet.

Wylie's performance in *Generation of Vipers* has a similarly subtle strategy. Wylie understands that what makes prophecy persuasive is not that it knows the Truth and everybody else has somehow forgotten it. Prophecy doesn't imagine that it has to inform you that there's something "stiff-necked" and generally wrong with the people; it assumes you already know that. It doesn't seek to convince you; it seeks to move you to conviction through the transforming emotional power of its

---

* Actually, the phrase "generation of vipers" is identical to John the Baptist's outburst against the Pharisees in Luke 3:7, which makes me wonder if either of them ever really said it. It's probably just the formulaic abuse of the first-century Christian cult in its bitter war of words with the Jewish temple priests.

harsh poetry. What makes prophecy persuasive is the music of vitu-
peration. Or, as Wylie puts it simply, "My technique is to invade the
reader's feelings."

Wylie understood the music of prophecy as a *novelist*. That is, he
understood it *ironically*. What his title says is, "I am not a prophet,
therefore I will speak most prophetically." Unlike the prophets/poets,
who imagine that divine Logos or the muse is speaking through them,
the prophets/novelists do not need an association with a superior principle, a God, in order to claim legitimacy. For the novelist, language is
self-authorization. The only authority this language has is not its Truth-
fulness but its continually renewed forcefulness. Sentence by sentence.
Wylie writes as if prophetic language were one of these Midwestern
weather fronts where warm, moist air rises up the vertical face of the
cold front and then pours down in a self-perpetuating display of power
and abundance. He argues, in effect, "Lord, let it rain down on me."

Such a way of thinking and such a strategy is alien to the media-mind
that is, disgracefully, mostly responsible at present for social commentary in this country. After all, there is no shortage of books critical of
American culture. Books of political commentary and current affairs
are an important part of what's left of the book industry. Few of these
books, however, are written by people you would mistake for a novelist
or poet. By and large, our works of social criticism are by journalists
and they're written to an industry standard. They're mostly a matter of
partisan bickering written in a style that can't fail to be understood by
reading clubs that meet at the Starbucks café in the local Barnes and
Noble. Editors, agents, critics, and readers all agree: a book is a failure
if it is not understood. Which ends up meaning that it fails if it tries
to provide an understanding beyond what is already well understood.
Thus, books have become the enemy of understanding.

What to do, then, with a writer who seems eager not to be understood? In fact, Wylie seems to be in a hurry to demonstrate that he is
not worth understanding because he is "wrong." According to editorial
assistants, book reviewers, and people who write letters to the editor, to

get something wrong—even just one small thing—is to cast doubt on the whole work. Wylie's purpose, much to the contrary, seems to be to cast doubt on doubt.

The most glorious (and funny) instance of this in *Vipers* is Wylie's claim that there is no such thing as a curveball (and this from a man with a background in physics, an advisor to federal science commissions). In a footnote to the second edition (1955), Wylie acknowledges somberly that many readers had informed him that, in fact, curveballs do curve, to which he replies, "Baseballs do curve, sometimes, a little, but . . . they do not and cannot 'break.'" Wylie speaks to his reader as if he were Hamlet mocking Polonius for seeing the shapes of whales and camels in the clouds. Very like a curveball!

Wylie's purpose is not to be "right" any more than Jesus' purpose was to be lawful. His purpose is, as he says, to "bash the phony ikons." It is anger, not facts, that makes him write. He is the temple priest enraged with the setting of idols on the altar, and furious that the congregation can't seem to tell the difference between God and a golden bust of Caligula. But who argues like this now? Do I need to point out that the bashing of phony ikons does not require data from the Census Bureau, reports from the Union of Concerned Scientists, or the Center for Disease Control? Never once does Wylie use the phrase "in a recent study" produced by the Center for Whatever. For Wylie, rightness or wrongness is not the point (especially if rightness is the domain of economists, demographers, and statisticians). What Wylie does seem to understand is Nietzsche's liberating claim that "if one is sufficiently rich for it, it may even be a joy to be wrong." Like Nietzsche, Wylie is "much too right." A good fact checker would delete half of this book without ever suspecting that its greatest virtue might be that it is richly wrong.

Wylie's superficial critics misunderstand him in other ways as well. For instance, Jonathan Yardley (reviewing the first Dalkey edition of *Vipers* in 2005) complained not only about his wrongness, but also complained (with the effortless obtuseness for which he is well known) that Wylie was merely imitative of H. L. Mencken. What Yardley doesn't get is that what makes Wylie like Mencken isn't Mencken, it's Nietzsche.*

Wylie claims that he's an advocate of "dynamic psychology" in the school of Freud and Jung. But the psychoanalytic influence here is hardly worth commenting on beyond Wylie's obsession with "instincts." What he's really interested in, for good and bad, is the human animal, and the great philosopher of the human animal was Nietzsche. Like Nietzsche, Wylie is appalled by the mob spirit, what he lambasts as the "common man," whether Christian or good German or the average boob under the thumb of the boss. What Wylie advocates against the common man is the "vital man," the "rebel against stupidity." Wylie is a Nietzschean vitalist. This is the force (or "will"), the determination to live in personal strength, that generates what Nietzsche called "loyalty to life." It is to this spirit that Wylie is most faithful. It is also for this reason that Wylie cites Matthew 12:31 in the book's epigraph: "All manner of sin and blasphemy shall be forgiven unto men; but blasphemy against the spirit shall not be forgiven." For Wylie, it is the vital and the intelligent that must not be blasphemed, and yet every waking and sleeping moment of the culture he observes is just such a blasphemy.

Wylie rails against the roles available to us—Christian, common man, mom, businessman, congressman, military man—because they are forms of death. They call to us as our common life, our community, our nation, our family but they are really just death-in-life whistling to us, hailing us from across a familiar street. This is Wylie's politics and his religion. His is, admittedly, a sharply modernist perspective (never mind that he calls modernist literature "contrived and infantile"). Wylie's criticism is a very personal and spiritual refusal of a world

---

* Of course, there is the minor problem that Wylie refers to Nietzsche as a "decrepit half-wit" and assumes the half-wit notion that Nietzsche was somehow a co-conspirator with Hitler. An example, no doubt, of Wylie's joyful indulgence in wrongness, all in spite of the well-documented disdain Nietzsche felt for anti-Semitism, militarism, nationalism, and Germanism in general. Unhappily, these were exactly the things that Nietzsche's first literary executor, his sister, endorsed. Speaking of half-wits. But now I'm behaving like a fact checker.

that believes that life's richness is a matter of staying on the right side of the demographic median in income, education, longevity, and retirement portfolio.

It is the Wylie who is loyal to life that still speaks to us—in spite of it all! In spite of all the wrongness. Even in the nineteen-forties and fifties Wylie received plenty of angry criticism for his creation of "momism." "Mom the human calamity." The "hen-harpy." His reason for condemning American womanhood? "I have been a *clerk* in a *department store* . . . I have watched the flowerhatted goddesses battle over fabric." This he calls the "Supreme Evidence." To say that this is wrong says very little. To say that I have no idea what he's talking about doesn't say much more. But I didn't work in the department store. In the end, the point isn't "mom" and it certainly isn't the department store. The point is a refusal to be taken in by what is merely "right" because what is right flies in the face of everything you've actually experienced. That is "the one terrible flaw of our lives today": the discrepancy between what we claim as right and what we are.

Nevertheless, in a world transformed by feminism, it's hard not to wince at some of his generalizations. Yet Wylie would surely argue that any form of ideology (what Nietzsche calls the "Moloch of abstraction") makes us stupid to our own experience and stupid, therefore, to what we really are. This holds, difficult though it may be to hear, for feminist victimology as well. But let's take an example that is less vulnerable to Politically Correct orthodoxies: there is hardly a person on these shores who doesn't believe that the division of labor is necessary and good for the economy. But that conviction makes us exactly stupid to the fact that we actually experience the division of labor as boredom and emptiness and futility. We claim to be prosperous with the highest standard of living in the world when in fact we're just bored. But then, as Wylie shrewdly observes, economists aren't interested in measuring boredom: "nobody is making boredom tables."

As for "mom," I'm happy to agree that he's wrong about her, but I doubt that a Saturday trip to the local shopping mall would prove that he's wrong. And Wylie knows it.

Wylie is also gloriously wrong about Marx. "Marxism was bunk," he writes. And yet in the chapter "Businessmen" he reveals with a pungency Marx would have appreciated that the foundation of capitalism is hypocrisy:

> Starting with the thesis that competition is the essence of democracy . . . the businessman undertook two main lines of bastardization of that truth. First . . . was the elimination of competition wherever possible and by all means imaginable. Second, was the establishment of the notion that business competed only with *itself* and never with any other requirements of mankind. By means of the latter absurdity, business was able to kick around and decimate the people and their needs with virtually no punishment.

Here, Wylie puts himself body and soul in the tradition of Ruskin and Thoreau and Marx. To this day, conventional economics will argue for the genius of the market without so much as a pause to consider what the logic of markets leads us to assume about what it means to be a human being. It means humans are consumers or labor commodities but they are the object of ethical reasoning only as an afterthought. As Wylie puts it:

> Any procedure that was technically legal, or could be made so to seem, became the businessman's definition of ethics and, thus, the public definition of morality. . . . That is like saying suicide is the best life insurance, but it is the current American way of business.

This fundamental truth about the capitalist mind is being brought home for us tragically by the Chinese entrepreneur who contaminates our pet food, toothpaste, animal feed, and even our Viagra with toxic filler. But for the businessman, it's only about poison if someone dies, otherwise it's about profit margin. So the game is to take profit as close to the poison line as possible. When on occasion profit spills over into poison (i.e., someone dies), there is a wild wringing of hands (and, in China, death sentences) but soon back we go in search of that ideal balance between profit and death. And this is not something peculiar to the Chinese. The Chinese learned their cost-cutting strategies and their ethics from America. How else could we describe our own industrial agriculture? Just how much herbicide and pesticide can we put down before it starts killing something more than bugs and pig weed? Plummeting bird populations are "incidental." Sick humans complain more, so they move from the incidental category to the "externality" category, to use the despicable jargon of economists. An externality is something that is outside of the market apparatus (like environmental degradation) that should be considered and in theory will be considered one of these days when budgets and the requirements of a "healthy economy" allow. Of course, this is all the domain of the "cost/benefit analysis" overseen with loving kindness by accountants and legions of liability lawyers. It is the world according to economists that Wylie detests. For him, the idea that profits and life need to be balanced is hypocritical, and destructive, and the people who believe it (most of us, after all) are morons.

It is a good and remarkable thing that Philip Wylie's *Generation of Vipers* can still speak so powerfully to us. But it makes me wonder if it was not something like the end of the prophetic tradition in American book publishing. Where are the visionary iconoclasts of the present? Of course, the enemies of righteousness (book publishers included) have always been many. Wylie's book, like all prophetic books, is a call to the faithful remnant to stay loyal to life, to what is honest, to what is just, in a context committed to death, hypocrisy, and injustice.

— Curtis White

Introduction

SOME WHILE AGO MY PUBLISHERS INFORMED ME THAT THE TWEN-
tieth printing of "Generation of Vipers" would soon go to press.
They asked me if I would like to amend it in such a way as to bring it
up to date. "Vipers," as the book is called by its fans, was written thirteen years ago. It is not "dated" but it does exhibit the lapse of time:
much that is mere prediction in the text as it stands has become history.

However, I feel that the re-writing of a book of opinion is a kind of
cheating; it is not comparable, for instance, to the revision of a scientific
work. What an author asserted in 1942 shows, in 1955, how wise
(or foolish!) he was in the past; so he ought now to stand (or fall)
on the fact of what he wrote then. The continuous revision of history
to suit the insights or prejudices of the present is craven and nefarious
—an enterprise suited to characters in "1984" or to demagogues.

I told my publishers I would read "Vipers" (I had not read fifty
pages in a decade) and thereafter, if any comments came to my mind,
I would make them—as footnotes. Somewhat to my surprise, it turned
out that I wanted to add or to exclaim about something at fifty-odd
points. A number of these "exclamations" relate to the now-demon-
strated accuracy of predictions regarded, at the time "Vipers" first
appeared, as bordering on insanity. It is, of course, "human" (in a low

sense of the word) to take pleasure in saying, "I told you so." But I have a better reason for drawing attention to my record as a Jeremiah, which I shall explain later in this introduction.

"Vipers" has had and is still having a strange history. It was written —I should say it was dashed off—between the twelfth of May and the fourth of July in 1942. That was the year after Pearl Harbor. World War II had commenced. But the period of "phony war" prevailed in Europe, action in the Pacific had hardly begun, and the American people were apathetic. I had come home to Miami Beach after a stretch in "government war information"—ill, discouraged and frustrated. This book represented private catharsis, a catalogue of what I felt to be wrong morally, spiritually and intellectually with my fellow citizens. Since it did not enter my head that millions shared my vexations and anxieties, that they would read the list and remark over it to this day, I did not make—alas!—that careful literary effort such an audience has the right to expect.

Indeed, my principal feeling on re-reading the book was one of regret that I had not gone over a hasty manuscript with patience and with care—to make it easier to understand, more "definitive" and better documented with the sources of theories and ideas.

My publishers (then Farrar and Rinehart, now Rinehart and Company) reacted to the manuscript with some shock. I have since been asked, hundreds and hundreds of times, how I "managed" to get so much "criticism and truth published in America." The question has always discomfited me. It implies that a great many persons take it for granted that our country enjoys no actual freedom of speech. It should be pointed out, then, that such haunted notions are false and disclose the very kind of fears which, if held widely enough, *do* lead to censorship—by general default.

While my publishers did not by any means agree with every contentious and dissenting opinion in my manuscript, they asked only that I delete one or two libelous passages and one scandalous item. I was not an "important" author to them in the sense that my past books had enjoyed large sales. But Stanley Rinehart and John Farrar, for all the blood flowing from their personal icons, published my book without tremor or quibble. They knew it would mightily offend many highly placed individuals and many powerful minority groups. They thought, perhaps, (as I thought) that it might offend *everybody*. But they brought it out with utter aplomb and their usual skill—in January of 1943.

They did this, I might add, in the face of doubt expressed by some of their readers and the violent assertion (made by a famous "liberal" who was shown the manuscript) that the book was "fascist" and should be suppressed. My publishers, as much as I, were annoyed that a "liberal" would suddenly clamor for book suppression!

The first edition was of four thousand copies, a number commensurate with sales of my previous books and one I thought high for the current treatise. Even before publication, however, I began to have an inkling of what was to come. An extraordinarily praiseful letter was written to Farrar and Rinehart by Taylor Caldwell, who had been sent a pre-publication copy. A wire also came from Earnest Hooton, the late Harvard anthropologist, which wound up: PUT OUT THE LANTERN OF DIOGENES FOR HERE BY GOD IN THE PLAIN LIGHT OF DAY IS AN HONEST MAN. And, on the Sunday before publication, Walter Winchell (with whom I had long labored in the "Stop Hitler" movement) highly recommended "Vipers" in his evening broadcast. The four thousand copies melted fast enough.

The book has now sold more than one hundred and eighty thousand copies and its recent annual sales have approximated five thousand.

Criticisms were mixed but never neutral; reviewers went out of their way to commend the book or to seek terms of scorn that matched my own. The response of *readers,* however, was awesome—and remains so. This may be partly owing to the fact that I invited correspondence in the forematter of the book. People possibly hesitate to write to authors for fear of being snubbed by silence; if so, my casual invitation undid that restraint. In the first year after publication I answered more than ten thousand letters.

They came from every sort of American—from soldiers and sailors

and marines overseas, from ministers of the Gospel and Middle Western farmers' wives, from day laborers who "read the book five times
over with the help of a dictionary," from young people in college and
high school, from moms and pops—the very people I had indicted—
from industrial tycoons and newspaper publishers and the presidents of
banks, from college deans and generals and admirals, from Aldous
Huxley and the late Harold Ickes and Hedy LaMarr. And more than
ninety-five in every hundred *liked* "Vipers"!

In the years that have passed since then I have heard from fifty
or sixty thousand people. "Vipers" has become a kind of "standard
work" for Americans who love liberty, detest smugness and are
anxious about the prospects of our nation. It has been studied by
scores of Bible classes. It has also been proscribed by Catholics. It
has been quoted in unrecorded dozens of other books; it is "compulsory reading" in hundreds of college English and journalism classes.
In 1950 it was selected by The American Library Association as
one of the major nonfiction works of the first half century. It was used,
during the war, as an instrument for "briefing" those British officers
who were to have contact with our troops, on the nature and neuroses
of *genus homo, race Americanus.* And it no longer seems possible for
any author, lay or scientific, to discuss motherhood and mom without
noting that the dark side of that estate was defined earlier by me.

Those are but a few of the vicissitudes of "Vipers." I daresay this
new, annotated edition will augment their number and their be-
wildering nature.

Two reactions to "Vipers" are common enough to warrant brief
discussion here.

A great many people have asked me, often with evident anguish,
this question: Are you sincere?

It is easy enough to reply, "Lord, yes!"

A far larger number of people appreciated my sincerity. And that
number increases hourly, in potential, as it dawns on one American
at a time that our situation in the Atomic Age is progressively of so
dreadful a danger as to make it certain that, somewhere, somehow,

we Americans have failed to achieve even a vestige of our goal of security. But the people who thought or feared that I was insincere are worthy of particular scrutiny.

Some may be, of course, merely literal-minded: persons who cannot believe that a man who will make a joke is really serious about anything—especially if his joke partakes of gallows humor. I suspect, however, on the good grounds of myriads of communications, that many are people who have so often felt themselves fooled or kidded or betrayed—by politicians and by supercilious authors—that they have grown skeptical of everybody's integrity. They would *like* to believe that, when a man lambastes hypocrisy, he is disgusted and deliberate—not just having private fun. They would *like* to feel that when a man stands up in their midst and yells, "To hell with it!" he is morally indignant—and not just trying to attract attention to himself. But they dare not. It is sad to learn that many Americans evidently feel within themselves a sense of being so often "sold out" that the most passionate sincerity puts them in quandary: they want to believe it— but they hate to risk being made suckers one more sorry time.

They are discouraged people, cynical without knowing it, robbed of self-confidence, intimidated, not very capable as citizens—and they are numerous.

A commoner and even more sobering reaction to "Vipers" concerned its concentration upon criticism and derogation. That was intended to stimulate constructive thought. I would not damn a traditional idea or circumstance or attitude that I did not believe could be improved: if I will not re-write history neither will I resent or regret the past, as do so many frantic authors these days. But to criticize or anathematize what men believe *now*, and are doing and saying *now*, is another matter: it is the *only* way to bring to the future any hope of betterment.

For a little thought will show that no improvement can be made in any object or idea until a criticism has first been made. If there is no criticism, if no fault is found, the object or idea will be regarded as perfect, or as not subject to favorable alteration; its status quo will

thus be assured automatically. A better mousetrap, or a better automobile, or a better concept of freedom, may *seem* to occur as inspiration; but no such "inspiration" is possible unless the inspired mind has
first perceived the existing mousetrap, automobile or concept to be
inadequate.

Criticism, that is to say, and the *doubt* out of which it arises, are the
prior conditions to progress of any sort. The intent of "Vipers" was and
is to provide a body of exactly that sort of criticism, that sort of doubt
and self-doubt.

The *critical attitude*, however, is mistrusted in America, for all its
fundamental place in any pattern of progress. Formal criticism as such,
while allowable, is regarded as an exercise of "longhairs" or "egg-
heads." All criticism is thought by millions to border on subversion
especially when it becomes criticism of America or of popular American attitudes. "Boost, don't knock," has replaced the Golden Rule as
the allegedly proper means to the American Way of Life.

That is partly the result of the infinite boosting of advertising along
with the "chamber-of-commerce mentality" of most businessmen, and
partly the by-product of censorship imposed from within (and often
from without, by minority pressures) on our mass media of communication. Three whole categories of national behavior are very nearly
immune to criticism in mass media—as I have proven by a sociological
experiment performed since the writing of "Vipers." These "sacred"
areas are: *sex, business* and *religion!* Such extensive "sanctity" leaves
very little room for the critical function in the press, radio, TV, movies
and magazines.

The result is to keep the American majority not just intellectually
*un*critical but *anti*-critical. This situation means that to progress even a
little, Americans must behave in a somewhat schizoid manner: hiding
from themselves that they are "knocking" and not "boosting" wherever they find a need for improvement. We do not even say, "Chicago
is a big slum," when we want to clear its slums; we say, "Let's make
Chicago even *more* magnificent." In such ways, even when we are
self-critical, we delude ourselves about the value of the critical func-

tion. A poisonous self-infatuation ensues—a blind bullheadedness, un-warranted by reality.

To people with that orientation—people who imagine that the "right" approach to any problem *must* involve optimism—"Vipers" was a great shock. For "Vipers" suggests that downright pessimism, in this day and age, may be a more fruitful source of national improve-ment (and even a surer road to mere survival) than all the compulsive optimism the public can pump up concerning its wonderful self. In this book I am plainly out looking for "what's wrong" and, during that pursuit, not interested in "what's right" or "what's magnificent" —whether about Chicago, or USA or common man himself. That many things are "right" is acknowledged—and ignored. For if the "wrongs" I see be great enough (left unexamined) to undo us all (and I believe they may be), they deserve our concentrated attention.

That *deliberate* fixation of my mind appalled many readers. They could see no "hope" in a book written to indicate *which way real hope lay.* "If what you say is true," a great many wrote me, "there is no use going on." And those same people often continued with the statement that they agreed with what I said! Three or four times, in the past thirteen years I have had to rush to the telephone or the telegraph office to get in touch with correspondents whose despondency, after reading this book, was so great that I honestly feared they meant to carry out plans for suicide described in their letters. I talked to one young lady for an hour while she sat on the window sill of a high floor of a Manhattan skyscraper with a copy of "Vipers" on her lap!

It was necessary to persuade such people that a mere vista of diffi-culties, however huge and horrid, is not an excuse for abandoning human effort—let alone life itself. Such reactions are extremely *child-ish.* Unfortunately, many people are just that infantile. A great many Americans have given up moral and intellectual effort in behalf of their country simply because it is hard to be moral and to reason.

The way most such persons "give up" is to decide they are "for" everything they consider "American," just as it stands, and "against" whatever they deem "un-American," and to demand that all of us conform to their particular set of delusions. On the high level of subjectivity, such people are traitors to America: they have not fallen asleep but *put themselves to sleep,* while standing guard over liberty. For if liberty has any meaning it means freedom to improve—i.e., that the right to knock is equal to the right to boost.

To people who became enraged by what they called the "negativism" of this book, I usually gave short shrift. Quite often—to my astonishment—they took my bitter words to heart, re-read the book more thoughtfully, and went forth in their communities to tilt with local dragons! Where the book struck home to individuals, they often wrote to say as much. I have on file, for instance, the confessions of numbers of "moms" who learned here how they had perverted motherhood to selfish ends and who pledged reform.

So much, then, for the vicissitudes of "Vipers" and so much for the responses of people who have read the book and written to or talked with me afterward.

I would wish—if I were a wishful person—that I'd had the foresight to estimate the interest in this random work. It is one thing to sit down in a mood of disappointment (mixed at times with toxic glee) to write, for one's private satisfaction, a bill of particulars against the antics of one's fellows. It is quite another to have that intemperate version of sincere heresies receive such a profound response from a huge, perpetual audience. Had I been able to foretell my future as an author I would surely have been a better one in the pages ahead!

"Vipers" is an important book to many because it looks into a variety of truths often overlooked. To other people, it has importance because it tends to keep open the franchise of freedom: "If Philip Wylie can say thus-and-so in print, why then, before God and as a sincere American, so can I." It has helped many to learn to *think,* for thinking involves the critical method employed here, before it can become "creative thinking"—as I have explained. It has had value as a continuing counterbalance to our dangerous American habit of thinking too well of ourselves—of making self-infatuation the pre-condition of what is deemed "patriotism."

But to me, the main value of this effort is usually disregarded. I said, earlier, that the new footnotes often point to a "prophesy" now proven accurate; and I said I had a better reason than gloating for those notes. I have.

Most of the observations and criticisms in the book derive from the application of the theories of "dynamic psychology"—that is, from a use of the psychological insights of Sigmund Freud and Carl Jung. Those theories concern man, his nature, his motives, his personality and the way his "mind works." They are well understood and highly regarded by some people. Modern medicine is coming more and more to appreciate, for example, how right Freud was in postulating the effect of inner conflict on bodily health. Arnold Toynbee, for another instance, has illuminated the whole of history by showing how men have followed psychodynamic laws which were discovered by Jung through studies of the individual. But the average layman, however intelligent, however well-educated, has little understanding of the *philosophical* implications and intellectual values of this very new and not yet very exact branch of science.

It is my hope that by noting here some few of the places in "Vipers" where I showed an insight in 1942 that was not commonplace, but that proved to be correct, I may draw attention not to me but to my *method.*

The test of *any* scientific theory is its accuracy in predictability. A theory is first "given," then "checked" by experiments; if they "come out" as predicted by the theory, the theory itself is accorded credence: it becomes "scientific," a "law of science."

Using the American scene and the state of the world for "experimental material" thirteen years ago, I applied psychodynamic laws. That so many of my "experiments" tallied with, or approximated, subsequent reality (when the great bulk of "prediction" in identical areas was different or contrary—hence fallacious) tends to show, I believe, not that I am a peculiarly bright, prophetic, intuitive or mystically gifted author but that the theory by which I guided myself was far more "correct" than the theories commonly employed. Since "predictability" is a scientific, rational or logical test of *any* method, I hope here to bring new attention to *psychodynamic* methods. For today's hideous history was made by the attitudes of yesterday, the attitudes of 1942 and attitudes a thousand years older than that: much of it was predictable when the attitudes were properly understood.

In 1955—a year far more threatening to American freedom, American security and even to American existence than the year 1942—I would like more people to come to understand a science by which useful insight into what may happen tomorrow may be had, through a special scrutiny of what we are doing—and thinking—right now.

There are numbers of dire predictions in this book which have not come true—*yet*. If enough of us understand the logical concepts which make such disasters foreseeable, I think the lot of us might be led to avoid them. It is this thought, that hope, about which I am *most* sincere:

The learning of science, logic, reason and especially the logics of dynamic psychology, by enough men and women to prevent the needless squandering of a great nation, in which I am one citizen, and the needless death of a great, free people, to whom I belong and whom I try to serve because I love them.

Philip Wylie

South Miami, Florida
December 7th, 1954

Generation of Vipers

All manner of sin and blasphemy shall be forgiven unto men; but blasphemy against the spirit shall not be forgiven—whosoever speaketh against the eternal truth in the spirit of men, it shall not be forgiven him, neither in this world, neither in the world to come—Either make the tree good, and his fruit good; or else make the tree corrupt, and his fruit corrupt; for the tree is known by his fruit.

O generation of vipers—!

—JESUS CHRIST

CHAPTER I

Catastrophe, Christ, and Chemistry

A Preliminary and Prejudicial Survey of a Modern, Christian Nation at War, with Notes on the Church, on Science, and on Economics, the New Mysticism.

IT IS TIME FOR MAN TO MAKE A NEW APPRAISAL OF HIMSELF. His failure is abject. His plans for the future are infantile. The varied forms of his civilization in this century are smashing each other. In universality and degree, the war he has finally managed to perpetrate surpasses every past similar social disaster. The United States of America is still intact, but its material safety is by no means guaranteed and its psychological future is in black doubt. Plans for what is called the defense of the democracies involve a city-by-city holocaust resembling an Old Testament act of Jehovah.

The war* began at a time when society was rapidly disintegrating. American and British democracy had held itself from the center of a chaos which was described as the great depression by a series of stop-gap borrowings and other slip-witted expedients which no sane man believed could be indefinitely maintained. Some nations froze their societies into absolutist schemes of life. Such freezing, in an individual,

---

* This refers to World War II, of course. World War III, now in its middle-incipient stages, will obviously bear an even closer resemblance to an "Old Testament act of Jehovah."

3

or a state, or a species, is the inevitable precursor of extinction. The way of hand-out and tax-patching was the step before the last one. Only a fluid and realistic society is evolving. None of the contemporary societies was realistic.

War is, of course, another expedient. It represents an unreasoned and inarticulate attempt of a species to solve its frustrations by exploding. A variety of outcomes can be expected. Some wars reseed populations and, after a gestative period, instill new vitality into stale regions. Some wars destroy the victor, the conquered nation, or both, and thereby simply erase angry causes from the planet. Some leave the combatants exhausted enough to *think,* if they have stopped short of total ruin, and to advance their future by the exercise of reason and goodwill, motivated by the shock of what has happened and the obviousness of what the sick populace requires. But most wars are inconclusive; the psychic trauma which they produce leads to a false era of apparent altruism and peace; old grudges, hypocrisies, greeds, imbalances, jealousies, superstitions and fears slowly erase the briefly necessary sense of safety. War comes again.

We Americans are planning the peace, already. Aside from the utter fatuity of the fact itself, our plans, as announced to date, show so little understanding of the causes of the war we are engaged in, that anybody who contemplates them must realize the peace in view would be as hopeless as the last one.

We may not win. Or, we may win under circumstances which will make us too dulled and enfeebled to carry out any plan. Or we may win after suffering such ghastly punishment as to turn our altruistic purposes into revenge. Or, again, victory may come so soon, and so easily for the United States of America, that we will sit like a benign Dutch uncle at the peace table and hand out Sunday School rules and diplomas to the infuriated peoples of Europe. We did that the last time.

We have set up as peace aims such ideas as the world-wide institution and maintenance of the "four freedoms"; and the implementation of an "Atlantic Charter." I suppose, when Washington or Winston

Churchill gets around to it, there will be a "Pacific Charter," also.*
These aims are unselfish. The emotions of the men who subscribe to
them are decent. But they are fantastically naïve aims.

They assume what almost every Briton and American assumes: that
civilized man has reached the edge of the dawn—that goodness and
virtue and nobility are *almost* ready for universal realization—that
we are a Christian and a scientific people who need only a few more
years and a slight increment of intelligence in Parliament and Congress to produce a millennium. Our concepts of our own constitutions
and our own ideals of freedom include perfectionism, or something
near to it. We believe that we, as individuals and as the inhabitants
of states, shires, townships and nations, are wedded to human dignity
and acquainted with truth.

One could point out that Germany was, until recently, a so-called
Christian nation. Catholicism and Protestantism were firmly rooted
there. Germany, indeed, has produced more than its share of martyrs
and protesting reformers. In its churches, the same gospels were
preached that the people of London and New York hearkened to, on
Sunday. It sang the same hymns and practiced the same rites. Its Bible
was interchangeable with our own. Germany, too, was a great "scientific" nation. Until the beginning of the last war, a quarter of a century
ago, Germany was the *leading* exponent of science, both applied and
classical.

In ten years, Germany exorcised the church for all practical purposes, substituted a widely practiced and self-acknowledged paganism,
put a stop to every branch of classical science save that which was

---

*As I write (September, 1954), this "Pacific Charter" has come into
a state of murky being and Churchill recently made a quick trip to
Washington concerning its architecture. I did not foresee, however,
that the Prime Minister would be by this time more or less opposed
to *any* arrangement which would offend Russia—owing to an Utter
Vulnerability of the British Isles which, nowadays, amounts to military
nonexistence.

deemed fruitful to the war effort, and set up a state policy denying the holy tenets to which the democracies paid lip service.

From that, and other similar national regressions, a detached citizen of the world might draw the conclusion that our own premises and practices were shaky. Such an observer might infer that neither Britain nor America held over the bones of barbarism much but a rotting cloak of clericism and a deceptive scientific advancement. The lesson is so plain, as a matter of fact—the analogy so exact—that it ought not to be necessary to examine any other aspect of man's current society than the German in order to find the causes of our universal despair. However, owing to the basic flaw in the modern approach to consciousness, no list of parallels between Germany and, say, the United States, however long and explicit, would convince one single American that Americans need to worry themselves about such immediate future possibilities as Iowa pogroms, the national glorification of instinctualism, the enwhorement of American womanhood, Boston church raids, and a federal Gestapo.*

Americans think Germans are foreigners who live in funny-looking cities and have little locomotives that couldn't pull a line of boxcars up the foothills of the Rockies. University professors, scientists, medical men, pompous doodles, many of whom hold Heidelberg degrees, think that about the Germans—even though they trouble themselves to invent in addition a latent, inherent *difference*† between Germans and

---

* These matters (with the possible exception of Iowa pogroms) have come to be the occasional worries of some millions of Americans.

† During World War II it was generally assumed that the "differentness" of the Germans would remain self-evident for some centuries. Genocide alone, taken as a national principle, gave Germany a distinction shared in kind and scale only with the Soviets. Today, however, owing to a fearful need of allies to stand against the red tide, those Hitlerian eccentricities have been glossed over. Men like Dulles have fitted Germany into the "defense picture" (against the remem-

ourselves which they describe in elaborated terminology. Thus, to use the German analogue for the purpose of showing how near the United States is to barbarism would be hopeless. Acting on the assumption that we are different and better, we, the American people, educated or unlettered, hold to the asinine premise of "thank God I am not as other men," above all other postulates.

But we are as other men, exactly. Of one blood, one species, one brain, one figure, one fundamental set of collective instincts, one solitary body of information, one everything. Superiority and inferiority are individual, not racial or national. Only deliberate, human breeding over periods of thousands of years could alter that fact. However, since our ability to learn by projection and parallel has been stifled from the top to the bottom of our society, it will be necessary to demonstrate the shakiness of our civilized fundaments and the thinness of our Christian veneer by taking an attitude slightly unlike the usual approach of ourselves to ourselves.

This shift of viewpoint will provide much illumination, both profound and superficial, although there is nothing new about it. It is a shift to an attitude that has been tested by millennia. It has never been found wanting. It is not my personal and private attitude. To say so, after reading this book, will be to revert to the nonsensical postulate that you are not as other men. Not, in *this* instance, as *I* am. Unluckily for the comfort of the hour, but luckily for the history of man, the spread of the theory of human differentness invariably precedes the pratfall of the proud.

I am going to write somewhat about the world but mostly about you —your home and kiddies, mom and the loved ones, old Doc Smith and the preacher, the Brooklyn Dodgers and the Star-Spangled Banner

---

bering reluctance of France) and words like "Dachau" are losing their emotional impact. This change in viewpoint is one more evidence of the emotional nature of our age which, if it stemmed from the principle of *laissez faire* before the War now surely has the earmarks of that even more urgent motive: *sauve qui peut.*

—in short, the American scene. But I am going to ask you to look at it through my eyes, and through the eyes of certain far wiser men than I, whose sight I have borrowed, as you can. For a great number of pages, I am going to examine, with you, the debit side of our ledger. Some people will think this is unpatriotic and some will be certain that it is dangerous. But none can deny that we are in a horrid mess and all will agree that to remedy disaster and to prevent its recurrence, it is essential to study the true causes, no matter what they may be.

I happen to believe, after much study, hard thought, and a variety of miserable experiences, that the attention of modern man has been so far diverted from nature and reality as to make the even momentary refocus of his eye a difficult proceeding. I can only try—with such faculties and facilities as I possess. I am proud of mankind for his good points. I am deeply concerned over his blindness to his evil attributes. I beg you to attack them with me in a mood of honest urgency and courage, the mood of a man, say, who submits to a perilous operation because his only chance of existence depends upon it.

We have cancer—cancer of the soul.

Religion has failed. Indeed, its widespread adoption and the holocausts which followed strongly suggest that religion, as we have known and thought about it, will never reappear importantly in the councils of man. Germany, as I said, was religious. So was Russia; so was Italy. But the behavior of Germany is in no way different today from the behavior of Japan, a country known to be heathen, barbaric, and full of grisly mummery.

Some time ago, the organized churches of the world took a body blow from science. Science revealed their orthodoxy as sham—a business largely pagan in origin, and partly cheap psychology in practice. The subsequent retreat of the church, or its demoralization, had a more sinister effect upon people than is generally imagined.

Science has not actually stricken any real human ideal or philosophical hypothesis from the realm of possibility. It has made no startling discovery in the field of good and evil, right and wrong, decency and obscenity, courage and cowardice, altruism and nihilism, or the relation of man's consciousness to the preultimate ingot which blasted itself apart into a cosmos. Few scientists, in fact, have studied such matters, and those who have done so, with a handful of exceptions, have produced nothing more than a vast literature of measurements of objective human behavior. The handful who proceeded deeper into the investigation of man's personality have written a small but amazing collection of books which show that psychological honesty, put in practice even before the invention of the internal combustion motor, produced truth then, as, indeed, it always must.

But the truths uttered in antiquity were not sorted out from antique error by the church, or the scientists, or anybody—and nearly all old thought was thrown away by bright new man in his brave new world on the unscientific principle that some old thought was manifest rubbish, therefore all of it could be ignored. It is a peculiar fumble, typical of the last century and a half. No doubt Archimedes uttered as much nonsense in his life as any man; but his investigation of displacement led to conclusions which are still accepted. Sound old values in the material world have been maintained. Equally sound old values in the world of human personality have not. Jesus Christ, who probably also uttered much unrecorded nonsense in his time, clearly conveyed a great deal of truth. We retained Archimedes' law but not Christ's. I will show you why, in due course.

Such Christianity as we professed—forms, rituals, buildings, mottoes on our coins, and the like—obviously has not been enough to save our world from horror. Instead, out of a Christian era was born the uttermost horror of man's hard story—the hellishness of these days and the hellishness—largely unrecognized—of 1930, 1920, 1910, and 1900. For, in our years of peace the seeds of war did not lie dormant; they grew grotesquely everywhere in the land and only the blind failed to see the crop. Unfortunately, practically all men were blind.

You have considered this a Christian nation, all your life. Our constitution implies as much. But a minute's thought might have shown you years ago—decades ago—that the United States of America was not in any *real* sense a Christian nation at all. Numerically? Less than half the people had even a nominal church membership. There goes the sacred majority. Dogmatically? Those who belonged to churches belonged to so many different faiths at swords' points with each other on matters of creed and technique that even the definition of Christianity crumples to absurdity. You laughed over the medieval theologians who argued about the number of angels who could dance on a pinpoint—and then deliberated petulantly on whether or not proper baptism consisted of a sprinkling with Holy Water, a complete immersion in a small swimming pool with the preacher in rubber boots, or a mere symbolic laying on of a minister's hand wet in something that came unblessed out of a faucet. Even if you personally avoided these mighty encounters, your fellowmen engaged in them, wherefore it was up to you either to stop their nonsense or take the consequences of it. Religion in our Christian land was mostly puerile fiddle-faddle before science kicked it apart.

The kick—or the repeated kicks—which made it inescapable to all but abject dupes that "the things that you're liable to read in the Bible . . . ain't necessarily so" had no refining effect. The dross of sentiment, fable, error and fundamentalism (which was everything but fundamental) was not discarded for the pure gold of exquisite logic and insight which remained in the Scriptures. The whole business was thrown overboard. And the church did not try to retain *any* integrity, because its bishops, priests, canons, and ushers had never known which parts possessed integrity. Nobody had shown them. They tried, rather, to meet the iconoclasm of modern religious criticism by a process of adaptations which have brought them to a position that is tragic, repulsive, and very funny.

On the contemporary pulpit, shrouded for Sundays, there is apt to be a bingo wheel for weekday lotteries. The service house of the up-to-date church is a combination basketball court and dance hall. The symbolic blood of the Lamb is still sipped on Easter, but on other days the punch at the ladies' aid is sometimes spiked. Where the Buchmanites have left their spoor is often a "modern approach toward sex living" which leads to all sorts of miscellaneous gropes in the gloom, neuroses, and confessional orgasms. Not yet a place of open assignation, assignation is the next logical step for the church—as it was once a primitively logical part of temple routine. A bolder clergy might revive it. But the desuetude of the church is such that in recent years few bold men have been attracted by its "challenge." The real challenge was too profound for the contemporary undergraduate even to know about. The superficial challenge was too silly for him to accept. Mentors became, as they always do on a decaying social limb, the maladjusted, the weak, the misfits, the confused, the dangerously well-intentioned, the squirting extroverts, the cloyed, the greedy, and the exponents of laziness—pipsqueaks, in short.

Millions of human beings have been emotionally exalted, "uplifted," or even, sometimes, worthily instructed in small affairs, by the church. But the over-all uplift was deleterious in the end because its source, its mechanism and its validity were not understood and the very incomprehensibility of the elation set up an equal decline, adding one more factor to the schizoid world of modern people—one more bump in our now established set of infinitely superimposed cycles of manic-depression.

The church has failed. It failed to create an individual philosophy acceptable to an "educated" modern man. It failed to enlist an American majority. Its component parts failed to agree with each other on any basis. So our Christian civilization is neither Christian nor civilized. Look at it.*

---

* It did not occur to me, as I wrote the foregoing passage in 1941, that orthodox religion, by 1955, would have become a new refuge for masses of Americans who, out of sheer panic, had refused to look at themselves or to study science. I was well aware of the coming "atomic age" and its horrifying probabilities, but I was not able to perceive then that unconscious fear would shatter the common sense of multitudes.

I did not realize, that is, how the chief menace of communism would be seen as its "godlessness" and how, in magical countermeasure, "god-

The failure of science is even more grotesque.

A detached brain, contemplating science and scientists these days, could scarcely stay maddened lampoons and inspirational japes. Science did away with the church by throwing it into widely accepted default. That certain truths which had long ago given rise to the church might have prevented the occurrence in no way alters the fact. Mankind abandoned the true with the false and made his place of worship into a joke because science had revealed that not all its ceremonies and offices were "rational." The average man was shorn of his Sunday lecture, his conscience, his logarithms of right and wrong. "Intellectual" men stamped upon the grave of religion so that the ghost would never rise: the business was done with, they decreed.

Science made almost no study of the thing it had destroyed, or of the vacuum left in the spirit of man by the confiscation. Science, by God, was science, and religion was positively not scientific! Down with it!

What science did achieve is no secret. Science took the atom apart. It put together a relativistic definition of the tangible universe. It ruled out as nonexistent all elements it could not detect by machinery, even though man is preoccupied with such matters throughout his days. That renaissance, enlightening in its way, was accompanied by a thorough pulling of the blinds in half the human house. What you could see through the front windows was scientific. What you were not allowed

---

liness" would become more or less consonant with "Americanism"——how even an actual pledge to God would be added by the Congress to our pledge to the Flag. It is a lapse for which I apologize (and one for which I have tried to make amends in the years between). But who could have imagined, early in World War II that, as the American need for clear and detached thought became imperative, Americans would be frightened *away* from thinking, from science and from scientists—abandoning their one decent hope to gain the presumed sanctuary of godliness? In this connection, one recalls Stalin's acid query about the number of divisions possessed by the Pope. God surely will not do what man could and should and will not.

to examine through the darkened rear windows was not merely nonscientific—it simply did not exist. No medieval theologian ever touched off a sophistry of greater magnitude!

The results of scientific endeavor piled up, however, in such variety and size as to be convincing evidence of the efficacy of the method. On the outermost fields of speculation, science did not reach any conclusions much more satisfying to the average man than some of the postulates in, say, the Vedas, which are at least three thousand years old. But the new measurements satisfied the scientific passion for description. And, if the Aryans of 1000 B.C. somehow got onto corpuscular and radiant speculation—if they meditated the firmamental origin in somewhat the same terms as Abbé Le Maître—it is nothing against science that it should derive the same notion and express it even better, ninety generations later.

Shunning the difficult terrain of the intangible and the impalpable, science undertook the tangible and the describable. It was not only easier, but it was fashionable. The renaissance of science took place at the beginning of a European age of trade. A man of wealth was then, as usually, more of a personage than a man of wisdom—and many brave commercial pioneers had the foresight to perceive that science could be turned into a tidy thing. Born among a materialistic people, science consequently throve on matter and even its purest forms were usually subsidized to create more wealth or, at least, subsidized by wealth in patronage.

Science set out to increase worldly goods. Classical men in the business may grow black in the face denying this, but—so far—science has contributed virtually nothing else to mankind and I hold that a ninety-nine per cent total of circumstantial evidence is fairly convincing. Man's physical senses were extended enormously by science. The degree and the speed of that achievement are, indeed, the most common sources of our contemporary vanity; they form the whole preposterous case for the claim that we are civilized. No other attributes of man were, in any way, either extended or vitalized by science. Man's personality, his relations with other men, his private ethics, his social in-

tegrity, his standards of value, his love of truth, his dignity or his contentment, were not even potentially improved by the scientists—if the
almost unknown work of a few men be excepted.

The effect is, of course, alarming. (At least, I am alarmed by it.
And I hold that any man, these days, who does not live every hour in
a condition of alarm—however detached or icy—is either a traitor or
an idiot.) The electron tube, the locomotive, the internal combustion
engine, the suspension bridge, vaccine and the glass giant of Palomar
were turned over to the cruel bumpkin of the Middle Ages and his pal,
the naked bushman leaping around his tribal fire. True, those characters were stuffed into good waistcoats and somewhat circumscribed by
municipal law—but inside their heads they were living fossils—obsolete in the presence of their accouterments—intact specimens, in so
far as science had anything to do with their psyches. A few suits of
clothes, some money in the bank, and a new kind of fear constitute the
main differences between the average American today and the hairy
men with clubs who accompanied Attila to the city of Rome. The behavior of Attila's boys has been duplicated by millions upon millions of
Nazi soldiers and laymen, in detail. They are Western men, remember
—scientific and Christian, like ourselves. Each acted from an environment as modern as that of Chillicothe, or my own city of Miami
Beach.* Each had studied science and each had gone to church—each
of millions—and yet each was able to embrace rape, murder, torture,
larceny, mayhem and every other barbarous infamy the minute opportunity spelled itself in letters acceptable to him.

Americans are no different, underneath.

In another passage soon to appear, I propose to point this out more
graphically. Here, I merely wish to indicate that the science-built world
of engines and laboratories in which man lives has grown up apart
from man himself. Science has not instructed man—it has only implemented him.

A very proper sense of confusion has thus fallen upon mankind. His

---

* We have since moved to the country.

elected representatives do not understand the gadgets and machines which have come into being, or their consequences, or their social implications, or even the reason for the existence of many of them. Soil erodes away. States become dust bowls. People are unemployed and famished. Prices rise. Bread grows scarce. The radio blats away all day and night without the dimmest notion of responsibility for the effect of what it says. Men and women harbor in their houses machinery the workings of which they do not have the intelligence quotient to learn to comprehend by any possible means of instruction. Men and women drive automobiles which are so much better and more dependable, as natural objects, than the minds of the drivers that the net result, aside from universal escapism, is a homicide total higher than that of all our war casualties put together.

But science continues irresponsibly to tender new tools—airplanes, for example—and it is not bright of science. There is nothing wrong with the tools. The trouble is with the people. I would declare no truce against discovery. But I do suggest new lines for scientific investigation. Men unequipped internally but overloaded by objects are sure to stumble and fall to fighting. Again—one should not hand loaded pistols to the youngsters in a day nursery; but that is the learned procedure of this century. The proliferation of goods mounts and mounts again. Avarice, imitation, the lust for money, power and glamour—all primitive and unrestrained impulses—control the consumer public. The demented dogma of classicism reimbues the scientists with the urge to continue the proceeding irrespective of all result. And so they burn late oil, to freedom's glory—or Hitler's.

Our boots are not merely seven league: they stride the globe. Our eyes see through light years. Our ears hear voices from every city on the planet. Our biceps tear down cliffs. In every material sense, we have reached the end of the legends, the finale of the fairy tales. All the physical imagining of man, when he was limited to the power of his own body, has been realized. But not any good whatever has come of it—only the greatest evil man has yet endured.

During the decade before the onslaught of the current war, society was very near to collapse, and one thing was certain: in that prewar society of ours, not one per cent of the population really understood the material advances of their time, and of that one per cent, scarcely a man in ten thousand was giving any large part of his effort to an *intelligent* study of the hysterical dilemma. I say intelligent, advisedly. There were myriad panacea-makers but almost none mentioned as the cause—individual man.

Science had convinced itself that *only* the field of matter, or energy, was worth exploring with its new instrument: truth. Not one physical scientist in a thousand made a suggestion for attacking the manifest shambles of the individual. Salvation was expected even by the savants from a loosely associated group of pseudo-scientific quacks who called themselves economists or sociologists. The plans of those persons, probably, will go into the formulation of the next peace—making that peace as unrealistic as its numberless precursors. For this is the era when man subscribes his whole body and soul, in so far as he can, to materialism, and farms out the remnant to somebody called an economist.

The economist poses as a scientist and is so accepted. He tries to view man as a consumer of goods, and nothing else. Economic reasons, he says, start wars, set up national boundaries, build churches, create cities, destroy nations, and bring plagues of locusts. The correct economic system for the manufacture and distribution of goods, according to these wizards, is all that is needed to make life one long throb of happy motoring. Here, disguised as science, is the mystical motif—the witch-doctor prerogative—religion in its worst sense. Through such be-all-ism, economists have become the clergy of the twentieth century. In them we have placed our faith.

There has never been a democratic school of economics. Instead, in every democracy, are many schools, all interested in narrowing democracy, rather than in promulgating it. None agrees with any others, even concerning a definition of terms. On every public problem our great economists (and there are no mediocre economists—as Marcus Goodrich once pointed out—which, in itself neatly implies the absurdity of economics) solemnly take all possible sides: the positive, the negative, the converse, and the contraposite, which is logical as a device, but gets the public nowhere.

However, even where there is one system, the theory of the amenability of all man's problems to fixed trade rules breaks down. We have before us two notable examples: communism and fascism—the left and the right. Both are economic systems, basically. Both are absolutist —one compelled upon the state by the people, and the other compelled upon the people by a small, impassioned group which declares itself to be the state.

Apologists for communism explain that it broke down in Russia because Russia was not an industrial nation. That seedy and specious argument needs no more rebuttal. The Soviet itself has furnished it. Communism broke down because men are not created equal, do not work equally, cannot be paid equally, do not have equal social and financial deserts, will not produce their best effort in a society that is not competitive, and cannot be made to work long or hard or with brilliance if they are not permitted to own, possess, buy, sell, and do business with each other.

All the illuminating work of Pavlov on dogs merely seemed to show that dogs were machines; but none of it undertook to destroy the instinctual patterns of dogs. Later work of the same sort, attempting exactly that, showed that when even the best-conditioned reflexes of pigs were set in conflict with their instincts, pigs had nervous breakdowns and went insane. The Russians *had* to quit trying to squeeze human life into the patterns of Pavlov and of Marx because men have instinct, too. Men are not machines. A few months of Marxism showed with ghastly clarity that his economic theory, which depended upon the presumption that men could be made to operate as ants do, was phony, and Russia abandoned communism.

Fascism is, of course, old stuff. Communism was, too, but Marx knew little of anthropology. In any case, he was so furious at the outrages of nineteenth-century industrialism that he was unable to think lucidly. Fascism is communism compelled by state violence and put to any use for which the state sees fit, from the doling out of candy to the citizenry to the enactment of war upon the citizens of other states. Absolute dominion of a powerful people by a minority always produces national aggression. The psychology of that phenomenon is simple in essence even when it is complex in expression. A king and his nobles, or a Hitler and his unsqueamish satraps, having snatched the power, must brandish it to emboss the fact on the local populace. Next, they must protect their luster by impressing outsiders, lest a peripheral human titter undo them. Conquest is a most impressive procedure. It is useful to them, also, to start wars as a diversion; the people would study the high cost of tyranny, if they did not. War is by far the most diverting exercise man has thought of—and for such reasons, aggression goes hand in hand with autocracy.

Fascism—or rightism—is in essence the legalization of larceny, as has been said. That is why we find the czars of our American monopolies have rightist tendencies. A monopoly, being a strict contradiction of nature and acceptable only as an emergency measure, requires the legalization of larceny for its maintenance. All living things are in competition to live at all times—even man—and even man today—but truces are essential for mutual tolerance. Fascism, like monopoly, denies the right of truce. Plundering at home is quick work for every totalitarian administration. Plundering abroad is a constant temptation. So fascism—or state capitalism—will always be neighbor-raping.

The economic system of theft has one immense advantage: it works. But it also has one great disadvantage: it works only while there is something to steal. Thus, if Germany or Japan conquered the whole world, the winner would take all *—including the problem of man and science, unsolved, and further boggled by whatever medieval nonsense

---

* This is the point overlooked by many erudite but foolish people who nowadays assume that we—and the democracies—ought to have let Hitler conquer Russia. To those of us who cannot manage to select amongst tyrants a preferred foe, let alone a preferred American führer (or commissar), the point seems cogent.

would be added by the Germans or the Japs. They would be nowhere
—which is to say, they would be, at best, just where we were when the
war began, and at worst, some thousand or more years behind that,
which in truth, is not very far.

I do not mean that a thousand years is a short time in biology or ge-
ology—although it is. I mean that man, except for his possibly fatal ac-
cretion of machinery, has really advanced almost not at all in the *last*
one thousand years. Even the dreadful specter of Hitler's Tausend-Jahr
Reich is, in that relation, tiddlywinks. If we in America were busy
spreading through our population some powerful forward step of consciousness, we might look selflessly at the Hitler proposal of a millennium of slavery as a most dismal threat. But we are not busy with anything more valuable to mankind than private security and prosperity.

We could be.

The proposition I wish to make could and would start just such a
movement and give rise to exactly that result: a general increase in the
consciousness of man. It is a simple proposal. It has been made over
and over for many thousands of years by thoughtful people. It has not,
however, been put forward, so far as I know, by any popular contemporary author in terms acceptable to the average doctor of philosophy,
high school graduate, or reader of the New York *Times*. I am going to
try here, by various means, to set forth an old and basic idea in such a
way that it can be understood by that travesty of wisdom and catastrophe of misguidance, the modern educated man.

All I shall suggest is that man—individual man—enlarge his attitude toward himself.

In order to do so most rapidly and effectively he should use the tool
at hand: science. He should employ the scientific method for the purpose of studying himself and teaching himself what he learns about
himself. He should apply logic and integrity to his subjective personality—just as he has done to the objective world. He would find that
laws parallel to physical principles rule his inner life. He would find
that truth cannot be escaped within, any more than it can be escaped
without. He would learn that when he kids himself, or believes a lie,

or deceives another man, he commits a crime as real and as destructive as the crime of deliberately running down a person with an automobile.

Our civilization has not yet even dreamed of applying science to *itself*. Science is exact. It measures and weighs. It admits every error instantly, when error is detected. It understands that knowledge is fluid and changing. It recognizes the relativity of data. It perceives that objects are not at all what they appear to be and that their nature is bizarre and changing. It knows that nothing stands still. Only the principle of fluid integrity, of eternal openmindedness, is fixed, in science. Everything else can be dismissed at any time by every scientist. The objective world, viewed by him, holds no dogma save that one: I will pursue the truth, and the truth only, because all else is by definition false, and I am a mind of too much dignity to limit myself by awarenesses based on falsehood.

The great American oaf—be he college president, bank teller, race track tout, or missionary—assumes that he has *already* been converted into this state of mind by science. The number and excellence of the products of science on every hand lead him to identify *himself* with the scientific principle. His civilization is scientific. So he is.

No more pitiful fallacy could be imagined. An automobile represents an immensely greater body of honesty than the salesmen who sells it or the jerk who drives himself to doom in it. Most men are literally too crooked with themselves to be allowed to drive cars. Since they *are* allowed—cars contribute their share of calamity to man. The integrity of thinking and acting that enters into the radio set on the common man's bedside table is a thundering rebuke to the reliability of the cluck beside it and the macaroon singing over it.

Man must now approach himself, if he still has a chance, with the detached and sincere passion he has applied to the world of things. He must give as much energy to his soul as he does to his job. And the best men with the best brains must research as feverishly into themselves and each other as they have into atoms.

The blame for Armageddon lies on man. And the millennium will come only when the average man exhibits a scientific integrity about *all* he is and does—instead of half of it. Many a psychological Archimedes has put signposts on the hard road man must follow if he is to avoid self-destruction and come into his own. A few very great modern scientists have added to the lore. Indications of what man may expect of himself are everywhere at hand. But most men must first be persuaded that the task lies ahead and not behind—that we are infants, still, with loaded guns for toys. Toward that persuasion I shall now set myself. I have said that we civilized men are still medieval—cruel bumpkins and dancing savages. I would like to elucidate that point, first, because no other can be made until it is somewhat accepted.

CHAPTER II

Subjective Feudalism

A Teleological Ramble with the Author.

HISTORIANS WILL WRITE ABOUT AMERICA OF THE YEAR 1940 somewhat in the manner of the following paragraphs, presumptively selected at random:

"During this period, the United States had not yet entered into the so-called Second World War. It is a period representative of the medieval way of life as it developed after the beginning of mechanical knowledge. . . .

"A more brutal and degraded era can scarcely be imagined. The cities, teeming with millions of people, were constructed largely of brick and rock cement, reinforced by steel. These and other heavy materials were fabricated with much imperfect combustion, which, abetted by the fires used for the heating of warrenlike abodes, filled the air with smoke and other noxious vapors. Solids in the atmosphere were measured by tons per square mile and visibility was almost nil, at times, in many of these infestious metropolises. Houses and buildings were set side by side in square blocks, without relationship to each other and without any plan or specific reason for their being in any given place. Ramshackle slums nudged towering 'skyscrapers,' and residential areas were indescribably mingled with the smoking, clamorous factory districts. The streets were filthy. Garbage, papers, animal excrement and vile sludge were sluiced from them periodically into open sewers which debouched into any convenient river or harbor so that the waters, too, crawled with flotsam.

"Some measures were taken to protect public health, but very few. Owing to superstition and religious prejudice, certain diseases which could have been controlled were not even 'discussable' in fashionable circles. About five per cent of the population suffered untold misery from these plagues alone, despite the fact that the 'science' of that remote and repugnant era was adequate to have blotted them out in the space of a year. Medical care was available to the lucky among the poor and to the very rich. A large, neglected class between those extremes suffered from all manner of untreated communicable diseases and evil conditions. Legless beggars rolled down the thoroughfares, exhibiting their rags and their dripping lesions. Half of the beds in all hospitals were occupied by patients with 'mental diseases' and half of the benighted creatures who reported themselves ill to the medical profession also suffered from nervous rather than actual complaint—facts not to be wondered at, in view of the conditions under which people lived in the dark ages. . . .

"The sports of these people were cruel in the extreme. One of the chiefest among them was a contest in resistance to blows. In this sadistic pastime, the contenders, standing before tens of thousands of screeching, orgiastic onlookers, wrapped their fists in pads and undertook to beat each other to insensibility. The man who was able thus to batter senseless every challenger was known as the 'heavyweight champion' of the world. These bloody battles often produced in the participants a permanent state of idiocy which the public regarded as hilariously amusing. The sight of two men hammering each other in this fashion —occasionally, indeed, to death—was doubtless some psychic compensation to the ordinary man for the formidable and revolting circumstances in which he was forced to live. . . .

"Cruelty was common to many other sports and torture was a recognized method for 'extracting the truth' from witnesses or suspects in criminal actions. The American instruments for this inquisitional procedure were generally not as crudely elaborate as those used earlier in the

Dark Ages for similar purposes—but their effect upon the victim was identical. In one collection are rubber hoses attached to broom handles, which left no traces of the lethal beating they could administer—hot, bright electric lights, which were played on the victim while food and water were withheld, whips, matches, which were applied lighted to the hands and feet, and artificial brass knuckles which officers of 'law enforcement' donned in order to shatter the flesh and bones of a suspect's face for the purpose of compelling confession. These are all to be seen in the American collection. The European collection includes so many diabolically ingenious instruments of torment that one forbears to list and describe them. . . .

"A good portion of the population kept its senses partly drugged by the ingestion of alcohol, and the use of hypnotics, opiates, and the like. It is not to be wondered at, although the effect was terrifying, especially since medieval man of the twentieth century operated millions of self-propelled vehicles. These were clumsy but swift; they raced through the streets of his cities and the roads connecting them, under the guidance of all manner of morons, fools, physical incapables, drunkards and drug addicts. Loud horns were attached to them for the purpose of warning all and sundry of their approach—but, though the continual din of these horns may be imagined, often enough, a child, woman or man was struck down by the reckless passage of such an apparatus. Often, too, the operators dashed themselves, their passengers, and their vehicles to pieces.

"Incredible as it may seem, the annual death toll among twentieth-century Americans from this single cause approached forty thousand and the number of persons injured annually reached one million. That is to say, each year almost one per cent of the total population was either hurt or killed, in or by vehicular traffic alone! Historians are agreed that the foregoing single statistic expresses the nadir of man's irresponsibility to man—hence the figure represents the abyssal date of the Dark Ages. . . .

"Along the stinking, obscure and clamorous streets crept every figure familiar to students of those appalling centuries. Contemporary with Freud and Einstein, amazingly, were the garbs and the customs of a world that should have vanished long before them. Nuns passed, shaved of head as they had been for hundreds of years, sworn to sexual chastity and suffering the inevitable psychological consequences, averting their eyes from the clamor and the horror, fingering their symbolical beads and muttering meaningless prayers in Latin—a language that had been 'dead' for a thousand years. Priests and ministers in similar costumes could be seen. In some cities, on special occasions—all manner of citizens dressed up as animals, men as women and women as men, and as mummers, clowns and other demonological or escapist figures. Members of secret lodges, with traditions and ceremonials kept intact for hundreds of years, paraded in the costumes of the Near East to their tomblike places of conclave. At night, other secret societies, in bed sheets and pillow slips, rode on horseback anonymously to lynching trysts and torture rendezvous. . . .

"The favorite novels of these people dealt, not surprisingly, with deliberate murder. The killer, at the end of these tales, was invariably caught and usually committed suicide immediately upon apprehension, a sop to a nonexistent morality. Other forms of entertainment, including periodicals of the most banal sort, motion pictures, serial 'strips' which appeared in the newspapers, and continued dramas on the daily radio, dwelt incessantly with such infantile themes as the sudden and unexpected accession to wealth, the selection of an obviously ill-educated and untrained female for a wife by a figure of worldly prominence, the finding of treasure, and—also inevitably—upon murder, torture, horror, monsters, bastardy, seduction, and other crimes.

"Nudity and promiscuity were prohibited by law. Nevertheless, for advertising purposes, the figure of a near-nude woman wearing a blissful expression of manifest sexual ecstasy, was standard. A psychologist will not be surprised by such findings. Medieval man, suffering from the impossible restraints placed upon his behavior by the church reformations, expressed in myriad symbolic titillations the biological activities which were so strictly circumscribed by law.

"The law was, of course, evaded. Indeed, a cursory examination of twentieth-century law makes the student wonder if the whole body of it was not created more to line the pockets of lawyers than to protect the citizen—for it is full of incredibly obtuse phraseology, of contradiction, of loopholes and injustices, of irrelevancies, of unenforceable dicta—of all manner of savage nonsense, in fact, save natural law and simple rules for public behavior. . . .

"Except for courses in the mechanical sciences, which were extremely advanced, and the parallel, in their later time, of the engineering knowledge of the ancient Egyptians, the university curriculum was not much different from that of five hundred years before. Various religions were taught, and also the law, which, in America, was based on a body of three-century-old English common law. Latin and Greek were diligently studied, although for what reason one is unable to determine at this distance. Foreign languages were taught, as they had always been and still are, to some degree—but there was little thought, in the various institutions of learning throughout the world, of hitting upon one universal language. Some colleges used the metric system and some the English system of feet and inches, pounds and ounces.

"The colleges themselves were ponderous stone buildings, usually segregated from the populace, and many were for men or women but not for both. Great learning was attributed to pedants who were still debating points that had been without relevancy for thousands of years; thus an 'authority' in Sanskrit, a very ancient language, was regarded, inside a university, as the intellectual equal of a chemist or a physicist. The education of young people had very little to do, it may be seen, with the life for which they were being prepared, and every sort of bigotry was proselytized by one or more colleges. History was written and taught without any regard for fact, but only with the motive of nationalistic 'face-saving.' Graduation ceremonies were held in Latin; the professors and students, in their black robes, under their flat, black mortarboard hats, kept visibly alive even among the so-called enlightened classes both the specter and the spirit of the ages of darkness against which, presumably, education above all else should have struggled. . . .

"The people of this black and benighted era were so confused that their dismay found an expectable expression in their arts. Atonal music, discord, disrhythm, and the admission to symphony orchestras of ringing doorbells and machinery noises typified their state of mind. Under the pretense of being 'abstract' or 'advanced,' artists without ability of any sort covered canvases with daubs, mists, swirls, spirals, cubes and half-envisioned objects which had, admittedly, no significance. These 'paintings' were solemnly criticized by a special body of men whose sole function was just that; they were purchased for large sums of money and soberly hung in the principal museums. Literature endured an equal battering at the hands of writers who, obviously unable to find order in the foul, frenetic world around them, tried hard to emulate and reproduce chaos. Books of poetry, and, indeed, long novels, may still be studied today, which have no sanity in them save capricious and incidental associative relevancies of the most contrived and infantile nature. The grievous gulf between medieval man's engineering skill and his ineptitude at being manlike is thus reflected in the art of the woebegone period as vividly as it is to be seen in his crammed and caterwauling psychopathic wards. It was, indeed, as close to doom as man ever brought himself. But the seeds of enlightenment present in that vile soil would not sprout; they were not allowed to. . . .

"The brutishness and filthiness of the people was equaled only by their ignorance and credulity. Every mind was clogged with superstitions that had to do with ladders, black cats, hunchbacks, the new moon—an infinitude of objects. Yet, the people believed themselves to be enlightened—the strangest superstition of all! They indulged in mass myths of a great variety. Everybody, for example, 'loved his mother'—it was a tenet, and a man would smash your jaw if you said your mother was a back-biting hypocrite—although, likely, in that age, she was. Moreover, public opinion would stand behind the man who had smashed the jaw of the critic of his mother—rather than behind the man who had told the simple fact. Again, it was believed, in large areas, that prostitution was a device necessary to keep 'good' women 'pure.' The 'home' was said to be sacred and each man's house was regarded as an inviolable castle. This superficial sanctity of person was carried to such excesses that no precise records of human beings were kept, so that criminals often could not be identified even when caught, babies were lost track of, men died and were buried in nameless graves, and a victim of amnesia was frequently irrecoverable in the screaming, smoke-drenched welter of a large city. . . .

"Life in rural areas, excepting for the benefits of machine-powered tools and automatic transportation, had not changed since the time of Julius Caesar. Rural people were close-mouthed, clannish, and suspicious of strangers. Unlike factory workers, they would not band together for mutual protection, and were therefore at the foot of the economic ladder—a poor, ignorant, starveling huddle of farmers and tenant farmers, inbred and degenerate, often to the point of near-idiocy and albinoism. Indeed, in some rural areas there were villages in which half the propulation was pink-eyed, white-headed, 'touched,' or definitely insane. But even sanity was relative in any one place in that epoch. It is likely that a man from a Missouri farm, brought to a great eastern city, would have been regarded as insane no matter how carefully he had tried to behave and express himself—and city-livers who appeared in the rural areas were invariably the butt of ridicule and cruelty, due to their inability to comprehend and adapt to that sullen environment. . . .

"The halls of state were filled with the representatives of these people, who had an elective government. Popular interest in making money with which to purchase the products of factories so far surpassed interest in rational government, however, that the people either refused to take the trouble to exercise their voting franchise, or, if they voted, did so in a cynical acceptance of the knowledge that at least half of the candidates were running for office not so much to govern as to graft, or to abet the graft of some large corporation or some powerful person. Out of the total moneys paid in taxes, at least a quarter was exhausted by deliberate waste, by theft, and by other forms of chicanery.

"Permission to avoid many laws could be purchased. Thus gambling, for example, although 'outside' the law, flourished by the paying of intricate tribute to politicians holding elective offices. Men elevated to executive positions, under such circumstances, could not be expected to be either judicious or honest. They were neither, as a rule. Recorded proceedings of the governing bodies of large states which controlled the destinies of millions of people show that the representatives often lacked even an elementary knowledge of geography, arithmetic, logic, grammar, law, business, or trade. Following a leadership that was often corrupt and nearly always self-seeking, they voted as they were told, and spent the rest of their time in ribaldry, drunkenness, whoring, and shooting spitballs at one another even when in legislative session. . . .

"The average citizen of the abyssal epoch, if he appeared magically before a modern man, would have to be approached with great care. In and on him would reside colonies of the germs of various infectious diseases—fungi in his feet—bottle bacilli in his scalp—various cocci in his mouth and on his skin—and other bacteria and viruses inside him. He would be anointed with a harsh perfume dissolved in alcohol, the purpose of which was to hide the smells of dirt and sweat incurred by his clothing, and the odors of sulphur and carbon which pervaded his hellish cities. His apparel, stemmed from garments originated hundreds of years before his time, and still littered with vestigial traces in the form of tabs and buttons, would not cover him evenly or properly. Shoes of animal hide would stiffly box his feet—which would be misshapen because he had worn such shoes all his life. If he had been walking on his own streets, there would be upon his shoes in small quantities the excrement of horses, dogs, cats, birds, and other creatures. He would quite possibly be thick-tongued and dizzy from the effects of a few ounces of alcohol taken internally, but he would stoutly maintain himself to be 'sober.' If anything untoward happened, as you viewed this man, such as the falling of a fork on the floor, or, possibly, the sudden appearance of a white horse or a cross-eyed person, he might mutter, 'Bread and butter,' or cross his fingers, to ward off the evil of the omen.

"He could tell you the name of the city from which he had come and many facts of a superficial nature concerning it. But he could supply no exact information about any of the methods of its construction, power sources, water supplies, sewage disposal, or other such simple facts. He could give you an index of the items in his house, but he could not tell you how they had been made, of what, or how they 'worked.' He would have a blurred and absurd idea of the history of his nation and none at all, to speak of, concerning the history of other countries. He could name the 'heavyweight champion' of his era and give you encyclopediac information on the subject of other sports, which would be of great importance to him. In the world of enterprise, he could tell you with detail about one small aspect of one department of one business, such as the selling of ladies' shoes in a 'department' store, but about all other businesses he would be hazy. His knowledge of art would be nil. But he could unwind an infinite number of the 'plots' and describe the myriad tawdry characters of the illustrated newspaper 'strips,' radio 'serials,' magazine stories, moving, talking pictures, and other escape fictional devices with which he had glutted most of his free waking hours.

"His moral sense would be fantastically garbled with prejudices, superstitions and religious taboos. He would tell you his home and his wife were sacred and his 'fidelity' thereto beyond question. Indeed, he might, as previously indicated, offer you physical assault for any question of it. And yet, as an average man, he would have spent a considerable amount of time trying to find opportunities to be 'faithless' to his wife, *i.e.,* to cajole miscellaneous women into copulating with him. The rare coincidence of the chance and a coercible female would have caused his actual 'indiscretions'—as he would put it—to be so few in relation to his feeble wishes as to make him feel 'righteous' in the assertion of his 'fidelity.' Most, if not all, of his behavior-thought patterns would be approximately analogous to his statement of categorical fidelity and his actual record.

"Any rigid insistence on explicit factuality in the exercise of this man's thoughts as they related to his literal behavior would drive him into a hysteria or a bleak melancholia, depending on the type of his personality. He would be so accustomed to his warped attitudes that actual torment would not evoke a coherent statement of whole truths from him. He would be, indeed, incapable of letting himself imagine the truths about himself—a pathological liar—a schizoid personality —who lived in a world of small, seedy dreams.

"Such would be a fair glimpse of the average medieval man. He would have many more faults—many other vices—eviler smells, perhaps—and he might also evince great virtue on very rare occasions. For the rest—a modern geneticist would not let him breed, and a meat inspector would not pass him." *

---

* Nearly fifteen years have passed since the date given for the foregoing, slightly tongue-in-the-cheek description of "medieval" man. On reviewing it, I find no occasion to revise it upward but, rather, the contrary. In matters of health, sanitation and the like there may have been improvement on the order of, say, one per centum. In the matter of the suitability of cities for human habitation there has been marked deterioration. Some, like New York, are now crowded beyond all bearing; others, like Los Angeles, are rapidly poisoning their own climate; nearly all have come to use great, flat walls of glass in their architecture which—considering the nature of future warfare—remarkably attests my theory that modern city-dwellers have an impulse, innate but unconscious, to destroy their metropoles and themselves in the most bloodsome fashion possible.

Besides, latter-day barbarism has taken man further from thought, back to the old, futile rituals, and added to the burden of his days a geometrically growing, unstoppable Fear (of himself and his hidden intentions) which he currently tries half to camouflage and half to acknowledge by admitting (at long last!) this to be an "age of anxiety."

Anxiety . . . !

CHAPTER III

A Footnote to Chapter Two

IT MAY SEEM THAT I HAVE HEAVILY WEIGHTED THE IMAGINARY balance of history against pop and the folks. I freely admit that some other historian than the one I have quoted may well write with a certain studied praise of our times—looking down a long nose and belittling even as he compliments. But *our* enlightenment will surely be discussed just as we discuss the enlightenment of, say, the Egyptians: "They were amazing engineers to build those pyramids! They made paper, and stained glass, and even a few things we can't duplicate today. But, of course, they were simply barbarous. They split people in two with big knives—alive—and they had hordes of slaves. Their religion was savage and cruel and their idea of sport would make your blood run cold. They didn't have any justice or equality and they killed literally millions of human beings to get their work done. And of course, all the work was for nothing, anyhow; what earthly *use* are the pyramids . . . ?"

And so on.

They will be saying the identical words, no doubt, when Boulder Dam, long since silted up, is disinterred. It generated electricity, they will say, to light fools the way to dusty and so forth.

They will surely say the same thing when some eminent archeologist, stumbling upon the faces of four presidents carved on a Dakota mountain, will decipher their names, dig up their dynasties, and find out a little about their accompanying wars.

The life of the common American will seem most dismal to them— even as it does to the common American, whether or not he knows it. All our gallantry and courage will be dryly wrung out of our doings; a more real set of motives will be ascribed to them. The thirteen colonies rebelled not to win freedom but to avoid taxes. The army at Valley Forge dyed the snow with its bleeding feet not because of any necessity but because of the grafting shoemakers and the nitwitted sloth of Congress. School children in some far future will study this war not as human experience but as a series of campaigns which, for all the difference it will make to them, might have been fought with lead soldiers and tin airplanes on tablecloths. Our heroism is not in vain, I know. But the future will pay scant attention to it as heroics.

The future will point, like mathematics, to the one terrible flaw of our lives today: the discrepancy between what we are able to accomplish by objective honesty in the material world and what we fail to do in the world of behavior and attitude because we will not treat them with any sort of honesty or objectivity whatever.

Every hour makes the flaw more apparent. Every passing day widens the gap. And a species, like an individual, cannot maintain itself when its physical accouterments are no longer geared to its behavior in its environment. The awful machinery of defense and offense possessed by the great dinosaurs was operated by a brain the size of a nutmeg; in that, no doubt, is their raison-d'être-non-plus. It may well be the same with man, who has got himself into the identical situation—though with no need for it: man's brain is big enough; he does not use it rightly.

CHAPTER IV

A Psychology Lesson, a Study, and a Sermon

A Psychology Lesson—A Second Study of the Church in the Light of the Lesson—and a Sample of an Unpreached Sermon.

DR. CARL JUNG, THE ZURICH PSYCHOLOGIST, HAS SOLVED ONE OF the greatest enigmas concerning man. The fact that most scientists have paid very little attention to Dr. Jung's solution is of no particular moment. Most scientists have never heard of it. Of those psychologists who have, many are so preoccupied with the measurement of conditioned reflexes as to be unable, intellectually, to find room in their heads to understand what Jung has said. A few, of course, have studied the theory and found it sound.

It requires a specially courageous personality to appreciate the idea: Like all laws of psychology, it is at first rejected on sight by most persons. That is because most persons have ignored, disobeyed, or debauched all psychological principles for so long that they find it expedient to disbelieve in them categorically rather than to accept them at the cost of much private chagrin. Freud was the first to make *that* discovery.

Jung's law has to do with man's instinct. The very juxtaposition of those two words—man and instinct—sends certain learned jackasses into a spin. If they were as scientific as they pretend to be, they would never spin about anything. Indeed, their spinning is logically construed

34

as a demonstration of the truth of Jung's premise and not of their own formalized bigotries. A man who is sure of himself doesn't blow his top: the very state of being sure precludes the blast; but top-blowing is devilishly instinctual.

In animals, the presence of instinct has been demonstrated beyond peradventure. But man, possessed of an ego into which he forever tries to stuff his whole awareness, denies that he has instincts because to admit it would deflate his ego by restoring some of its contents to his history. Through some magic that lies outside the field of known biology, he claims, instead, that he has evolved beyond instinct. A careful study of ontogeny in relation to phylogeny would suggest, at least, that he will outgrow instinct at about the same time he outgrows protoplasm.

But, even if he grants the likelihood of instinct, where, man asks himself, do his instincts repose and in what way do they express themselves? Dr. Jung finds the answer by looking at all manner of men in all ages and in all conditions of society. He expects the evidence of instinct to be modified. Man has the power to reason, to feel, to evaluate, to guess, to imagine, to project himself into nonexistent situations, and to articulate his resultant ideas. In him, therefore, instinct might not necessarily express itself as the raw impulse of the beast. The very number of alternatives which his brain is capable of suggesting might conceivably alter, camouflage, or even refute any given instinctual impulse. But evidence of such impulses must be there, according to any normal hypothesis.

Moreover, the fact that the evidence does not appear in toto at the moment of birth does not refute man's instinctuality, although some mustached Columbia females, finding that an infant's only discernible instinct is a fear of falling, have triumphantly used the experiment to show the nonexistence of instinct in human beings. Apart from the fact that these women have used the proof of one instinct to show the existence of none—which is addled—there is the fact that instincts appear in all animals as they mature and not at their birth.

Jung has shown that human instinct has been translated into *legend*. By studying collections of ancient legends and by studying primitive people as well as the folk fictions of various contemporary societies, Jung has been able to demonstrate that there springs up invariably in every group of human beings, however isolated in time and space, a set of myths in which is found an elaborate pattern of identical premises, identical characters, and parallel situations which come to identical conclusions.

Because of his articulate speech and his power of projection, man has *personified* his instincts. Primitive man acts with a consciousness of being "in" his legend. He gives himself a name related to the representative of an instinctual quality; a personified god or hero controls his destiny in every particular proceeding; his compulsions and taboos originate, he believes, with these legendary characters, or gods.

Jung has called the figures "archetypes." Their universality is recognized, uncritically, by all of us. They appear in every ancient literature, whether of the Greeks or the Norsemen or the Hindus or the American Indians. Primitive men, cut off from other men for thousands of years, produce archetypes of matching pattern, by themselves. Societies in every climate, every continent and island, and every period of time, have always originated these figures. It is, on examination, not difficult to understand the mechanism by which man has translated his instinctual knowledge into personalized figures with histories which reflect the immutable quality of his instincts. The process is inevitable, in an animal with a brain.

The discovery is one of the most useful and enlightening of our age; or rather, it could be if it were widely understood and if the logical implications of it were employed by society. For the archetypes are the picture-memory of the wisdom of the breed and there are as many of them as there are human qualities and problems.

Foremost is the Hero. The Hero is a god, or a good man, a strong one (stronger, of course, than the aspiring mortal), and he is generally engaged in performing a hard task in order to win immortality or a beautiful woman or both. Perseus and Theseus, Loki, Achilles, Samson, Paul Bunyan, Ulysses, Hercules, and so on. The heroes, be it noted, had flaws. Loki was full of mischief. Samson tangled with Delilah.

Achilles had a weak spot in his heel. Ulysses had his long voyage and its disasters. Theseus first failed to lift the stone—and Hercules had to shovel a lot of manure before he was promoted. Here is the universal picture of instinctual man struggling toward virtue and running head-on into the slings and arrows of bad luck, personal fallibility, and, more subtly, the energies which automatically oppose every force in action. Myriad gods and heroes of savage tribes endlessly repeat that same pattern.

Again, in legends, the duality of woman is depicted either by two equally important archetypal characters or by one woman who is both good and evil. Man's attitude toward woman as it is expressed in his entire recorded history was embedded in his brain before there was writing, and even before men built fires. Eve demonstrates that fact—and the still more sinister figure of Lilith—Salome, Venus and Helen of Troy, Juno and Sappho, Freya, Circe, and a hundred more. Magic and sorcery are closely associated with women; primitive man could interpret in no other way the compulsion of his powerful sex instinct toward beauty and the frequent disenchantment which followed.

Among many archetypes, as cogent and as universal, are the wise old man, the witches, everyman—who is small, bent and gray, the devil—on whom with unerring accuracy a thousand races have fixed the horns of the beast, death, and so forth. The serpent is always wise, for a reason that contemporary man would be enlightened to understand. There is wisdom on the Tree of a thousand folklores, for another and equally good symbolical reason. The pattern is incessant and inescapable. Instinct in man was expressed by personification, deification, and in short, by what he came to regard as his creed or his "religion."

No student of ancient history can doubt that in man today are the same impulses which burned in him millennia ago. That is, nobody should doubt it, any more than one should doubt our cave-inhabiting ancestors had hands and ears and noses.

Of course, people do profess to deny the idea. It was necessary to deny it (and here I illuminate, by another degree, an earlier disquisition) to make the Marxian theory of economics seem applicable to mankind. In that case, either the assumption had to be made that man was born naked of any impulse whatever, and all he was had been poured into him from his surroundings, or else Marxism was bunk. Of course, it was.* But, for quite a while, a considerable school of socialist anthropologists, geneticists, and the like attempted to codify Marx's nonsense. They failed so dismally that, in the end, they were kicked out of even the most tolerant learned societies. Their papers evoked laughter because they flew in the face of so much demonstrable fact.

The tentative Soviet effort to abolish human instinctuality was a reasonable project, however, compared to the treatment it has been

---

* For reasons of belief and principle, of theory and of personal experience, I am opposed to communism and have been from the very days when so many of my literary colleagues—the liberals and liberal-intellectuals—were not so opposed. The basis of my opposition is more knowledgeable from every viewpoint and (dare I say so?) far more real and profound even than the fundament upon which rests ordinary clerical opposition. Yet, because I believe there is just as much of the identical "bunk" in orthodox religion as I note here in the secular passion called communism, because of my mere apostasy—because of my exercise of a right without which Americans no longer belong to America—I have been sometimes publicly called a "Communist."

That would be ludicrous if it did not connote the unfree, prejudiced, anti-rational and altogether baboonlike hunger for headless conformity which this book was written to decry. Communism is not people but an idea; it can be effectively "fought" only when it is understood thoroughly (a goal we Americans now propose to evade) and when a superior, more effective, realer and more modern philosophy is offered as an alternative (which philosophy has been given us but which we nowadays too often ignore or even debauch). Let the reader note, then, that I am not only untainted by communism but free of the taint which makes certain conformists so label me—certain rotten-egg-heads whom we must laugh off the stage lest stupid persons scream them on.

accorded by the so-called ethical thinkers and moral leaders of our own society. It was Jung—not I—who showed the development of primitive religions out of personified instinct. But let me now carry that method into an examination of what we call religion today and of its relation with instinct.

When the scientific investigation of matter embarked on its recent zoom, its effectiveness was so startling that a rejoicing world took it up as the primary cause. People, as I have said, made the farcical assumption that because their machines were efficient and honest, they, too, partook of those qualities. The Christian religion lent itself readily to this masquerade although, as Christ taught it, there was no element of perfectionism in Christianity. His efforts were to make people try to be more conscious of who and what they were, and to live according to the wisdom stemming from that increase of consciousness. His parables were all archetypal.

But, in the early part of the Middle Ages (assuming, still, that this era is the center of the Middle Ages) a schizoid process began in Christianity which was fulfilled with the dawn of the age of scientific reason: dogmatic perfectionism replaced growth as a psychological "must." You had to be chaste, or to give one tenth of all you made, or to go without meat one day a week, or to say so many Ave Marias, or to put a nickel on the drum. If you failed, you were penalized, according to a precise scale. The Reformation shook down the mercenary angle of perfectionism, but it increased its psychological aspect. You had to be spiritually perfect—or else. Or else you would go to hell. Or you'd be obliged to live in penance. Men like Luther, Calvin, Knox, and others put the bar so high that nobody could vault over it.

The bar went even higher outside churches, when the scientists forced themselves to admit that they couldn't get anywhere with anything unless they agreed to deal with the truth, the whole truth, and nothing but the truth. Religious morality, already a leprous garble, could not compete with such standards. Hard upon the unspoken acknowledgment of that, many honest-minded human beings became agnostics, or, at least, turned in their pastoral letters.

The preachers and priests could not stand before their flocks and demand that each individual reckon with himself, his character, his manners, morals, dealings with his neighbor, and attitude on international affairs, with the same exquisite integrity which the scientists were applying to objects. The people would probably have massacred ministers for suggesting it. The church would surely have collapsed from the revealed weight of its own disintegrity. Those scientists who still held church memberships would doubtless have led the drive to prevent anything like a scientific investigation of the church—since the church was a repository of their instincts and they were neither proud nor even certain about their behavior on instinctual planes. Indeed, like ordinary men, they knew damned well that what they secretly thought would not bear the light of day, since it was congruent neither with cold common sense nor with the accepted dogma of perfect behavior.

This mess was resolved, after a fashion, by expedients. The onus was in some cases passed to Christ. Certain churches let his death atone for generations of license. A system of vicarious punishment was set up in these churches. As if no man had ever endured pain before, Sunday after Sunday the sweating congregations were made to suffer the agony of Jesus on the cross. Now, painful as crucifixion may be, billions of men have suffered as severely for a much longer period than four days. But a man who is needled agonizingly once a week feels, if he is no careful thinker, that he is entitled to some compensatory pleasure of the flesh. So, suffering with Christ on Sunday, he is able by a psychological ruse to obey instincts of his own the other six days, almost uncritically.

Numerous similar rationalizing processes could be detailed. The worst is the most general—the one that gulped the camel—the one which assumes that there is as much perfection in the soul of the twentieth century lout as there is in a geometry theorem. The happy acceptance by the church, the organ of collective instinctuality, of that idea undid the church and, in the process, unhinged the common man's capacity for introspection.

Unable to compete with the standards of science in its own sphere of subjectivity, the church simply discarded all mention of that part of instinctual behavior which is decidedly nonscientific, irrational, and dangerous to peace and reason. Unwilling to carry on the arduous and nasty business of casting out devils, it merely turned its back on the devil.* Man is good, it said categorically. Sin was no longer preached, but goodness only.

The people, beholding the real millennium of goods, rejoiced exceedingly (and smugly) upon being told there was at hand a similar millennium of the soul. The cloacal welter of evidence to the contrary was shushed up by a new set of fancy conventions variously called forbearance, tact, manners, purity, holiness, sanctity, tolerance, and so forth. Another batch of citizens walked out of the church when they were told they were whole. They knew it was a lie. Their archetypes

---

*Here is another example of the imperfection of my use of the psychodynamic method for making predictions. Since the oldtime religion (or something akin to it though even more violent) *has* come roaring back amongst the fearful, the unfree and the demented, the devil, too, has been restored. His breath smokes from the pulpit and sulphurs the revivalist tent. He is literally reincarnated over TV every Sunday. And the latter-day Satan has taken to politics: he is a Communist. If you don't believe it, tune in Bishop Fulton Sheen. The devil nowadays is also said to be allied with science and scientists, by some. As usual, he is closely associated with sex—and the recent outbreak of "sex fiends" resembles the proliferation of witches, centuries back. In fact, the new devil is linked with so many human activities that the pious, in an effort to put him down, seem to be preparing for themselves a license to commit all folly, all mayhem and every massacre of sanity.

What an odious spectacle it is for this century! And how little men realize that, when they set out to "get" Satan by stamping on other men, they become, not servants of God, but demon-worshippers and, themselves devils.

made it plain that nobody could be whole save for a minute at a time, and that emancipation of spirit is to be had only at the price of everlasting introspection and watchfulness. But it was a few who left the church. The remaining many turned it into something like the rest of their environment.

This amounted to a self-canonization of some thirty million people of the U.S.A. They are Right—and they do not hesitate to tell you so. Behind the mask of these good, virtuous, sacrificial and holy American people, instinct has gone on working exactly as it always worked. Men are murdered. Children are seduced. Public officials are corrupted. Thieves steal. Churchly men have invented forms of theft so subtle that the law has no means of detecting and punishing them. One I know, for instance, sold what he boasted was a mere nostrum and people who relied upon the nostrum died in hordes. The Christian was, of course, a mass murderer. But, under the new plan of accepted perfectness, his kind are not punished. They build fine houses and are widely respected.

The system spread from churches and into them. Greed, expressed as civic pride and municipal improvement, threw up the hideous and planless cities. Business was accorded a sacred right of secrecy. Men howled with wrath when any un-American finger of justice tried to point out the ways by which large corporations or unions of laborers had piled up fortunes. Lurching ignoramuses seized the benefits of science and administered them as radio companies or power and light stations, without any real knowledge of electricity, of the public, or of themselves.

On and on the negative instincts led the disguised chase. The practice of laws became in a large part the practice of concealing robbery. A business apprenticeship consisted in training a youth to be a Fagin. Even a doctor might be practicing medicine or he might be practicing any crime that suited him—for profit. The scientists hired themselves out to the businessmen and searched only those corners of nature in which lesser brains thought there might be quick money gains. A tradition of integrity in the central government for a time hampered the process of irresponsible acquisition, but men soon set about to put in the government persons whose identification with noble tradition would be less embarrassing. Eighth graders, with hair over their ears, gangsters, perverts, thugs, bullies and scumskulls of every sort, so long as they were either purchasable or preoccupied with some personal crotchet that did not interfere with the plunder of man by man, were recommended solemnly to the halls of state by big business leaders, lawyers, doctors, soldiers, and the rest of the blind and grabby retinue of people whom the church had blessed and confirmed as perfect Americans.

These unholy rascals died protesting their virtue and the vast benefit of their presence on the earth to other men. With blinders on their motives, seeking all pleasure, all luxury, and the avoidance of all pain, bent on piling up the profit that would make paradise purchasable, the American boosters, the sponsors of progress, multiplied confusion upon confusion until the tangle underneath their society at last turned even the external parts into a strangling boggle.

There was one curious though inevitable effect of the process. It consisted in the slow, unnoticed erection of a gigantic wall which the people of America were compelled to build in their minds to shut out the ghastly spiritual view. We have been thrust some ways around that wall now, into the midst of the most disastrous business man has ever engaged in. But high in the minds of most of us stands the wall, still: the wall which keeps us from seeing that the *reason* for our planetary paranoia lies inside each single individual—and not in the system. In the days before perfectionism, when the church still recognized sin, sermons were preached on the foregoing topic. They were personal and accusative. Like this:

You are to blame. You—and you alone.

You have made the choice of folly, along with the rest. You have built the wall that will not let you see the truth about yourself. You are the one who is good, complacent, a booster, and not a critic. But all the old archetypes are functioning. You know it, somewhere in the dark depths of yourself. Still you cower behind your wall, never facing the full and awful measure of your own greedy and sinister insides—insisting tediously on your perfectness.

You won't read the papers and collect in your mind the full pile, year after year, of each three hundred and sixty-five days' worth of human brutality, greed, stupidity, cruelty and barbarism. *You* will not allow yourself to realize that the Chinese burning alive in gasoline* in Nanking are your responsibility. *You* will not dare to think that you may be similarly consumed, but you may be. The screaming men who roasted on a tanker outside my door the other day may be you—should be you—*will be you*. Lustfully, you consume the news, printed and broadcast, of ax murders, kidnapings, drug addiction, police beatings, lynchings, stonings, riots, revolutions, battles, tortures, sodomies—lustfully, to satisfy the part of you behind the wall, which must be satisfied somehow. But this you never relate to yourself. Should an example of it actually touch your life, you will use your wall to mark off the example as an atrocious and wanton blow of meaningless fate. You do not see it as an ineluctable expression of the instincts you have said do not exist. But you are Attila. You are Salome. You are every man on every rack—every moaning and foaming gobbet of flesh in history—every good impulse and also every evil one. By denying the existence of the evil in you, you have forced upon it an autonomous existence and it has marched clear around the globe and it is ready to consume you.

Ignorance is not bliss—it is oblivion. Determined ignorance is the

---

* This reference is to certain atrocious Japanese methods of making war. Since I wrote it, of course, we have cooked a million or so Japs in napalm, which is a form of gasoline, and left some other thousands mere man-shaped carbon stains on radioactive sidewalks. These achievements make it even harder for us Americans to acknowledge, humbly, the terribleness we share with others. Indeed, most of us seem able to declaim brightly that atomic weapons "must never be used in war," without noting the eternally attached shadow: that they have so been used, and that we did it.

hastiest kind of oblivion. Yours is the most inexplicably determined in all the swing of the centuries. So your oblivion will be the greatest.* You who are worried about the possibility of socialist concessions in your precious capitalistic system would do better to worry about your chance of being alive at all. The blasting of Germany to defeat will not solve your problem. The bottling up of the Japs in their islands will not change the score. Peace will do nothing for you save to arrest, temporarily, certain specialized liabilities of sudden demise which threaten you and your family.

Only an honest effort to live in accordance with the choices you could make among your archetypal patterns will be of any use. Progress hardly exists. These are the beginnings of retrogression. Only you can stay it. And none of the values by which you have lived can be maintained if you wish to accomplish the deed. Man does not live by bread alone. And your anxiety has been entirely to get bread (or even stones) into the mouths of other men—at a profit that will keep you full of cake. It won't work. The pattern of nature, inexorably implanted in human instinct, completely expressed in thousands of years of legends, is the compelling pattern of existence. That is the raw material of yourself. You cannot omit any part of it from your personality with security, for if you do, that part will grow independently into a free-moving chaos and pursue you into hell. That is not merely conscience. It is the Law.

Our jungle is chrome-plated; there is no other difference. In the black dazzlement of it, let us next examine some specimens—one of a myth, one of an attitude, and one of an institution.

---

* A simple statement, derived from laws of cause and effect, not differing much from the thought that those who live by the sword shall perish by the sword. It was regarded by nearly everybody, a decade ago, as the author's "gross and unwarranted exaggeration" and an example of what *The New Yorker* called "tub-thumping." Several years later, the same journal published John Hershey's "Hiroshima," and nothing else, in a single issue——a very magnificent, if unwitting amends.

CHAPTER V

A Specimen American Myth

IN ORDER TO PERPETRATE UPON OURSELVES THE MONSTROUS half-consciousness by which we have been living, we have, perforce, developed bastard legends. These legends suit half of a human personality, most admirably. Their development, as such, was unconscious— for we chose unconsciousness by our act of spiritual self-aggrandizement and the repudiation of the dark half of our heritage. The phenomenon, to wiser and more detached observers than most of us, in itself supplies an amusing description of our fallacy. Like the worship of any false god, it reveals its counterfeit nature by what it omits —even though the worshiper chooses to regard it as whole.

The modern American, to express the bulk of the thought above in a single phrase, has rejected the critical method for himself. He applied it to ions and bugs. But upon the portals of his cities he engraved that limitlessly emasculating motto: "Boost, don't knock." No scientist could synthesize without first analyzing. But man believed he could promote himself all right by slapping together his activities without any criticism whatever. From that, one can deduce that his legends must necessarily have at least the appearance of being beyond criticism. They must have a perfection and an absoluteness which the hardier-minded peoples of the past were too honest to ascribe to their heroes and nymphs.

The brief discussion of the relation of legends to instinct in Chapter

46

IV and the note on the rationalization of our instinctuality, together with the sermon, were to prepare your mind and heart for some words on contemporary American myths and archetypes. Let us look at Cinderella.

In the original Cinderella story, the heroine was a slavey. She suffered the taunts of her gadabout sisters without complaint and stuck to her job. Her fairy godmother came along with a shoe that fitted, and the gal won the Prince. The philosophical notion behind that altogether solid story had nothing to do, really, with Cinderella's winning of the Prince. He was, in that sense, a mere symbol, as was his wealth. The story is an allegory for the idea embodied in the mythical jewel in the toad's head. It is a statement of the fact that out of the dross and discard of egotistical man may be plucked the real and priceless valuables of life. "The stone which the builders rejected has been made the cornerstone." The possibility of finding a worthy Cinderella *in that background* is the moral.

Not so in the magazine-movie-novel-radio version. Not so in the American version. Our rags-to-riches theme gives scant attention to the virtues rags may conceal; it deals mainly with the lucky escape from rags. The American version of the Cinderella story, retold ad infinitum in the magazines, by the movies, and on the radio, puts all its emphasis on the reward. Each story opens with our heroine having a hell of a time. Along comes the Prince. Fade-out.

Nor is any attention given to the second thesis of the basic Cinderella legend, viz.: that a Prince, wanting nothing but the best, searched long and ardently to find it, and at last discovered it hard at work in a homely environment—and *not* among the thoroughbred court ladies who presumably surrounded him. Those ladies, the legend implies, were hypocrites and uptown whores, gabbling twirps of the Social Register type, not worth the time of the earnest Prince.

But, as we have translated the story, the object of Cinderella is to get into the Social Register. Originally, she had no object whatever but to mind her business and perform her drudgery well. That was the point.

The error of our interpretation could be reduced to terms which I believe even a behavioristic psychologist might understand. The sex libido of the Prince (in the original version) was somehow attuned to integrity and a high sense of real values. He repudiated the court phonies and set out to find the McCoy. Eventually he did, in a lowly spot where hard work and unselfish devotion had made her into the sort of creature who would respond satisfactorily to the uplift urge of his conditioned reflexes. Since nobody wishes to be married to a brassy tart destined soon to turn into a vengefully destructive middle-aged harpy, it may be assumed that the conditioning of the Prince's reflexes would have enabled him to pass the aptitude tests of Columbia University.*

---

* Here and there in the ensuing text I made somewhat slighting references to Columbia University. Several hundreds of readers, not all alumni of Columbia by any means, have written to enquire what I have "against" that particular institution. In this case, as in others exhibited by my correspondents, is to be seen a very characteristic American infantilism: the identification of *any* slight or *any* criticism as *total* rejection.

Columbia has much to be proud of and I have nothing personal "against" the school whatsoever. I have never even set foot on its campus. I merely employed its name (as *most* readers appreciated) in a symbolic fashion. Through its Teacher's College, as everyone should know, Columbia has espoused (and nationally promulgated) the "progressive" methods of education, based by the late John Dewey on the notion that he, at least, was pretty much conscious of human motives —or, minimally, of a means to explore them with "laboratory" techniques. Dr. Dewey ruled out (and tediously scorned) any idea that psychological process might be largely unconscious, or that man might be motivated mainly by animal instinct.

Since Dewey is dead and his "method" is coming a more appalling public cropper every day (which, however, does *not* imply a need to return to the old methods he so effectively discredited) it may be some-

In the modern debauchment of this theme, the reflex of the Prince is not important. He is conditioned, presumably, to yearn for a gal, and that is all. Accessories to the yearn may be a dulcet voice, bright eyes, an acromegaloid chin, or what not. Mainly, though, he is a moneyed man who wants a girl to sleep with him under the legal aegis of marriage. The important factor to us is Cinderella's conditioning. It is decidedly *not* to go on dutifully sweeping the floor and carrying the wood. She is conditioned to get the hell out of those chores. There is, the American legend tells her, a good-looking man with dough, who will put an end to the onerous tedium of making a living. If he doesn't come along (the consumer must consequently suppose), she isn't just lacking in good fortune, she is being cheated out of her true deserts. Better, says our story, go out and make the guy. In other words, we have turned the legend backwards and our Cinderella now operates as her sisters did.

Of course, in spite of our capitalistic society, there are not enough Princes to go around—so most women actually must settle down to a compromise of major dimensions. That they will have to make such a compromise is not entirely concealed from them. But the American woman, after some twenty years of investiture in the American Cinderella story, is scarcely conditioned for the mathematical destiny to which reality must and does ascribe her.

There are as many effects visible in our society today from this fiction as there are people. We have enshrined, not the earnest search of the Prince, which is a positive force in the story, but the girl's reward. And we have turned over most of our fixed wealth to our women. Woman spends it. The absurd posturings of chivalry (and they were superficial, for the most part, in the age of chivalry itself) serve to bloat the nonsensical notion of honoring and rewarding women for

---

what unfair of me to let Columbia University stand here as a symbol for the exploitation of academic prestige in furtherance of manifest folly. So, if "Columbia University" offends you, substitute your own alma mater—or anybody else's.

nothing more than being female. Cash is heaped at the feet of the sweetheart, the bride, the wife, and especially "mom." Since money does represent a crystallization of human energy, this gave females an inordinate power. The church helped in the process, too, because it is easier, by and large, to wangle sesterce out of women, who usually have less sense and ambition than men, than to wangle it out of men, who often have ideas of what to do with money that lie outside those of the church. The women, demanding to be made Cinderellas, have seized the cash allotment and various agencies have helped them do it for various reasons.

Since wealth will purchase only material things and since the pseudo Cinderellas of the U.S.A. have come by a great bulk of the wealth, it is interesting to look at our material civilization from that standpoint. Woman is the biological partner who makes and maintains the home, supposedly. But she is equally susceptible with man to sloth. Science and industry, slavishly following the commands of her liquid assets, have turned the cities into exactly what one would therefore expect: (a) markets for home-consumed goods; (b) markets for the sale of goods to make home-keeping a minimal-cinch; (c) markets offering female vanity-goods; and (d) minimal-cinch homes.

A city is that. The proudest part of its proudest street is its row of hat, dress and department stores. Its best residential area, in the newer cities, consists of penthouses and classy apartments, where living for female adults has been reduced to its easiest form and, just incidentally, living for children is almost impossible. Around this area are miscellaneously scattered the factories which produce the things the women consume, and the abodes of the citizens not fortunate enough to live on, say, Park Avenue. This is a lazy female pattern. General Electric, General Motors, General Foods, Alcoa, and the United States government consult the female-demand pattern sedulously, and conform to it rather than to any other. The corporations turn the pumpkin into a Chevrolet. The government builds roads for it to palaces—movie palaces.

Another effect of the reversed Cinderella legend, which is nearer the heart of modern society than Christianity or science, may be found in escape. Unable to achieve any semblance of the legend in reality, women pursue it in fancy. This is why there is such a daily, weekly, and monthly infinitude of fictional production. A woman on the grubby floor of a three-room Oklahoma shanty can, through the so-called miracle of radio, and by means of projecting herself, enjoy vicariously the whole experience of Cinderella even though she is literally in the exact spot where Cinderella's story commenced and will never get away from that spot.

The moving pictures, through actresses, created another set of Cinderellas for the housewife—live women, hence more interesting than storybook characters—who were actually engaged in the business of marrying Princes, taking booty from them, living in palaces, and the like. The extraordinary popularity of the Hollywood "gossip" column and the "fan" magazines shows the penetration of this escape device into the mores and habits of American women.

Men also "escape"—although less constantly and generally than women. The unrealness and infantile unreasonableness of most wives is, alone, a sufficient cause for a wish to escape. The fact that men are, largely, engaged directly or indirectly in the fabrication of materials (which women will purchase) is another urgent reason for escape. Man, acting on an instinctual plane, will work his head off to supply necessities; he will work, too, to manufacture such luxuries for himself as he has the energy to contrive and such luxuries for his wife and his family as he feels are deserved by them on a real and not a Cinderella basis. But all the men in all time, working together with all their instincts and energies, would never, in realistically conceivable circumstances, have fabricated, say, a department store.

But work of any kind, even on women's goods and household nifties, is natural to man; the mere doing of it rescues him in part from the degeneration that accompanies everlasting fantasy. Man goes to the office and the factory. Woman, whose hands for tens of thousands of years never stopped tending babies, feeding fires, twirling flax, and pushing broom-handles, are idle, at last, by the million. If the machine age had emancipated those hands for some less trifling tasks, there would be no reason for this book and there would be no war. But the machine age merely cut off the hands. War is restoring some of those hands. If I were a labor leader, I would think hard about that. But, most likely, after the war the ladies will go back to their clattering cipherdom.

Woman as an idle class, a spending class, a candy-craving class, never existed before. Some women in the category instantly set out to compete with men in their own activities. The fact that many have succeeded does not, in itself, prove any more than the undeniable fact that many men have been able to give other men sexual satisfaction—an act admittedly the prerogative of women. After the original Cinderella was enthroned in the palace, it is doubtful if she set out to instruct the national courts, train the guard, select the priests, and reorganize the peasants. American women think they can do that. Perhaps they can. They have, merely, shown no sign of the possibility yet. With nine tenths of all females either escaping into imaginary Cinderellaism or trying, somehow, to become Cinderella, we have enough trouble on hand, without borrowing it from the future.

The idea women have that life is marshmallows which will come as a gift—an idea promulgated by every medium and many an advertisement—has defeated half the husbands in America. It has made at least half our homes into centers of disillusionment. It is as responsible for the absurdity of keeping up with the Joneses as the bare instinct toward conformity—because Mrs. Jones is trying to keep up with Cinderella. It long ago became associated with the notion that the bearing of children was such an unnatural and hideous ordeal that the mere act entitled women to respite from all other physical and social responsibility. Woman, indeed, has capitalized heavily on that theory ever since Cinderellaism and chivalry allowed her to conceive of it. She does so still, in spite of the fact that modern medical practice is able to turn most childbearing into no more of a hardship than, say, a few months of benign tumor plus a couple of hours in a dental chair.

The main waft of the current, gathering inertia from itself, pours over us all the mighty river, butterscotch on top, and underneath, sewage. Boating about on it is the child wife, the infantile personality, the woman who cannot reason logically, the bridge fiend, the golf fiend, the mother of all the atrocities we call "spoiled children," the middle-aged, hair-faced clubwoman who destroys everything she touches, the murderess, the habitual divorcee, the weeper, the weak sister, the rubbery sex experimentist, the quarreler, the woman forever displeased, the nagger, the female miser, and so on and so on and so on, to the outermost lengths of the puerile, rusting, raging creature we know as mom and sis—unrealists, all—flops in the impossible attempt to become Cinderellas, shrill ones, pushing for more yardage in the material world, demanding only that the men, obviously no Princes, at least make up in some small way by acting like Santa Claus who has become, also, an Americanized archetype.

Women possess most of the wealth. Most of the acts of man are performed to earn back some of this money owned by women—in order to give it to other women. A matriarchy in fact if not in declaration, America would do well to inspect its physical plant in relation to its imaginings about itself. Amazons might have piled into Manchuria and Ethiopia to stop the Japs and Mussolini when they could have been stopped by a few sharp blows. But Cinderellas, in our accepted, national sense, would never do any such thing. They would frown and buy new hats. They did. Their men did.*

---

* The state of America's "Cinderellas" has, of course, steadily deteriorated. To be sure, as they marry, they are getting out of the city into the suburbs. But they have taken along branches of their department stores; the drugstore has become a department store and so has the grocery, now called a supermarket. Alarmed research workers have lately studied the habits of Cinderella in the suburbs, in the Leavittowns, and so on—profiting, doubtless, from the path broken for them by the foregoing.

Mrs. Cinderella—*they* find, not I—is depersonalized and disindividualized. She regards her husband as possibly temporary and refers to him as "current." He uses similar terms for her. Marriage is regarded as a kind of musical chairs. The standard for the children of these couples is based entirely on things—gifts and gadgets; huge suburban toy stores help the Smiths keep up with the Joneses in this. Nothing—no *thing,* that is to say—is deemed "too good" for these overencumbered kids, often on their second mother or father, or even on new sets of parents altogether.

In these mechanized "developments"—where the only cattle are human but every abode is a ranch house—the intellectual norms are rigid. The principal norm is to be without intellect. Thinking, studying, serious reading, the arts, the pursuit of ideas are taboo; persons who engage in mental activity are regarded with suspicion, fear or ribaldry and treated with social exile. Conformity is the word for home; every critic or dissenter is invited to one party, only.

These growing hordes of suburbanites are church-goers and do-gooders who, nevertheless, have no theology, and mixed ethics—which is to say a notion that what serves their private ends is acceptable, however crooked, so long as they are not caught out. Their concept of "good" is congruent with the bodily well-being of themselves.

Cinderella, since the War, has tried in this way to make a package of herself—and to package life. Hence her outer aspect is neat, tidy, clean, attractive. But the families themselves (the research people find) are rootless, uneasy, emotionally insecure and without deep gratification. These wretched persons have reached the end of a Nineteenth-Century Utopian dream: they live in the true paradise of Economic Man. They do not know it, but they are the disturbed and disturbing proof that Marx was an ass and the gigantic upheaval in Russia is utterly in vain.

For it is not the package that needs (and always needed) attention. It is the content. Inside these Cinderellas, beneath the bright containers, a few residual juices of life remain (with vacuum all around) and these skimpy juices, upon the slightest heating from any emotional source, expand and often explode the whole.

The goal of security, seen in terms of things alone and achieved in those terms during the least secure period in human history, has predictably ruined Cinderella: she has the prince, the coach, the horses— but her soul's a pumpkin and her mind's a rat-warren. She desperately needs help.

CHAPTER VI

A Specimen American Attitude

THE ICONOCLASM WITH WHICH THIS BOOK COMMENCED, TO-gether with the subsequent sampling of a myth, an attitude (and, presently, an institution) may seem to the reader random and extremely arbitrary. But to bash all the phony ikons of Americans, and to examine all the myths, attitudes, and institutions which need overhaul, would take more books than have ever been written. Since, however, I purpose to suggest the entire galaxy is wrongly apperceived and idiotically revered, my method, perforce, is like that of the Gallup poll—a cross sectioning. And my literary technique is to invade the reader's feelings (his values) as much as his reason, which will be explained in due course—as to explain it beforehand would be to reduce the efficacy of another stratagem of mine.

It is my hope that the many-angled cross sections in the early portion of this volume will persuade the reader that his good opinions and right thinking rise in a large part from quicksand and that the dogmas and thoughts of some of his fellow men are even more ill-founded. Such a realization is disheveling. But the chaos of our society is the product of the dishevelment of our ideas; my disarrangements are to show the need for courageous rearrangements. When, later in these pages, such specimens of mental nonsense as I have elicited here are applied to sample types of American citizens, the whole purpose will emerge.

This chapter, dealing with a specimen American *attitude*, might well be borne in the minds of those readers who cannot retain more complex prefaces as the ideal illustration of the many ways in which we have deceived ourselves, rotted out our moral character, and very nearly wrecked what little subjective civilization our ancestors bequeathed us. It is ideal because it is typical and universal. It is ideal, also, because it discusses a body of grotesque and grisly bunkum which Americans accept as truth, honor, and nobility but which is really savage hypocrisy. I am going to talk a little while about sex. The American attitude toward sex is exactly that of priests engaged in human sacrifice.

Sigmund Freud, after a lifetime of purely scientific investigation, decided that the sex instinct was dominant in modern life. Other psychologists have been inclined to ascribe to different instincts a power equal to that of sexuality, but none of any merit has denied that the sex instinct is one of the three or four prime movers of all that we do and are and dream, both individually and collectively. These gentlemen should know. All others by comparison, are amateurs—and as a rule —prejudiced amateurs. With our national penchant for viewing the delay or diminution of an unwanted event as its negation, we have taken modifications of Freudianism as proof that Freud was a fool and evidence that the hard tasks he implied need not be undertaken. In spite of Freud's work, today as before, a State Department economist, let us say, and Westbrook Pegler, are regarded as authorities on sex the equal of any—though they would hardly be regarded as skillful surgeons. The analogue is, unfortunately, most accurate.

The subject of sex is still envisioned by the American public as one which belongs in the realm of private conviction rather than the realm of natural law (and, therefore, science). Freud's studies weigh, in the prejudices and vanities of the Iowa yut, with no more significance than the maunderings of a New Deal economist or the Catholic biases of Pegler. That is as if evolution, reproduction, instinct, morals, behavior, genetics, eugenics, and so on were as simple and trivial as flavor— as if an opinion on sex were like an opinion on vanilla, chocolate, and strawberry, and everybody had a right to his own, however inconsistent or chaogenic the aggregate might be.

Such is obviously not the case. To make it seem so is to frustrate a giant compulsion and thereby to drive it to autonomous action within the human mind. There it works blindly, against the proposals of men as often as for them—a raging torrent of reality denied and ignored. Our American way of dealing with it is comparable to pouring vanilla on the issue of a blast furnace. It wouldn't flavor the iron even if it weakened it, and it would certainly not turn the iron into ice cream.

We present ourselves to each other as the inhabitants of a highly continent society, monogamous, virginal to the altar, each bride and groom sworn to forsake all others, and one and all so delicately sensitive to the manifestations of sex that we arrest persons for going nude and teach our children about storks or flowers rather than people. Slews of our most highly esteemed men and women are constantly at work protecting the morals of the young. Numerous otherwise satisfactory men are thrown into prison for half their lives because of acts of coitus they performed with females under ages that vary from sixteen to twenty-one, in different states. What is called lewdness and salacity in various forms of art and literature are denied the use of our mails; the authors thereof are also occasionally jailed. Innocence, which, on examination, appears to be neither more nor less than ignorance, is everlastingly lauded by the populace.

Such is the iron ice cream. The man from Mars, looking first upon us, would doubtless decide that we were trying to do away altogether with reproduction. A second look might even convince him that our estate was so horrible as to make the move extremely sensible.

What we consider "morality" invades the waking moments of every life, ceaselessly, in all the above forms and in the form of countless other repressions. There is nothing wrong with repressions, ipso facto, so long as they are homogeneous with what is real. But America's sex repressions have little to do with what is real. Our very pretense of "virtue" is denied by the facts—for we are not continent, chaste, or faithful at all.

A recent survey of drafted men showed, for example, that more than three quarters of the unmarried men from time to time had sexual relations with females. That statistic, all alone, means that every human being in the United States who talks or thinks about the chastity of the nation is uttering or pondering the veriest bilge. There is no such thing; to think there is, merely makes a fool of the thinker. It is like the "curve" in baseball * which, apparently does not exist, or exists only microscopically. The facts could be easily demonstrated once and for all by science. But generations of sports writers would go on absurdly describing "curves," even if they were forever proven to be mere subjective crookedness.

In another survey, designed to show the relative chastity of American women, and conducted by a leading women's magazine, the results were so "appalling" to the editors that they omitted from the publication of the study all figures relative to female unchastity and marital infidelity—privately justifying the omission, I might add, by the fantastic statement that publication of it would have a demoralizing effect upon the young women employed in their own offices! Still—so many boys fornicate that the girls must.

There was until recently a notion current in the general population that prostitution had been wiped out in America. Its mass appearance in the vicinity of army camps has shocked those who believed in the alleged extirpation but they still contrive to spread the myth that the tramps reburgeoned with the Draft. Actually, not only is the vast majority of the men unchaste, and a large minority of the ladies, but America is overrun with whores and has been for the last decade and a half. Anyone who has read *Designs in Scarlet* knows this to be the case; any reader of that book who doubted its accuracy could have

---

* An extraordinary number of persons took exception to that innocent comparison. It is therefore pleasant to be able to report—it is a sign of *progress* to relate—that baseballs do curve, sometimes, a little, but that they do not and cannot "break." Thus science carries us ever onward toward basic Truth.

checked it by casual investigation. A study made in Chicago some years ago provided another true picture of Americans as feckless fornicators. All honest research reveals the fact. A recent public announcement of the FBI in Florida that 270 out of every 1,000 men in the armed forces had become infected with venereal diseases within a few months of arrival again makes clear (and ghastly, if accurate) how far our behavior exceeds our pretensions and how little we care.

An extraterritorial but encroaching sexual procedure is still further threatening the absurd images of those who believe we are sexually "virtuous." I refer to rape, legitimate bastardy, and so on, as practiced by our military enemies. If they win, of course, everything we know any meaning of will go by the board and all the pretty girls of America will be ravaged time without number, as well as many ugly ones, and some men. But, even if they lose the war, their doings in that field will enter into the body of the human race. We may be able to get the lecherous Japs out of China and wall them up in their islands. But we will not thus solve China's problem of their bastards.

In the case of the Germans, the problem will be even more astonishing. There will exist in the middle of Europe for the next few decades some twenty-five million men, at a conservative estimate, who have been taught to sow their seed in every female, for the greater glory of the fatherland. The impulse will not die with surrender. Matching them will be millions of German women trained to breed with any soldier, together with millions of other women—French, Polish, Czech, Russian, Greek, Norwegian, Dutch, Belgian, Yugoslav, and so on—who have been forced to marry German soldiers, or to sleep with them, or who have been pressed into the sex-service of troops and civilians, as streetwalkers and as stock for whorehouses. A German defeat will release them upon Europe, if not America. Presumably, the forced harlots will be repatriated; they will not fit into the prewar moral postures of their nations: harlotry is an easy means of livelihood and a habit difficult to drop altogether. It is my expectation that a collapse of Germany and its occupation by the troops of the United Nations will precipitate widespread rape of German women—an expectable, understandable gesture of revenge by men who were vexed at having their wives, sisters, and daughters dragged into Berlin bordellos while they were fighting for liberty.

The incalculable smugness of the American of this era is nowhere better illustrated than here. In the face of unassailable evidence of the rise of mass degradation and rapism upon the planet, our national reaction has been a half-doubting, half-face-averting, "Tchk!" Nobody has thought of the long-range consequences of the business— but the long-range consequences will have to be faced by us, if they are faced at all, and if they are not faced, they will work out their own effects upon the sexual and social attitudes of our boys and girls of tomorrow. Meanwhile, it is against the law to interfere, in Norway, if a woman screams at night.

Whoring, raping, and statistical unchastity may not be the proper introduction, for some readers, to my thesis that the U.S.A. is technically insane in the matter of sex. Let us, therefore, consider it from a more folksy aspect. Why is it that most of the young men, and *almost* most of the young women, have gotten to sleeping with each other in our land—even though our land pretends they have not? How did it come about? Where does it go on? Why is it that the average upper middle-class husband cannot honestly sign a certificate of his fidelity, and his wife, in a large percentage of cases, has kept her person no more "sacrosanct"? Why *are* we an unchaste nation?

The answer, in broad generalities, would include such statements as, first, we were never especially chaste as a nation, anyhow; second, *people* aren't very chaste and never tried to be, except in small groups with specialized religions; third, people who once had religious scruples against fornication have lost their morals, including all such precept; and fourth, modern enlightenment has made it clear to a great many persons that taboo systems, such as the Victorian, were the product of diseased minds, of toadies, and of cheats.

There is another answer, besides. It is simple truth to say that, in this year of grace, any couple with reasonable intelligence, a moment of time, a little information, and about two dollars in money, can cohabit the night long without serious danger of catching a venereal disease, even if the agent is present, and without fear of impregnating the female. Every self-determined holy man and woman in the country, and most of the mere macaroons, can protest from now to doomsday that our sex morals and our sex laws are contrived of higher necessities than those which have to do with the spread of disease and the production of offspring. The protests are witless, in the main. The bulk of our so-called morality is the product of the reproductive aspect of coitus and of its long-standing function as a spreader of germs.

The removal of those two imminencies automatically produced a new era in the life and times of man. Disease is still spreading and females are still being unwillingly impregnated, but neither is necessary any more. The effort of the masses to prevent their continuation grows more powerful with every hour. Its ultimate success is inevitable. Moreover, one is able to state, not as a prediction but as a mere assessment of scientific procedure, that the methods by which individuals can control reproduction and prevent the spread of disease will swiftly become simpler and less expensive. Hundreds, and perhaps thousands, of brilliant men are working on the proposition, which is far less complex than many they have already solved. In five years, or perhaps ten, your daughter, sister, mother, aunt, cousin or wife—in order to prevent conception and keep herself free from the risk of infection—will have only to swallow a pill, take a powder, or get a biennial hypodermic.

Some persons have envisioned this destined state as altogether charming. In *Brave New World*, Mr. Huxley foresees a terrestrial population which produces its new members in bottles and uses its sex function entirely for pleasure, promiscuously and incessantly, teaching erotic play to children, and discussing in crowds, openly, the bedroom proficiency of individuals, as if it were a public physical skill, like ice skating. Conveniently for Mr. Huxley, there is no family problem involved in his scheme—owing to the fact that people are bred in test tubes. And Mr. Huxley has ruled out the possessive instinct, so that there is no jealousy. It could be ruled out, of course (and often has been by many societies of people, such as the Eskimos), but it would take a bit of doing—from a puerile start such as our own.

Rather than a Nirvana of the future, the new condition in our life and times may be expected to produce a pseudo retrogression, at least at first. Through the mere reduction of the sex act to one of no lasting physical consequence, it will return the instinctual psyche to the ancient social condition in which man did not know that there was any consequence of coition but pleasure. An examination of primitive peoples unaware of the results from their love-making would, if I am right, give us a very considerable clue to the possibilities of society in the immediate future. Since this book is designed to state the problems —not a pap of quick solutions—a series of alarms to unheeded fires rather than an attempt to put them all out—I will not enlarge much on the above notion. But I should point out that the tribes which have not known that love-making brought babies and buboes practiced every form of promiscuity and polyandry, of perversion and diversion, of witchery and buggery, and rape as well, so that one may assume there is to be no ipso facto emancipation for mankind in his new-found freedom from unwanted sex burdens, but only another opportunity for him to use his head and a fresh, fancy chance for him to make a botch of things if he doesn't.

Certainly some discipline, if only an aesthetic, will have to be imposed by future counsels upon the sexual behavior of the people. It should be incidentally remembered, too, that the doctors who have sterilized sperm and germ alike have also stretched the life span, and in this new era (so close to us that our children may live it) a huge percentage of the people will be middle-aged and senile: sex freedom is going to involve millions of antique rips, rakes, and the like. That, in itself, is a rather odious picture. Possibly it will suffice to permit every degree and type of promiscuity up to the arbitrary age of forty and to insist on a decent semblance of monogamy, at least outside professional engagements, for those older. In actual present practice, marriage is the only remaining bulwark against promiscuousness, anyway —and it is full of leaks.

One thing is sure. The pulpit cannot beat prophylaxis. It failed to beat even golf. The age of innocence is done for.*

I can imagine that, on the less negative side, the new emancipation will have many benefits. If our species is strong enough to preserve the idea of the home through the transition period, future marriages will be founded on much more solid stuff than evanescent physical charm. The restoration of a naturalistic attitude toward sex will do away with much of our insanity and neurosis. It will satisfy the major part of the normal desire for sex adventure and novelty as well as normal sex curiosity and experimentalism at early ages, thus releasing (possibly for better things) stores of adult human energy now frittered away in the sinister monkeyshines that deplete the lifetime of the average American. It will also, of course, lower the enormous psychical tension that exists between the sexes in our present society and thus obliterate in part a polarized source of much libido. The result of that, in

---

* This passage, it ought to be remembered, was written long before the sensational appearance of Dr. Kinsey's first "report." At the time of publication, it was categorically repudiated by various persons who felt that the "unfounded and outrageous lies" here set forth would do "great moral damage" to myriads. Of course, Dr. Kinsey and the rest have since made it plain that the data offered here amount to understatement. Our sex manners are muddier than I said.

I am inclined to take a whimsical view of such castigation, however. So many people (often of such eminence) have said I did not know what I was talking about! And, now, it appears, what I then discussed (so very frequently) was what they *would be* talking about, come five or ten or fifteen years. There are many matters in "Vipers" (and in other books I've written since) which, up to now, have not yet been bruited about—have not yet happened—have not emerged, so far, as plain and horrid Reality. The same people, by and large, are saying these *further* postulates are—unfounded, outrageous, tubthumping, hysteria, lies, and the like.

I wonder.

turn, will depend upon circumstances now unguessable: it might break the grip of the matriarchy or it might have the opposite effect of replacing man with woman in the dominant position; it might lead to a fervent and expanding society, full of reason and warmth and humor; it might lead to a degeneration into a vario-sexuality wherein erotic play made no distinction between the sexes whatever. The ancient Greeks were headed toward some such condition shortly before their decline and there is evidence that America is approaching it, in the increasing numbers of bisexual persons.

In that connection, we might note that America is still populated largely with male ignoramuses who stand ready to slug nances on sight and often do so—and who know about female homosexuality only as a shady and inscrutable washroom joke; but there is, nonetheless, an ever-increasing practice of homosexuality through all the country. It is common in the navy, the army, and in colleges both for men and for women. Discreet surveys have revealed that a very large portion of the upper-class and upper middle-class citizens of the nation have made one or more experiments in that form of erotic activity. The same incidence is rising in other classes. Psychologists have shown that the urge toward the experiment is thoroughly normal in the young, although its continuance in maturity may be regarded as infantile. They have also shown that many of the men who are inborn sluggers of nances are motivated by a sense of shame and fear caused by the fact that they have engaged in lifelong psychological battles to repress and to conceal miscellaneous homosexual urges in their own personalities. They have further shown that the true function of the homosexual aspect of every personality is to afford a base for psychological projections which will make the opposite sex understandable. Such demonstrations make it clear that homosexuality should be dealt with as a type of behavior important in relation to private neuroses and the birth rate—and a subject to be implemented in child study and child welfare. To treat it as a fiendish manifestation, like ax-murdering, is silly.

Americans generally treat it like ax-murdering. To them it is horrible, repulsive, loathsome, and altogether beyond the pale of thinkability. The fact that it goes on all the time means only that millions of people have dangerously guilty consciences. However, a guilty conscience is the penalty not only of those whose sex impulses have led them to include members of their own sexes in their amusements, but also the penalty of most living Americans in the realm of sex as we exhibit it. A guilty conscience is a terrible peril to the individual; collective guilt is a profound and imminent menace to groups. Our guilt is august.

For, not only do we have the pretensions of sexual chastity I have noted, and, alongside them, a national conduct in no way resembling our pretensions, but even the literally chaste among us are not permitted to go or be anywhere in our society without suffering multiform repudiations of their continence. If they are technically chaste, they are surely intellectually as promiscuous as dogs.

Their subjective lives are not "protected." There may be a few sects somewhere in the mountains who do not look at newspapers or magazines or listen to the radio and are able by such negations to avoid the bulk of our mass subjective promiscuity, but even they cannot escape all of it. If we were to admit that we are a sexy folk, always coveting currently popular movie stars, frequently on the make in bush and juke joint, constantly slipping into the bedrooms of our neighbors' wives when our neighbors are away, everlastingly reaching in our automobiles, and generally behaving the way we do, there would be no reason for such writing as this. But few admit it and most of those who do so make the confession only to inaugurate some sort of reform. To the sex "reformer" nothing is pure; he is therefore the lewdest man of all and his gospel is his lechery in action.

While we have kept hidden from ourselves the nature of our actual sexual behavior, we have made an open admission of it, subjectively. On the plane of suggestion, we have, indeed, turned it into a sort of goad, and used it for gross commercial advantage. Too many people have howled about the exploitation of libido in the movies, on the radio, and in fiction, for me to do more than cite them in this connotation. It is presumed that human beings can stand the schism between legal reality and imaginative incitation—represented by civil law and moral precept in the first instance and by lusty screen and radio glamour in the second. They can't, of course. High school girls don't merely ape the dress of the movie stars—they kiss like them—and they try to have the same tawny, tangled look after they have been slept with. So also the matrons. So the men. Those who do endeavor to maintain the schism often end up, as might be expected, with schizophrenia.

It is in a less suspect field than those above that I would like you to look for manifestations of our hidden sexuality: the field of advertising. In another portion of this book I have written extensively about advertising—with which, in principle, I have no quarrel. I do not have any quarrel, either (in principle), with the kind of advertising I wish to discuss here—but only with an attitude of Americans which makes it possible for them to absorb printed reams of it without realizing that it is changing their standards, impulses, morals, and fetishes and without considering the danger of trying to live on in the wretched pretense that they are like their Calvinistic and Victorian ancestors.

Year by year, since my boyhood, I have watched with approval as advertising became more nude. I like women. I like nude women. And I also like pictures of them. Year by year I have watched advertisements become more "frank." I like candor. Some of them, it is true, have grown concomitantly more banal and some ever more misleading, and that has disgusted me; all of them stick to euphemism, which is maddening to any person of taste; but the idea underlying them grows annually more discernible even to the obtuse and it is an idea which would best be expressed, in that forthright use of the vernacular of which all advertisers are enamored, by this slogan: Madam, are you a good lay? *

---

* This commonplace phrase gained lasting currency among the ladies and gentlemen aptly named "hucksters" by Frederic Wakeman. I am rather sorry I invented it, however. For its effect on the advertising profession has not been to show them the psychological sickness

Nobody has yet printed those words above a full-color double-page spread of the naked head and shoulders of a lush young woman obviously in the clenched ecstasy of orgasm. But innumerable advertisers *have* printed the head and shoulders or the whole torso of stripped, orgiastic soubrettes beneath the statement that a given product has rendered them more kissable, engageable, marriageable, popular at parties, and in demand for moonlight strolls—or caused them to be okay in the matter of feminine hygiene, breath, armpit and perspiration odor, or made their hair withstand the male test, God save us, of "nasal close-up"—or brought a host of new swains to them because of neater techniques during menstruation—or taken them to house parties where they were, according to serial cartoon illustrations, constantly in the bushes with boys. The products have transmuted ten thousand wallflowers into passionflowers. Various medicaments, pads, pledgets, salves, gargles, girdles, rinses, soaps, douches, rubber devices, elastic undergarments, negligees, cigarettes, automobiles, house furnishings, washing machines, kitchen appliances, cosmetics, deodorants, perspiration arrestors, booklets of intimate advice, dandruff removers, and hangover remedies have dismissed these handsome wenches from states in which nobody paid any attention to them and prostrated them in the illustrated position of copulative thrall, with (or, so far as the reader can discern, without) benefit of clergy. Since the implied purpose of every syllable of such copy and every expression on the face of every

they bred by exploiting love and sex and the undraped shape in an anti-sexual culture. On the contrary—to judge from what I see in newspapers, stare at in magazines and sometimes glimpse on TV—if I did anything at all by the exposé, it was to show the hucksters clearly what they had been up to, more or less unconsciously. With the guiding light I gave them, they and their ilk have now turned every billboard and even kiddies' comics into peep shows. Furthermore, it is the upper half of woman, the infant's half, that has gotten most of their attention and I sometimes marvel how it is, with all these misdirections sprawled about, that the birth rate has risen so.

such model, photographed or painted, is to startle the woman reader into an inquiry of whether or not her body is thoroughly prepared and equipped for nonrancid sex service, the slogan "Are you a good lay?" is the real one.

I submit this argument as unanswerable and recommend to any person who demurs a rapid survey of fashionable ladies' magazines, all of which will display enough samples of the kind of ad under consideration to convince the most skeptical.

There is nothing wrong in the wish of a woman to become a sexually desirable object. It is, indeed, her first purpose. There is nothing essentially sinful in erotic activity for everyone. And there is nothing wrong in reproducing billions upon billions of copies of young ladies in ecstatic postures. Canny advertisers, aware that most of today's young women and nearly all of today's young men are affably on the make, appeal indirectly to that statistical situation rather than to the conventional assumption that we are a chaste people. Few of us who are more than thirty years old know anything about the sex mores of those who are younger. The automobile is, for them, a detached, portable bedroom. In it they consummate their sex necessities by what they call "petting"—still naïvely assumed, by older folk, to be synonymous with "necking," though Havelock Ellis had other terms for it. Here, once more, youth is in the lead of middle age—having outstripped it.

But the profit-crazed advertisers compound only the *subjective* urge to extend and multiply promiscuous activities. Males may develop a certain tolerance to the incessant stimulus of the billboards, magazines, and radio commercials. Their boiling point, to use an obsolete phrase, may rise. And girls, growing up in the presence of national advertising, may be able to preserve the idea that they are not expected to accept every offer of ecstatic frolic, or to take money for their intimacy, but they can hardly escape the massive implication that they are getting themselves ready for it by every imaginable stratagem and artifice on the counter, and that they will be expected to perform it with Jack, and probably with Bob also. They have always been getting themselves ready for love, but, until recently, it was at least sketchily presumed to be the love of one good man only, or one at a time. The new behavior, which is the inevitable beginning of the new era, demands a fresh attitude for everybody.

Other, miscellaneous subjective effects of the ads, car cards, and lithographs could be noted by the dozen. A man who is married to an ugly shrew, as millions are, today lives in a distracting world which presents all sorts of manifestly available lovely young things. A girl who has caught a dull or detestable husband must reflect ten thousand times that with a little attention to her "hygiene" she would have done better. So reflecting, she must be prone to change her brand and try flirting with the handsome bachelor next door. Thereafter, one thing—as humanity discovered ages ago—leads to another.

Although few will admit it, the pressure of so much abjuration to coition must and does produce a nervous sex urge in everybody; it also establishes an unconscious background of expectation, so that modern daughters may be found to be "errant" without being victimized by classical family shock, and the sowing of wild oats by sons is taken for granted.

The beauty of the ladies in the ads, and the handsomeness of the men, must also set up a gigantic store of insatiety. The fact that the very business of being a mannequin is an invitation to sexual frigidity and that numerous nances operate as male models hardly enters into the minds of the beholders, who are led to assume, rather, that excessive good looks are a necessary correlative of satisfactory love-making. That is an unhappy assumption, because excessive "sex appeal" is rare; it is also a dangerous one, because it lies so far from the facts of life.

The preceding examples are random, of course. They will suffice. The Cinderella myth insists that blank gorgeousness is the one essential attribute of a mistress, consort, weekend pal, wife, girl friend, fiancée, and automobile collaboratrix. In the real world of spreading promiscuity, both men and women will find out that a modicum of especial and highly personalized attractiveness, coupled with qualities like intelligence, humor, sportsmanship, sensitivity, imagination, and, above all, a variegated skill at the actual business of love-making, are far more to be desired for a night, a week, or a lifetime, than the possession of lavish looks, which in themselves are without any meaning.

If public opinion would allow the advertisers to employ this far more honest and worth-while presentation of the problem of how to be a good lay, millions of men and women would be made far happier and much less neurotic, almost overnight. To some extent, the radio, to a larger one, the movies, and, on occasion, magazines, by their fiction, have implied that a girl does not have to look like a Christmas tree ball, or a man like the latest model of a roadster, in order that they may enjoy being in bed with each other. But the advertisers have not followed suit. I have seen no copy along the lines of "Hips too broad? Yes! Complexion a bit sallow? And how! Too tall? Of course! But she's a dilly!!! *Why?* Buy one box of Sap's Super-Soap and read the amazing free booklet that comes in the box: 'Tom, Dick and Harry took Frances to Bed.' "

Nothing of that sort at all—though a national situation has been set up, by the expenditure of billions of advertising dollars, which makes such data a must, if we are to end an era of reckless insatiety and altogether needless frustration.

Let us summarize what I have said in this chapter, bearing in mind that my figures are carefully chosen from expert surveys, that I could add hundreds of tables to them, and that I could write books from my own direct knowing:

About seventy-five per cent of the unmarried young men of America copulate with girls. Of the adult, single young women, hardly half are virgins. Harlots are ubiquitous everywhere in the U.S. An appalling percentage of a group in Florida in the service contracted venereal diseases, mostly from whores, in a few months, showing the fornicatiousness of our males and the proliferousness of our tarts (as well, incidentally, as their frightful state of health, which is due entirely to our national refusal to admit they exist and, in doing so, to demand decent care for them). In about half of the world's densely populated areas, rape is now common, and enforced prostitution is the rule. If we lose the war, we know this condition will be universal. If we win, we will have to deal with the resultant moralities of whoring millions, though we have not even considered that fabulous inevitability. Americans were always a hell-for-women folk; all people are; religion has no longer a strong enough hold on the population to set up sex taboos in more than a fifth of it, at most; an enlightened attitude toward sex morality has, for many, relieved extramarital coitus of social infamy; and—more important—in sleeping even with strangers, people do not need to contract venereal diseases and women do not need to risk impregnation. On the subjective plane, the major media of articulation in the land implicitly admit our sexual gregariousness. Advertisers in those media tend not just to condone it, but to promote it directly and indirectly, in hundreds of ways. The eyes and ears of Americans are incessantly turned upon sex reverie and fetish with the purpose of selling goods. But the real effect, unweighed and largely unrecognized, is to sell mass-produced libido.

Such are the facts. The mere erotic inertia of ubiquito-copulation is daily increasing the numbers of the nonvirginal and reducing the numbers of the chaste.

The effect of wars upon chastity has always been known. That this one will accelerate the abandonment of chastity in those who still possess it is as certain as moonlight.

Homosexuality, a more infantile form of erotic exercise, but one currently regarded by the moralists as the most heinous, is increasing. The agglomeration of tens of thousands of men in camps remote from the habitations of women will inaugurate a new spread of homosexuality in America, as it has in every war.

Brothers, husbands and sons, good Americans all, are busy as I write these lines, in the number of thousands upon thousands, seducing high school girls, sleeping with married women whose husbands are at war, contracting venereal diseases from millions of whores and amateurs, and dubiously practicing pederasty.

In the presence of such behaviors on the part of the male majority it would be logical to suppose that the public attitude toward sex, sex acts, and even sex antics, would be different from what it had been at a time even as recent as that of the last war. Indeed, one would assume there would be a spirit of great tolerance, understanding, and compassion in America. One would reason that the scientific advances which can save the population from disease and mass bastardy would be in good repute and general application. The common people are usually sensible about their mere peccadilloes; toward behavior which has become customary, they stand as welded champions.

Here, however, no such instinctually sound procedure has ensued. The people, common or self-important, are engaged in a violent vocal repudiation of that which they are simultaneously engaged in doing.

Such a condition—a disorientation of the mind in relation to the realities of its environment—satisfies the classic definition of insanity. That is why I say that our sex attitude is insane. That, too, is the peril which I see in the whole business—a peril that far outweighs the danger of *any* change in our mores or any plague of illegitimacy and syphilis. Such plagues are, indeed, symptoms of the national schizophrenia rather than entities in themselves and a sane society would stop them in a month. Since we are very nearly totally (although not quite hopelessly) insane in as fundamental a matter as our sex behavior-and-attitude, it can easily be adduced that we are insane in such less comprehensible and more remote acts and opinions as those appertaining to foreign relations, air transportation versus land and sea transport, gasoline rationing, the four freedoms, and the metastatic psychic cancer of fascism. All of it is curable madness. But no madness can be cured except by a hard individual choice to face facts and to deal with them only as such.

We are terrifyingly far from that procedure even in relation to sex; the distance in relation to grim and subtler realities of this world is proportionately greater.

In our civilian life, we start teaching the no longer operative sex taboos of a dead age both at school and in Sunday School. The white in our flag is still presumed to stand for purity and it is given out discreetly that "purity" means sexual chastity, though it was Christ himself who pointed out that, to the pure, all things are pure—a proposition no longer comprehensible to the self-styled followers of Christ. Our Protestant churches, and, even more especially, the Catholic Church, devote an incredible portion of their political energy—perhaps most of it—to interference with the sex mores of the great non-Protestant and non-Catholic majority. Such religious enterprises are therefore essentially fascistic and in no way democratic. But it is a fact that no law which runs counter to the exact letter of medieval Catholic dogma can be passed in any of our states, and if a sensible law infringes on the archaic attitudes of Protestantism, it cannot be *offered* in a state legislature.

The church has stood, a rock colossus of bigotry, in the path of ten thousand proposed reforms. Sane efforts to legalize birth control, the dissemination of birth control information, the manufacture of proper birth control appliances, appliances for the inhibition of the spread of venereal disease, public instruction in sex hygiene, free clinics for the treatment of venereal disease, the inspection and treatment of prostitutes, controlled prostitution itself, the publication of psychological and physical sex information, aid for unwed mothers—myriad attempts by sane men acting sanely on real problems—have been fought down by church-frightened legislatures and church-dominated courts.

Personal hygiene is a furtive business here, still. Determination of the number of one's offspring is still everywhere illegal, though everywhere practiced. A nation overrun with bawds does not have laws to keep the bawds even healthy. The automobiles of America's millions of families carry their youngsters into the night across the land and so carry millions to copulation—but it is ignorant copulation, and produces the minor American tragedies attested by the prodigious busyness of America's abortionists, hospitals, and asylums. Too many juke joint romances are consummated in cars, trailer camps, motels and hotels without clinical supravention or subsequent access to neoarsphenamine or sulphadyazine. The church is responsible for this. Its hierarchy, like that of the battleship admirals, would rather lose the nation than yield an article of a code no longer pure, a faith no longer true. They are, indeed, of the same hierarchy—that of the Dark Ages. Neither can help it. Brains and opinions can be obsolete as well as machines. We can forgive the pontificators because they don't know what they are doing—but forgiveness for working these monstrousnesses upon us will do nothing to get us off the cross.

The cross itself, in fact—the gold cross of Christianity on a fine gold chain—hangs around the necks of thousands of harlots in the whorehouses of these United States and most of those girls are there not by coercion, as the lurid newspaper stories have it, but by lazy choice, since it is remunerative work and often fun. Many of them live with their knowing families, in off hours. No doubt, white slave rings impress innocent adolescent girls into whoredom. But far more get into the business by design, often after a considerable amount of industrious job-seeking.

These days, it is impossible to draw any precise line between socalled loose women and professional prostitutes; the usual standard for judgment is that a loose woman gives away permission of her person but a doxy asks something material in return for it; that definition, as has been pointed out, would include many of the respectable married women in the Social Register, as well as all the somewhat less respectable women who are not in it but bestow their favors for quarters, half dollars, hundred dollar bills, bottles of gin, and evenings at the theater—although they would unanimously bridle at being described as trollops and prefer such designations as grammar school kids, working girls, actresses, wives, and college graduates.

However, our churches, courts, legislative bodies, and the fourth estate take the attitude that, by and large, there are no such people, and no such things happen, in America. Each one of endless cases that prove the fallacy of the attitude comes to their attention only to be regarded as an individual abnormality. There is a definite reluctance to keep statistics of them and such statistics are always loaded against truth by prejudice and a wish to create a false but chaster-seeming impression. The home is supposed to be another bulwark of this hypocrisy. Statistics we do not gather would soon show what the home really is today—statistics of abortion, miscarriage, childbirth, disease, shotgun marrying, and so on. Those statistics, of course, cannot be got. The people lie because they have to. We, as a people, stick to our lip service of chastity and virtue and throw away our lives to prevent truth from revealing how we are living.

The drafting and examination of our males for military service has, at last, provided us with the evidence which makes any further deception doubly lunatic. We now know at least one large chunk of truth about males. But our military attitude, and the attitude of some men in medicine and government toward our soldiers, is still as fantastically out of joint as it was in the age of innocence.

Gene Tunney, director of physical education in the navy, who has a long record for unearthly abstract, recently published an article urging chastity upon the sailors as the only way of life. The article was full of preadolescent boyscoutisms as well as of bogies which described the horrors of venereal disease in terms that should have died out in the land, along with such beliefs as that vaccination would raise a cow's head on your arm. One of the quasi-official textbooks for recruits, widely sold to young men entering the army, and published by an authoritative press—a horrifying garbage of "old sergeant's" lore—contains such assertions as that, if the rookie is unlucky enough to contract a chancre, it may be seared away with a white-hot iron. I doubt that the army medical corps is using white-hot irons for chancres, but if it is—there is another reason for public panic.

The USO, a quasi-official organization, is also sanctimoniously set against coition for soldiers, and goes to lengths to prevent the unsupervised contact of uniforms with dresses which are not just ridiculous, but a coldly passionate insult to the dignity of merely being human. Mature men are invited to the various social activities of the USO in great numbers and then exposed to female companionship under the scrutiny of everybody from tigerish viragoes to military police. They are allowed to dance the dainties about, to be teased and titillated, and then they are scourged into the night alone, as if they were vermin. A sullen, degraded, and obscene reaction to such an unconscious attitude—which holds women out as fetishes but not as people—is inevitable in a large percentage of the troops thus repeatedly provided with a feast of papier-mâché victuals.

The fatuous over-all attitude of the American public toward soldiers seems to be that they long for the companionship of women in crowded places and have no desire to encounter a woman alone under any circumstances. Possibly there is something mysteriously unique in my experience, but I have entertained scores of soldiers, sailors, and marines—privates and officers—and talked to hundreds—and I cannot recall even ten, offhand, who were not actively preoccupied with the purpose of finding a "dame." There was nothing platonic in the predilection of any of these men.

The huge military and naval establishment which sprang up in South Florida presented an illustration of the dismal gulf between American behavior and American pretension, which I had anticipated, and about which I had prophetically written, even before we had assembled much of an army. Florida provides an abundance of whores for its winter visitors and the delectation of its year-round residents. To them were added other thousands who arrived by train, trailer, car and airplane. Unfortunately, Florida's public health system is one of the most wretched in America, as I shall show elsewhere, and few of the whores in Florida have been inspected or had medical care. The appalling rise of venereal disease among the troops in the state is proof of the filthy-minded unrealism of the right-thinking citizens of Florida. Their see-no-evil attitude has spread disease through the general population until a soldier is hardly safer in bed with a banker's wife than with a tramp; only the very highest priced doxies in the state ever attempted to keep themselves clean—a measure, in their case, necessary for the quality trade.

Soon after the great establishment began to root itself in Florida, army and navy officers, alarmed by the venereal rate among their men, demanded the iron-clad closure of all houses of prostitution. The civil government did a fairly good job of padlocking bordellos—reluctantly, since the annual fines are a fat item on civic budgets and the graft keeps many solons in high tax brackets. Some of the girls were rounded up and actually shipped out of the state. Most, however, vanished in the tropical evening and set up business as streetwalkers. They reduced their prices, accommodated more men to make up the deficiency of income, and spread disease faster than before.

The men were then confined to areas. Military police swarmed in the streets at night, poking couples out of sand dunes and clumps of hibiscus. The girls took to attaching themselves to indigent families and entertaining soldiers as visitors, old friends, and relatives. Increased military heat scourged unwilling civil police; monastic regulations began to tell upon the professional trade—and also, of course, to sabotage the morale of the men by compelling them to live like penitentiary trusties. Then a new problem came into being—a new one, but one that is also very old. The gentlewomen of South Florida began falling ill with syphilis and gonorrhea. Police began to notice, also, a curious phenomenon: late at night, and on into the early hours of morning, swarms of school girls, some as young as twelve, were seen skulking about the edges of public parks. It was soon found that these children were prostituting themselves in large numbers to the soldiers and sailors—for very small sums of money.

A curfew was put on female minors. A curfew was put on bars, night clubs, liquor stores. The prostitutes were shipped away by trainloads. Suspects were jailed, fined, exported. Tens of thousands of men found themselves, presently, living in the midst of a paradise, a glamorous Valhalla, without any women. Although Krafft-Ebing could accurately predict the consequences of such a situation, no hypotheses will be necessary, because the consequences are going to be realized by living men—tens of thousands of men who came out of a society that was not accustomed to chastity—and who are having it thrust upon them by the congress, the surgeon general, the officers, the church, the courts, the newspapers, and all the other exponents of the great American hypocrisy.

Dr. Hugh Young, the Johns Hopkins urologist, was among those scientists whom Pershing appointed to handle the problem of prostitution for the American troops in France in the last war. Young's reports are available to any American who cares to read them. No attempt was made to stop prostitution. Every effort was made to inspect and treat prostitutes, and to keep them segregated and under observaion. Prophylaxis was compulsory. (Better clinical methods are available for the same procedure today. Men and women with syphilis can rapidly be rendered noninfectious. Most cases of gonorrhea can be cured easily in a few days. Proper caution, exercised immediately after coitus, can prevent all venereal contagion in the great majority of cases even when the infectious agent is present.)

Stations for prophylactic treatment have been set up in our modern army. They are good only if the men use them. But, even with the relatively imperfect state of clinical and therapeutic procedure of 1918, Young was able to report that his methods reduced the incidence of venereal disease among American troops to a point lower than it had ever been among any comparable group of *American civilians.*

Such rational solicitude for American prostitutes would have an even better result today. If, in addition, a periodic inspection and licensing of the men were required before they were allowed access to women, venereal disease in the army, navy, air force, and marines would virtually vanish—and in a matter of weeks. Nowadays, any girl or woman who decides to have an affair with a man who has been in the armed forces for any length of time is taking a not inconsiderable chance of exposing herself to infection. Tens of thousands of women, sleeping with their own husbands on furlough, run this chance. That is not an opinion but a statistical fact. A program we would set up automatically to stop chickenpox would stop syphilis and gonorrhea. There is no such program. There is no intention of having such a program. It may be that America will never be able to institute such a program.

Why?

Because, to do it, we would have to admit—all of us—publicly and honestly—that hundreds upon hundreds of thousands of American flowers of womanhood are whores. And that millions of noble American men get in bed with them—married men as well as single men and the old as well as the young. As Americans, we are unwilling to admit the existence of even one whore in our particular town; when one is found, we self-righteously hunt her down as if she were a cobra.

I submit, then, that our national attitude toward sex—which I wish to have you consider merely as a specimen of many similar attitudes—is so disoriented, so unreal, so prejudiced, and so wishful that it is not an attitude at all, but a hallucination. The mass hallucination of a whole people who have been hypnotized during their youth into believing the realities which they *know* are still, somehow, untrue—hypnotized by various good-sized, ruthless minorities whose life as organizations depends upon the maintenance of the chimera, even though the illusion may lead us all to dissolution.

It is considered sophisticated to regard this situation as funny. The violence it does to our moral integrity is largely disregarded. The relationship that its hypocrisy may have to the establishment in the minds of Americans of other great and equally paralyzing hypocrisies is not understood.

On our mantels reposes the most horrible of all family gods: the squat little monkeys who see no evil, hear no evil, speak no evil. Their worship is the deliberate espousal of outer darkness, the admitted will to risk being cast into it, and the identification with monkeys of the Father, Son and Holy Ghost. If we pay for our refusal to reckon with the facts of life by having them stabbed into the bellies of all the women of America by the Nazis and the Japs the price, in the fierce accountings of natural law, will be the right one.

At the other extreme, if our attitudes became realistic and our motives honest, we would soon exorcise from humanity the beast our own beastliness unchained. Man evolves upward to new verities. We stand in the presence of new verity for our libido and our erotic behavior. In the days when we could understand neither, and control neither, we were forced by our vanity to pretend to understanding and control. We therefore invented the laws, rules, superstitions, taboos, dirty names, repugnances, and secrets. Reality has swept away the need of them and even the vanity that begat the need. If we seize upon it, we can remove the fetid incrustations of ages from our sexual instinct; we can clean our bodies; and we can discover a more honest principle for love, emancipating it from its foul present place in morals, and ourselves returning to morality with the passionate earnestness which true morality demands. If we do not, we shall destroy ourselves, because we shall have chosen to be mad.*

---

*Since writing this chapter I have, among many other activities, spent a great deal of time in psychoanalysis. One of the reasons for so doing was a deep, intellectual curiosity concerning the process itself and any possible enlightenments in the process. (My report on that cannot even be summarized in a footnote and will eventually appear elsewhere.) But another reason, perhaps, arose from this chapter.

So many said, on reading it, that I was nuts, as to make me consider their claim gravely—and do what I could about it. . . .

Looking at the foregoing diatribe in a post-analytical fashion (with, that is, some Freudian insight into myself) I can see what my accusers meant. The perturbations of the American libido themselves perturbed me, unduly, it may be. But such new insights as I have gained—whether from analysis, Kinsey, or mere aging—are of only personal advantage. They by no means tend to persuade me that our national attitudes toward sex are any saner or wiser or safer than I said here.

I now feel that most of us have *already* "chosen to be mad"—that the choice was first made by our ancestors, long since—and that the recovery of our mental health will be a far more difficult task than, say, the fabrication of every single material item in the land—and that it will take longer.

CHAPTER VII

A Specimen American Institution

Lux et veritas. light and truth.

The school, excepting for its sedulous care in teaching the basic principles of the physical sciences—interesting, necessary, and pertinent though they are—is the instrument of stupidity and lies. Just as the church is the repository of man's instinct, including by fiat his sex instinct, which neither man nor the church knows what to do with, so the school is the organ for promulgating the secular traditions by which man has tried to compass and codify his instinct. He has always made the attempt, so far, through organizations rather than through individual effort. It is a pity.

The school is an organism which teaches reading, writing, and arithmetic. It does that so the pupil can communicate. These accomplishments should also be taught so the pupil can *think,* but few schools have stumbled upon that notion of education. A thinking child would not think much of school—which would upset the system. The next step in school procedure is to teach the child political geography. A notion that political geography is permanent is imbued in the pupil —though how that can be done these days is more than I know.

Thus, to the average product of the little red schoolhouse, or the big cement one in the city, the boundaries of Oregon are important and permanent—congruent, approximately, to the Atlas Mountains.

Here the sinister process unfolds. The Atlas Mountains are real.

Only the ages will change them—by erosion. But Oregon is a myth. It does not exist. Temporary posts mark its border—but even its border was once uncertain. Its size was once different. Oregon is only an idea. It is in no scientific sense a reality. Revolution, a referendum, or enemy action could change the shape of Oregon, the color of the people in it, its name, and its nationality. There will only be an Oregon—just as there will only be an England, in spite of the song—so long as a group of people are agreed to keep in mind that the name of a certain arbitrary area on the surface of the earth is Oregon, or England.

In Oregon (and Massachusetts, and Texas, for that matter) they will tell you that Oregon is a lot more. They will say it is a tradition, a way of life, a kind of people, an accent, or apples in the midst of a dank west coast morning. They will give you all sorts of arguments to prove that Oregon is *something*—besides an idea. But it isn't. You could replace all the people and still call it Oregon and all but the people who were dispossessed would agree it still *was* Oregon. Oregon, then, is a dream.

So, for another example, is a dollar bill. A dollar bill is nothing in itself. The idea of a "dollar," in fact, is nothing. Once, it stood for a certain part of an ounce of gold. Then the rules changed and you could no longer get gold for it. Its value was recently decreased from one hundred cents to fifty-nine cents. The "worth" of a dollar is, therefore, unstable and subject to change. The dollar itself is a piece of paper with silk threads in it and ink on it. No more, as such, than the wrapping of a cigarette package. A Confederate dollar, which once bought things, won't any more. A dollar is also a dream—one that exists only so long as men agree that it exists. If men even argue about the value of a dollar, its value changes.

It is not necessary further to elaborate that idea. But *how many* similar concepts have you, as a school-taught American, misidentified in your mind? You do not know.

A few years ago the American "intellectuals" (again a dream—this one, their own) turning from a futile bout with what they called "humanism" fell with glad cries upon semantics. Semantics deals with meanings. It is no wonder that the intellectuals, having thought so hard and written so much only to find tenet after tenet as carefully explained by themselves collapse in the face of reality, should suddenly decide to delve into the meaning of meaning. It is no wonder, either, that, having exhausted the superficial illumination which flows from the study of semantics, they did not pursue it back to the origin of all meaning, and find it in their own internal struggles. Such a step would have demonstrated that, in the real meaning of "intellectual," they were using *their* intellects for nothing more than antique theological rhetoric, dressed up as "science." The intellectuals have a spiritual wall against that shock which is easily as thick as the wall in the minds of the godly.

But even a superficial understanding of the meanings of words is a help toward thought. This applies, especially, to words like "state" and "dollar." *

Children should be taught above all else to make the simple distinction between real objects and arbitrary ideas, between real laws and mere opinions, between facts and mere rules or prejudices. They are not, of course, so it is almost impossible to find an adult whose mind has escaped from the vise of the institutional method of our schools. You may not find it hard to apperceive that Oregon is nothing, outside the heads of men. It will probably be more difficult for

---

*It was obvious to numerous readers of this discussion that I had not made myself familiar with semantics, that I was ignorant of Korzybski and Hayakawa and the rest. At their suggestion, I have made my way through some dozen or so books on the subject and so become aware that this field of "meaning" has been explored by men better qualified than I. And, while I emerged from my perusal with an assurance that semantics does not, as Korzybski thought, connote a philosophical system, I do appreciate it as a great, new instrument for reasoning. It will be a long while, however, before many people—even many teachers—come to see how badly their rigid symbols have bolted their brains together.

you to accept the fact that a dollar, too, is nothing except a loose agreement between people. You will be likely to quibble about it. (A dollar may change in value, but there has to be *some* standard; there has been money, even for exchange between savages, for ages; etc.) But if I were to suggest to you that no fact whatever was *necessarily* described by the following words, you might be even harder put: murder, vice, holiness, courage.

Nevertheless, that is the case. Your idea of each is, in fact, your own. You have not added much to them; perhaps you have taken a good deal from those concepts as they were originally given to you. But the original gift was crummy, for nobody told you those things were all opinions.

The little red schoolhouse would scarcely hand out for a school lunch an allotment of sandwiches, half of which were poisoned and none of which was labeled. Of course, owing to greedy boards of education and stingy or stupid lunchroom managers, school children are often served sandwiches which contain metallic poisons, botulus bacilli, and so on, and the tots die. But the schoolhouse *is* engaged in the steady business of passing out information, part of which is poison and part food, but all unlabeled. Half the people in hospitals are insane —the people who got the poisoned sandwiches. The rest of the people, sick from lighter doses of the red schoolhouse toxins, are trying to carry on the affairs of a great republic. A pretty sight, you must admit.

The kids are dosed and overdosed not only with opinions stated as fact but with opinions that are cockeyed and fact that is deliberately made into falsehood.

The teaching of history, for instance, which begins in the sixth or seventh grade, is a shoddy performance and all educators now alive should, in fairness, be given the noose and faggot for it. I don't mean, merely, such rubbish as George-Washington-couldn't-tell-a-lie, but the whole subject. Ancient history, dehumanized and fumigated, is proffered as a rote exercise in place and ruin identification, simplified battle plan, and old law. One long look at the murals of Pompeii would teach more ancient history than fifty years in such a classroom.

American history of the school brand is a disgrace to the human cerebrum. It is taught as if America, an infallible nation, rose through heroism from dire persecution, with a shining and untarnished escutcheon. This is not the stuff to give drips, because it compounds drippery. In the first place, its inhuman excess of virtue makes it unreal and thus very dull. In the second, it in no way educates. To the mind of a future voter, the contents of a school history book are about as valuable as a knowledge of all the formulas for all the emetics in Christendom. Think, for a moment, of a few of the facts.

America was founded by a multitude of discontented colonists and a handful of well-intentioned men and women who took advantage of a European war to free themselves of taxation. It was partly a godly land, but in larger part, a slave-trading, rum-tippling, whoring melee of lawless opportunists who couldn't get along in a more conventionally organized society. It stuck together because a few men with a few ideals, wily compromisers who failed to compromise, were backed in a civil war by the industrial half of the union against the agricultural South. In the American Revolution, our book-vaunted militia broke and ran a dozen times from Hessian mercenaries and British regulars. In the civil war, our record of graft and bad generalship, of draft rioting and governmental mismanagement was unparalleled.

The conquest of the West was, again, the most brutal, brawling page of exploitatious and irresponsible rapine yet written by any nation upon its own population. Just in the process, a whole cross section of ethnology was pushed off the map: the Indians.

Our part in the First World War might have been considerable— and costly in human lives. It was not, many though our monuments may be, and the multitudes of men who came back brought from the whole of Europe one idea that topped all others in spread and repetition: that the French were sexually perverse.

We, who high-hat the British for their Empire, have already taken the empire of a hundred whole nations of red men, together with assorted chunks of sod we lifted from Spain, Canada, France, and Mexico.

Such are a few of the nonglorious pages of history. Taught truthfully, they might startle the moppets into an effort to improve a society plainly in bad shape. They would give no smug sense of national grandeur and security. We need leaders to reform our world—but reform begins with evil seen—and not where the teacher and the book point only with perfect pride.

In these days of war, patriots are busy saying that the "debunking" which has been modestly attempted in the last few decades has so soured and spoiled the souls of the young that they have no patriotism at all, no eagerness to die for their land, and no earnest will to fight for freedom. Of the young now soldiers, there is no use to speak. They no longer have any choice. But the indictment squarely fits millions of civilians. It fits not because of honest iconoclasm, however, but because of the failure of everybody—the educators, the intellectuals, the debunkers, and the sleazy people themselves—to hunt up and substitute real values for the false ones which were taken away by the debunking.

Such, of course, is the "practical" danger of teaching history as our schools teach it: somebody will come along and kick the props out of every lesson, leaving a vacuous lot of routed thumb-suckers.

Somebody has proved that Washington chased women and Grant was a drunk, that Lincoln told dirty jokes and that there was no Betsy Ross. Where, then, are the young minds? Busy in war—without reason, anchor, philosophy, introspection, knowledge, integrity, faith, hope, code, or even sanity—fighting because Mr. Whiskers makes them do it—with a vague and moody hope that somehow, someday, things will be better—and everybody will be Cinderella or the Prince and eat candy always.

The most Lethean error of the eunuch moms who operate the little red schoolhouse for the politicians has been to forget death. Death is implicit in what I call integrity and what others call honor or even just responsibility. Death is not merely an industrial hazard or the result of careless driving. During the first half of our national existence it was apparent that demise in war was a social function and the sterner schools of that period taught the fact. Custard-like thinking, quibble, and the nature of momism have wiped the bold and bloody axioms from the slates of the youngsters. Japs, Germans and Russians are taught they may die for their respective countries. The Chinese are always decently aware of the imminence of death. The English, even lately, have entertained a dim realization that extinction was possible.

Not we. Dying for liberty, for an ideal, or for any other sound reason has no place in our curriculum. It is, to American moppets, the romantic, exhilarating and obsolete activity of a group of ill-housed, ill-fed and ill-clad people who once lived in this country, fought amid its unlumbered regions, and were called patriots. No teacher, for the past generation, has greeted her roomful of fresh young morning faces with the words: "It is almost inevitable that a goodly proportion of you will die for your country; arrange your thinking to suit that fact." Such a greeting would have done wonders in sobering the radio-movie-comic-strip minds and helping them to put first things first. A kid who grows up thinking he may be knocked off to maintain the public franchise maintains that franchise while alive—or is likely to try to.

But the Americans who went to the last war didn't consider dying. They sang about coming back. And those who are girding themselves for this one still hope and believe that by some miracle it will be over before any large-scale perishing takes place. Moreover, since they were reared without the background of necessary risk, they lack the emotional foundation necessary for the maintenance of ideals in the face of confusions, arguments, treacheries and follies. No effort has yet been made either by the government or the schools to re-establish that foundation; the churches have made an opposite effort; science is still too rudimentary to comprehend the need of it.

The result is that we are asking our men to fight for what they regard as antipathetic attitudes, in hundreds of thousands of individual cases. They believe they are being forced to fight to maintain the New Deal, or to pave the way for socialism, or to keep Roosevelt in office, or to create a militaristic nucleus which will later become a political bloc, or to save the British Empire, or to settle remote and irrelevant European quarrels, or to establish new and arbitrary rights for labor, or for any other of a dozen such ideas. The grisly corruption of labor, the indeterminate international outlook of the British leaders, the actual remoteness and irrelevance of numerous European squabbles, the occasionally rancid political history of army veterans, the many sophistries and casuistries of Roosevelt, and the unrealistic diaperism of much of the New Deal are not, and will never be adequate reasons for dying. They are merely fine reasons for political argument and heavy balloting.

None of them, unfortunately, has anything to do with the reasons for which we are fighting—reasons which ought to make every American ready to risk his life without hesitation. We are fighting because we have the best way of life yet learned by mankind and we want to preserve it. We are fighting because a couple of hundred million mechanized atavars have sworn to murder and enslave us. Those are the two existing reasons. There should be another: we should be fighting because we have the intelligence, will and dignity to sacrifice ourselves whenever mass retrogression threatens numbers of our human fellows. The little red schoolhouse never taught the last thesis and it has overlooked the preceding two for so long that our adults cannot discern their own interests any more. They will have to learn the hard way, now: by doing.

Small wonder we have no battle-cry or battle song—for this one! *

---

*Although World War II continued for more than three years, no noteworthy songs ever emerged. The ballads of World War I are, today, more frequently heard. The songs of the Second War were weak and dependent (God Bless America), fatuous (Praise the Lord and Pass the Ammunition), feeble-minded (There'll be Bluebirds over the White Cliffs of Dover) or childish in an effort to be martial (Off We Go, into the Wild, Blue Yonder). People frequently think that *post*war songs were written earlier; they tend to identify the lovely, romantic music of "South Pacific" with the unlovely facts of, say,

Our history is every human history: a black and gory business, with more scoundrels than wise men at the lead, and more louts than both put together to cheer and follow. This is the most moral war man every engaged in; and we have not enough moral sense left to see it.

I might say here, before we get deeper into this deep business, and while we are on an erudite subject like education, that I could fill this opus with asterisks; under the asterisks in small type I could quote a slew of cross references and supply recondite confirmation for each fact. That kind of business, a literary loading of the dice, is not germane to my method. If names come in, they will appear in the large print.

This aside on source references will serve, in connection with the discussion of schools, to introduce the name of Dorothy Thompson, one of the great she-sachems of the intellectuals. She has the virtue of being exceedingly earnest. She has had several sound, workable ideas, mostly of a retributive nature. She has the additional nuance of knowing always, in a superficial way, what she is talking about, and even that is rare in women. But she has the handicap, like any average product of modern educational methods, of not knowing *why* she talks about anything at all, or why anybody does what anybody does. She can answer the routine questions of who, where, what, when, and how. But when you ask why, she talks gibberish from the book.

"The three main props of western civilization," writes this precious example of what I'm discussing . . . "Christianity, Rationality, and Organized Law." There, forsooth, is the little red schoolhouse talking! If these are, in truth, the props of Western society, then Western society is done for. They *could* be. They aren't.

I have pointed out that not half the population belongs to a church. I shall later show why not one church member in ten thousand has

---

Guadalcanal. As the evils of Europe have been expunged and we have become friends with the Germans——so the dreadful combat in the Pacific has been Michenerized. Korea produced no music I ever heard of.

the faintest idea of what Christ was talking about. Our civilization, as this book is designed to demonstrate, suffers from *not* being rational and from not knowing that it is *irrational*. As for "organized law," whatever that is, there is no longer much relationship between our law and what we already admit about ourselves and there is no organization of the law, to speak of, whatever. Besides, law, in point of usefulness, exists only in so far as it is enforced. If American law or any other sort is enforced here, then, all these years, my nine senses have betrayed me.

The little muckers dawdle through school, getting such ideas as that our society is Christian, rational, and our law organized. They grow up and believe them. Then, whatever happens, they assume it is divine. Such is the teaching of fact and morality. Consider the teaching of art.

English literature (an art) is rubbed into the human American hide by the school as if it were a hormone salve. The friction continues after the grease has disappeared and the hard palm of the teacher goes on chafing until not one graduate in ten thousand, to employ again a useful and conservative figure, gives a damn for reading all the rest of his life. Pulp fiction, yes. But real reading—no.

We are a "literate" nation. But there are not a million adults in America today who could comprehend even this casual treatise. There are hardly a million who voluntarily read nonfiction books.

That is a satisfactory comment on the educational system, from the standpoint of the essayist. It shows that, in the matter of teaching English, either our schools are incompetent to deal with our moppets or else society has produced a gaggle of Dodger fans, impervious to any literary schooling.

English, it happens, is our only common means of communication. A recent scientific study of "successful" business and professional men has shown that the graph of their vocabulary parallels the graph of their success, but bears no relation to the amount of their formal schooling. From that and other abundant evidence it may be assumed that the English a person knows will have a very direct relationship to his success as a person, his usefulness to the state, and his peace of mind and pride of being.

The way to teach English would be to divide pupils by aptitude rather than by age, to insist on grammatical precision from the start, and to see to it that errors in grammar and in usage, as well as vocabulary failures, brought punitive deprivations. Rewards would not be made. To reward a child for the performance of a duty is to corrupt it with Cinderellaism. Life holds no such rewards. The first gold star a child gets in school for the mere performance of a needful task is its first lesson in graft. Discipline is essential. A man clumsy in syntax cannot express himself. A man ignorant of terms cannot learn anything.

Children who are unable to learn or who will not learn the exact use of the only tongue in which, probably, they will ever try to articulate their ideas should not be permitted to listen to radios, go to movies, or otherwise amuse themselves with the ideo-onanisms of our society. If this restraining practice is instituted early enough and sternly enough—if it is attended to at school and followed up at home—most youngsters will by the age of twelve have a sufficient sense of ease and confidence with their native tongue to proceed more or less of their own momentum in the employment of reading as a means of self-advancement, an augmentation of consciousness, and an interesting pleasure. The rest will behave foolishly all their lives, vote badly, risk wars, aid the unscrupulous, and so menace your peace, health, safety, and life.

There is no way to pound such an exacting skill as reading into the brain of the yapping barbarian which a ten-year-old is—save by physical deprivation or punishment. No motive but the physical will make sense to his undeveloped brain. Any pretensions on his part to loftier ideals, such as religious ones, are sheer fatuity, sly purchase, or the remembrance of racial ceremony, largely orgy, associated in his young but by no means tender consciousness with mayhem rather than manners.

Since there flows in our veins largely the blood of generations of people who have managed to survive by the low cunning and treachery necessitated by the unnatural aspect of all past society, some kids will be unamenable even to the physical system of compulsory education. Taking away their desserts or knocking them on the head will not enliven them to any effectual effort at serious learning, even of their own language. These people should not be permitted to continue their schooling along general lines. An effort might be made to reclaim some of them after they reach maturity. But most should be prepared at once for the sedentary handicrafts—work in the trades, in the factories, in the iron seats of farm machines, and at the pump handles of filling stations. They have no aptitude for learning, make no use of what they do manage to be taught, and are a waste of tax money. A group of that group, the least stable and reasonable, should be politically disenfranchised. No one in the entire multitude should ever be permitted to hold public office. And a certain small percentage of this dreadful offal, much of which regularly accumulates in the bleachers of our ball parks, should be quietly put to sleep.*

---

*There is now much ado concerning all these matters and especially juvenile delinquency—though no one else, so far as I am aware, has even ironically suggested that the most hopeless of the lot be put to sleep. The "home" is blamed for the misbehavior of youth—and then it is found that some of the nastiest assassins come from "good" homes. So the "school" is blamed, as if personality were formed there—rather than at home, well before any child reached school.

No one seems willing to confess that "juvenile delinquency" as it occurs these days is, quite plainly, proof that the "American way of life" itself is sick. The teachers, whom I have rather harshly treated here, are not to blame for their own lack of education, incompetence, genetic inadequacy, and so on. The goals of our society are such that only the less attractive and the less aggressive remain to teach—the social leftovers; and our general population is so well satisfied (consciously) with its cheesy objectives that it is content to have its youth "taught" by bevies of suggestible, spineless dimwits. That amounts in

That is, of course, real democracy. That is the true application of the plan to give every man an equal opportunity. Any other is a fascism of sentimentality, forever handicapping the abler majority with an incompetent minority, artificially made equal—the feeble-minded, warped, stupid, cruel, mean, perverse, deluded, hysterical, dull, depraved, and silly. There must be reason in our collective behavior soon, as all can perceive. There must be an end to a government of boobs, by boobs, for boobs. Because there are already more boobs in our society than wise men, or even than scrupulous men, and the machines devised by science are so exact, so productive, and so powerful that a government which is in the hands of boobs will as surely commit national suicide as a sixteen-year-old kid, blind drunk on a blind curve, doing eighty in a twelve-cylinder sedan.

The idea of universal education sounded sensible to the founding fathers. Universal education consisted, then, in teaching everybody the language, simple arithmetic, and the structure of eighteenth century society. Science was elementary. Industry was nil, as we know it. There is no such society today. Only a third of contemporary people, at a generous guess, are even potentially educable to the degree at which their judgment would be of any value to the rest of man, politically, socially, morally, economically, or any other way. There should be an equal opportunity to have this higher education. But those

---

essence to one more scramble for short-range, private gain at the certain cost—if the attitude persists—of national suicide.

To pretend to educate people—which we do—to "pass" every student (for the presumed sake of "personality") is to give all USA a gradual lobotomy, destined finally to produce vegetables, not men. By such means we are not even keeping abreast of the prejudicial system called "education" in Russia.

What is remarkable is that, here and there, a few able people still elect to teach; what is lucky is that even one good teacher in a lifetime may sometimes change a delinquent into a solid citizen.

competent to profit by it should not be held for one day to the standards of the whole. To do so is to impose slavery of the mind in the name of national mental emancipation.

An educated man does *not* go on all his life believing American history was hearts and flowers. He does *not* go on thinking that the Romans were purely ornamental people who wore togas and spoke ponderously in their senate. He does *not* learn his native tongue so badly that he makes errors in the use of it, does not know the main words in it, and has no adult wish, ever, to read any book printed in it except such stuff as wet dreams are made of.

Above everything, perhaps, an educated man can tell at once the difference between a fact and an opinion. He knows whether a subject is established or debatable. He knows, for example, that you can argue forever on what mistakes Spinoza may have made—but that it is foolish to argue at all about the height of the Sphinx or the weight of Mars.

The schools give pupils no such approach to life. Because universal education is a national law, they do not dare to. Nine-year-olds, backed by political drag, money, prejudice, and other blackmail power, make it impossible for schools to teach anything but gibberish. That reason, plus the sheer inability of two-thirds of every class to stay in the same mental games with the other, together with the peewee caliber of teachers as a class, has reduced our education to a public swindle, an assassination of sanity.

A teacher who said Washington was a whoremaster would be confronted by the D.A.R. A teacher who said that there was no scientific evidence of the existence of the Holy Ghost would be confronted by the Baptist Church. A teacher who said our militia broke and ran in countless battles would be confronted by the American Legion. A teacher who said contraception was a social and not a religious problem would be confronted by the Catholic Church. A teacher who said man was evolved from the lower animals would be (and was) tried in court. It happened not so many years ago in the sovereign, dim-brained state of Tennessee.

Yet, upon exact perspective of such matters our nation's future depends. We cannot even hope to plan effectively without knowing *all* the facts we can scrape together about our past. Science will serve only the avarice of molten asses if asses can outvote the wise. We will go on believing such utter rot as that we are Christian and rational and have organized law, if we go on trying to educate saps and thereby make saps of the intelligent. The result will be chaos. The result *is* chaos, in fact.

Most of our people have been taken with the idea of easy living. Because machines can produce so much, they argue, man must be on the threshold of a cinch. But goods, as I have said in one way, and will in another, add little real ease to life and the total worship of goods, in the end, takes away all peace and all security. A man who sets out to find the economic solution of today's problems is merely burning joss sticks to goods. In a world that is engaged in the reckless rush for mass-produced material objects there is neither room nor time for honesty, consideration, integrity of thought, introspection, or the operation of conscience. In such a world—democratic, fascist, soviet, whatever the form of government—there will be no security because security comes from man's trust of man—man's confidence in man—and the mills cannot manufacture it and the state cannot guarantee it. Only each man, working within himself to the best of his ability, can create temporal security. So long as the few basic hungers in man are contented, more goods cannot add anything even to that security.

But we are in a goods-mad world. Our statesmen tonight are trying to figure out how to make security out of this madness for things. It cannot be done. If we do not turn upon ourselves the terrible honesty our science has turned upon goods, we are done for. This war, this uprooting—the second—will be only a stumble on the path back to a new start in a new savagery far deeper than that of a thousand years ago.

We will probably win this one. Then what? Does anybody believe that trade treaties and economic agreements will point the way to the reorientation of man and the discipline of his instinct by his head and heart? Sure. Our school-taught public. But will they not, rather, point to some vast new competition of nations? Inevitably, they will.

When the sons of those who do not die now are grown old enough to die, the sour-breathed economic uplifters' peace will be decaying. These United States, secure again, goods-crazed again, suffering still the inevitable cycle of boom and depression, isolated again, may find the valiant Russians have taken the production bit in their teeth and are not only "plundering" world trade but storing up arms to make a conquest of the U.S.A. Or, perhaps, out of Tibet and Mongolia will come direful rumors of new weapons, new engines, new trade policies, new ways to invest and seize a neighboring land—and the sons of those sons will go out into the night in bigger aircraft, with guns that poison a cubic mile of sky with gas, and set about to restore "decency" where there never was much decency to start with.

Man's destiny lies half within himself, half without. To advance in either half at the expense of the other is literally insane. We are almost all, of course, as mad as hatters. Our statesmen, our scientists, ourselves. You. Indeed, if you go on reading this book, unless it makes you wiser, it will very likely cause you to cork off screaming to the nut factory. You belong there anyway and, deep inside yourself, you know it. A self-made fool, like most others who are professional lunatics—a spot of protoplasm—wet blather on a wet globe—at heart a murderer, a thief, a hypocrite, a desperate jackanapes—because you are ashamed to face the truth.

There is the Cinderella myth, which makes you spend your days in any sort of travail, however nonsensical, dull or destructive, in order to get together the goods which will enable you (you think) to be or to create a Cinderella, depending on your sex. There is the stork myth, which makes you believe all sorts of rubbish but keeps you from the horrible necessity of having to meditate on what is real. Such bilge and its promulgator, the school, which ought really to teach you a few scientific lies just to give you a start at primitive reasoning and which actually teaches you a pottage of data and no route to reason at all, are the stuff you consider your education.

There is just a chance, a slim, angry chance, that the disastrous state of things, these days, may enable us to notch ourselves forward a small inch on the road of our common evolution. Because, at last, we know we must do *something*. We might, in consequence, get a glimmering of what to do. We will not be able to pat out a nifty global recipe as easily as Dorothy Thompson solves an international problem on three sheets of typewriter paper. But we may start doing better.

To the extent that we have denied the power of our instincts—to the extent that we have really believed the extravagant piffle that we are Christian, rational, and legal—they have kicked us to pieces.

But to the extent that the wide world is a tortured, screaming insult to the very word "man," our instincts have been at work on the other side, trying to get the pieces back together. We have been frightened by the magnitude of our incompetence. The indecency of the danger that rides the night wind over every home has made us willing to yield a little of our tradition and prejudice if it will seem to promise something of security in the times ahead. But we are reluctant, still, to give much—even a few weekly gallons of gasoline—for the chance of ourselves and our families to survive. That is a measure of our stupidity, and of our slavishness to ourselves.

We are going to kill people—which is a relief. They are people, in the aggregate, more bestial and conceited than we—and that makes the relief a holy cause. We propose, in this moment of fear anyway, to share the world's goods a trifle more generously. That is a forward step. We are discovering, in a score of nations, that vivid life can be maintained without the accustomed luxuries and comforts. That lesson will have value if there is added to it the discovery that man's spirit can flame higher, and man himself feel far more noble, in the execution of his duty to other men than in the mere acquisition of junk at the expense of duty. But, looking back over history and looking forward at the peace proposals, no one can be certain we will learn, in this age, much of that last lesson—the only important one.

The pleasure-lusting halves of all the legends are finished, for the nonce. Across the planet stalk the evil archetypes in such plain view that all men have to admit their power. It would be good if we would try to remember them afterward, if we would take the skeletons out of our closets and put them where they belong—in places of honor at our future feasts; thus, at last, giving the devil his due and denying —nothing. They have been so carefully hidden by—the "educators"!

CHAPTER VIII

Common Man: The
Hero's Backside

"GOD MUST HAVE LOVED THE COMMON PEOPLE BECAUSE HE MADE so many of them."

I have noticed that when people hear that saw repeated, they generally snigger with a warm sense of self-appreciation, and grow a little less watchful of themselves—more overt—and, all in all, commoner. It is indeed a bland and balmy assumption that, intrinsically, the common man is a wonder beyond all other wonders, possessed of indwelling virtue, and automatically endowed by God with marvelousness. Anybody, stopping to think, knows the idea is rot—a sentimental, fatuous, and absurd expression of zero.

(*The rest of this book is about people—common Americans—Germans—Jews—professional men—women—and a great man, Jesus Christ. To explain people, I have explained more psychology. But it will make understanding easier if you bear in mind, from now on, that such thought, such evaluations, and such illustrations as follow will be intended to illuminate human beings.*)

Common man has in his lump the good qualities of uncommon men. What makes common man worthy of note is his occasional, individual rise *above* the commonplace. His ignorances and vulgarities are tolerated only because they may be supposed to overlie better qualities. Thus, in spite of our betrayal of every instinct we have, even American common men and women are still capable, in extremes, of rising to heights of courage, resourcefulness, and self-sacrifice, albeit

100

grudgingly. At least, some of them are, and most of the rest can be frightened into a show of compliance.

There was, at the beginning of this war, a grave doubt in the minds of many intelligent men concerning the loyalty and generosity of the common man. If the war lasts for any number of years, common man will unquestionably give many reasons for a recurrence of the doubt.

But common men are not, in any particular group, at any particular time, given as a whole to nobility of thought or of deed. Common men spend the majority of their free time and most of their excess energy in small, unpleasant activities which, in the aggregate, stay the advance of common man himself. Common men are greedy and superstitious, self-seeking and without trust—because they are not especially trustworthy themselves. They are clannish, narrow-minded anthropoids, hating work, hating novelty—but hating monotony also—backbiting, mean, cruel, grasping, insolent where they dare to be, and sullen, if not craven, in the presence of that which impresses them. The vast and vomitous outpouring of their vulgarity appalls and nauseates even themselves, at times, and hardly any common man is able to live with the others, even for a few hours, without some violent complaint, criticism, or reproach of his associates. The world of common men is worse than a monkey-world, because common men know better than what they do, to their consequent endless, bitter guiltiness.

This Bourbon passage, taken from context, would be invaluable to my opponent if I were ever to run for political office. A politician, be he president or county clerk, must forever blather about the virtues and magnificence of common men. For practical purposes, and not in public hearing, he curses and reviles common man more than most. The universal American custom of spouting the apotheosis of common man is, at best, a dangerous form of flattery, and more often a fearsomely hazardous form of universal self-deceit.

Poops and prickamice of every description have got themselves public offices, fortunes, and even what passes for literary reputations, by this tetanic exaltation of common men. People who should know better melt into a dither of sentimentality at the mere utterance of "common man." Indeed, in my lifetime I believe I have seen more facile expressions of sanctity follow the mention of common man than I have the mention of God. God, to most people who mention him seriously at all, is a professional subject, a stock in trade, and as such has a name to be bandied about. But the same voices shake with the sound of the words "common man." And that—is real vanity!

Now the words, to me, conjure up the fine things that have been said honestly about some common people and the fine deeds that certain common people have done. But they also suggest the terrible capacity that common people possess to be wrong and to do evil. It is common people who run off our many annual lynchings. It is common people who scream for blood at prize fights. It is common people who, acting concertedly, vote fools into Congress and the state legislatures. It is common people who fill the insane asylums. Common people massacre each other on our highways. Common people, mostly, fill our penitentiaries. Common people run our rackets. Common, no-good sons of bitches.

"God," the saying might also read, "must *hate* the common people because he made them so common."

Both constructs of the aphorism hold true. But, because it is an American convention to adore common people without restriction, I elect here to criticize them, as a lesson. A society which cannot criticize its masses is hamstrung—as ours is. For it is our American common people, and not the highly educated ones, who have chucked overboard the critical method and thereby cut loose the ship of state from its sounding machinery, its rudder, its glass, and its keel, leaving the whole business to drift where the blather of common men blows it.

Love of liberty is laudable and logically the chief political end of man, so long as it is hitched to responsibleness. Eighteenth century man, politically educated and understanding the major implications of what was going on in his environment, made a fairly responsible voter. Today, common man insists on his right to vote and insists, equally, on the right not to have to know what he is voting about. This folly is pitching all common men rapidly toward the rocks. The current war is a mere reef we are now grating over. What lies beyond may be the greater disaster.

There is no liberty for a man under any discipline except that which is self-imposed. The imposition of disciplines by the state is called fascism, or tyranny, by common man; and he hates it. By the same token, any nation which subscribes to liberty and then attempts to maintain a majority who have no discipline of themselves, is destined soon to be without freedom. Anarchy exists nowhere in nature. An asceticism, which is to say, a discipline, is imposed upon every living object by its environment and its instincts.

American liberty has been tentatively saved for the last few decades not by the self-discipline of its citizens but by their instincts, which had not yet been blunted quite enough to prevent the people from realizing imminent dangers at the eleventh hour. Twice, now, we have turned at the last moment and armed ourselves to prevent the discipline of ruthlessness—the next most powerful discipline to responsible liberty—from overthrowing us. This second time we came within months, and perhaps even weeks, as a body of common men, of a position from which not even our instincts could have extricated us. It is not yet utterly certain that we have escaped, but the presumption is that we shall.

What about the third time?

If the third time does come, it will come because we failed to learn the lesson of the other two—failed to make ourselves into what Dorothy Thompson says we already are: Christian, rational, and possessed of organized law. If the third time is allowed to come, it will surely take the measure of us, find us wanting, and wait only until our fallacies are big enough to dull our last collective instinct of self-preservation. Then you—or your children—will be the slaves of retrogressive science, serfs of the vandals, and whores of the Huns, as are a far larger number of people than the population of the U.S.A. this very moment.

The urge toward liberty is, of course, an instinct. Like every instinct, it has its obverse side. The obverse side of this particular coin is the absolute responsibility of each free man for every single use to which he puts his freedom. All the legends that represent liberty—or freedom of choice—show the punishment for its abuse: Pandora and her box, the servants and the silver talents, Phaëthon and the sun chariot, and so on endlessly. Man knows he can't get away with anything. He, as an individual, may appear to—but his fellow man always pays his debts at compound interest. We are, indeed, part of the *Maine*—as John Donne said—irrevocably bound up in it, and the commonness of common man, his baseness, his tawdry attempts at self-deception, and his deceit of others steadily erodes the ground that sustains us all.

Everywhere I see common people suffering for this knowledge of their willful, private shortcomings; I see them tormenting themselves and abusing their families because of their pain. However, fear of the prison wall—fear, even, of the hot squat, as the criminal often points out—is not deterrent to antisocial behavior, which is to say, behavior that lacks integrity of concept, motive, and execution. All the rotten little men around us in this world, embezzling dimes, lifting the scales as the grocer pours sugar, cheating their customers, lying about their assets, taking the money of the helpless, beating their wives, mauling their kids, wearing on their faces as fiercely as possible all the while a look of smug arrogance—all these are afraid of themselves and live in queasy terror. They may deny fear and scorn fear, but the blackness of it shoots around inside them somewhere. For man's instincts are more powerful than his pretensions; they will *not* be cheated. And the common man of this nation has, as a rule, by the time he reaches middle age, a carcass that is an engraving of internal penalties paid in part or in full.

Few men, indeed, are so mad that they do not know when they are doing wrong. But so avid is their pursuit of goods that wrongdoing has become an element of all they do. To protest that fact is idle. Our politics, our business—little and big, our professions, our labor, are smitten in every facet with a corruption occasioned by reckless determination to make not just a reasonable profit but all the profit that can be wrung from every enterprise. Our commonest man, emulating his superiors, forges ahead with a brick on the safety valve of his conscience. Think over *your* morning newspaper in that light.

It never seems to occur to people that, so far in history, the common men of every nation that has arisen on the face of the earth have, somehow, run it into the ground. It is not a lack of leadership that creates ruin where there was once a city, but a failure, at last, of common men to heed their leaders or, at the least, to elect to follow wise ones. Apparently, as soon as a society, or a state, or a city, achieves sufficient organization to make its existence profitable in money to large numbers of its people a process of deterioration sets in among them. They turn from the hard idealism of the founders to the golden pursuits of the incumbents and, presently, there is not enough discipline, or integrity, or asceticism, in the whole entity to maintain the positive forces and prohibitions essential for collective life.

Sometimes, as this process begins, the halls of state quibble while the common people ride around in chariots, and, lo!, the slaves rebel. Sometimes a barbarian horde descends and sacks the debilitated community. Sometimes a technological disruption brings a plague that kills the inhabitants: the engineers have no longer been able to build the proper sewers because of prior land claims of the merchants. Occasionally a hardier near-by race on the upswing of honest endeavor, sickened or sullied by a decadent neighbor, moves in and cleans up. Sometimes a nation merely passes stalely into nothingness, so that its population moves from well-engineered cities to huts, and lives forever in view of the ruins of what it once was.

In all these cycles of decay,* common man plays the only significant

---

* For a thorough consideration of "cycles of decay" Arnold Toynbee's "A Study of History" is recommended. At the time "Vipers" was written, I knew nothing of Toynbee's work. It is not surprising, however, that Toynbee's view of our current civilization is not very different from my own: we are amidst a "time of troubles" and we shall not measure up to its "challenge" unless we adopt a new and loftier belief.

role. The humanitarian impulses of his first leaders spur him to more idealistic efforts—which, presently, become mere economic efforts. Less humanitarian colleagues then exploit him. Common man, catching on, learns to exploit others. In a primitive economy the exploitation of human beings, except by direct enslavement, is a limited possibility. In a city, or a state filled with cities, it becomes an enterprise of great diversification. Common man, forever confusing progress with material gain, exploited and exploiting, begins àt that point to undermine his own community. State quibbles are more fun for him than hard orders—so he promotes quibbling. He keeps down his slaves, if he has any, by savage persecution; even as we keep down our half slaves, the Negroes. He buys a chariot he cannot well afford and rides around in it when he ought to be patching up the cloaca maxima. Then the Germans attack him. Or, perhaps, he just decays, like the people left in some New England towns or certain rural areas in the Appalachians, who bob and nod and leer and scratch for corn around the rattling shells of the homes of their eighteenth century forebears.

In our case, the great impulse of westward expansion has died out. Whether or not it can be renewed in a fresh impulse even toward the industrial exploitation of the whole planet, I am unable to say. That it could be restored to permanent viability and so establish the first enduring civilization on the planet—though by a long, costly, introspective housecleaning—I know.

But I suspect that our next effort as common men will be, again, exploitatious and world-wide, and that we will embark upon it with holy words and even, to some extent, with humanitarian purposes. So long as we exist in the way we exist today, it will not come to much. We can teach the people English, give them mines and factories, dominate

---

Toynbee puts it about that way; my words might be less elegant. But, in his concluding volumes, he acknowledges that his deep insight into human psychodynamics came in part from an attentive consideration of the work of Carl Jung——the same work which gave rise to many of these less scholarly utterances and predictions.

them and sack them in our own fashion, but as long as we are vulgar and unrestrained about it—as long as America's gift to man is Chicago* we will merely be spreading the seeds of another society exactly like the thousands upon thousands which have flourished, grown great and proud, faltered, become confused, and vanished.

For civilization is a subjective quantum, and our common people are not much more civilized today, in any important sense, than the Moors, or the Mongols, the Tartars, Huns, Etruscans, Mayans, or the Iroquois.

We should, perhaps, stop mentioning the common people altogether. For one thing, although every man and woman alive in a democracy *is* one of the common people, and although kings and queens, on scrutiny, have mostly proved to be devilish common too, such is the dizzy egotism of man that hardly any single person believes *he* is exactly one of the common people. His consciousness of himself, the supreme achievement of nature, is employed largely by him to feed and inflate a peculiar sort of vanity. The uses for which a consciousness of self are intended (of which this book contains many examples) are generally discarded by man in favor of the more pleasurable use of it to butter himself. This masturbation of the soul by the soul may be noted as an augury of collapse in the annals of all the faded civilizations of which there is a record: the people got grabby and went soft.

In consequence of this phenomenon of vanity, it is almost useless to analyze "common man": when you do, every man looks around in the crowd to find one, and when you praise common man, every person in the crowd puffs himself up for being one. Since it is going to be necessary for common men to go through hell if they are to survive as Americans at all—either the hell of self-discipline, or the hell of more wars, or the hell of being conquered and rebelling all over at some

---

*We have tried to do these very things abroad lately. However, it has turned out that America's gift to the world is not even Chicago, but merely Coca-Cola.

remote date—and since I, at least, prefer the path of self-discipline, and therefore feel that the common man must be criticized from top to bottom, I suggest a rejection of the term. It is solely a praise-phrase and as such no longer has any meaning.

There is another reason for abandonment of the sickly expression. We have got too much into the habit of thinking of ourselves as "men" and we think all too seldom of ourselves, each by each, as "a man." It is convenient, and even necessary, to refer to ourselves collectively, since we live together and have so split up the chores and luxuries of living that no single man is able to maintain himself alone even in a travesty of the style which society decrees. But, actually, little enlightenment on the nature of man is to be derived from a contemplation of *men,* compared, in a sense, with the amount to be had from the study of *a man.* This is a matter which I hope our scientists will investigate carefully in the future. They have largely ignored it—and the implications of it—in the past.

Men collectively, for instance, never have a joint creative impulse, and rarely, any kind of joint positive impulse, except when it is instilled into them by one man. A crowd of people never painted a picture, wrote a book, composed a song, or spontaneously hit upon the idea of doing much of anything else that was constructive. Even in primitive societies, doing or building is the result of conference in which individuals speak their minds. The acts of crowds, when crowds act at all, are almost wholly negative. Lynching and murder, torture, arson, stampede, stoning, persecution, heckling, fugue, rage, and other destructive processes are the frequent manifestations of gatherings of common people that, often enough, start for other purposes. True, mass rape and orgy could be construed as a creative act, but aside from that it is axiomatic that crowd behavior, if it takes any objective form, will take a fiendish one.

It is axiomatic, but nobody bothers to investigate the axiom. Most of the treatises on what is called "mob psychology" are the work of nitwits, largely either Marxists or Columbia Ph.D.'s. I have perused several shambling documents on the topic, and what they show, mainly, is that I am right to contend that we do not apply the methods of science to ourselves. To treat a crowd as an entity for the purpose of its study, as most self-made authorities do, is to take a very gross attitude toward subjectivity. It is a process equivalent to alchemy, which recognized a few elements of matter, in a rough way, but had not yet considered molecules, let alone atoms.

A crowd, of course, consists of individuals. The behavior of a crowd is the behavior of many individuals. The net effect of a mob act may appear to be due to one impulse possessed by all alike. There is a contagion of the spirit that is almost tangible when "Fire!" is shouted in a packed theater. "In a matter of seconds," subsequent reports will say, "the audience became a raging, hysterical mob." For practical purposes, it did. Anyone who has felt the rise of any violent mob emotion knows that it is a real quantity, perceptible to senses not yet catalogued by the wizards of science, and difficult to resist. But, in the face of mob uproar, there are usually individuals who try to quell the panic, or hysteria, or fear, or hate; there are usually other individuals who get under things or behind things and by keeping cool heads save themselves from being trampled to death.

The ability of plain, ordinary, self-respecting, controlled, godly, decent, patriotic, home-loving men and women to turn, suddenly, into fiends of hell—killing one another without remorse, dragging live people through the streets behind automobiles, cutting off their testes and making the victims eat them and then burning them to death —this quantum, which may be commonly observed in many a town or city in the U.S.A. in this year of grace, should make economists think a thousand times, and sociologists a hundred thousand, before they spend any precious energy laying out collectivist plans for the future happiness, or abundance, or what not, of humanity. Because in the samples of collective behavior which it exhibits the mob or crowd exposes not a phenomenon appertaining only to mobs, but a basic characteristic of the individual man.

Before its revelation, all the pretty schemes of governments and statesmen crumble to dust. Until the individual man has made himself a sufficient master of his own personality to be secure in the face of such temptations as that to which the "mob" falls victim, no society, no state, no economic system, no social program, will be safe. All will be subject to violent and horrible overthrow at the hands of common men.

The action of mobs is another exquisite proof of the argument of this book—that man is not yet the captain of his soul and that his destiny is therefore in grave doubt. What an individual can do in a mob shows many things. It shows that we live, always, side by side with our brute ancestors, and that all they have done we can do, plus refinements we are able to add by employing science. It shows that common man is still a fiend. It shows that good Americans are scarce because good people are scarce. It shows a need to reckon with ourselves on this bestial plane, collectively and individually, now and always. It shows that everything we call civilization, religion, enlightenment, modernity, knowledge, and hope is as thin as a one-molecule oil scum over the deep abyss of our instinctual nature.

The behavior of a mob in bloody panic is, however, simply a gross and extroverted evidence of all the other aspects of collective human behavior. As the people of a city, a state, and a nation, we belong to all sorts of mobs. In lesser degrees, a good part of our actions are mob actions. We are stampeded every week, because one or another of the mobs to which we belong has stampeded. We perform public murder, arson, betrayal, self-mutilation, and so on in the name of one mob or another, without thought of punishing ourselves and only the dimmest, briefest sense of guilt. We do these savage acts in the name of "public opinion" and we take our collective cue from "right-thinking people." Now the public has no opinion, but only its instincts; and people do not think, but only one person at a time.

All people exist for each single one. Every man is the center of all others, in so far as he is concerned. When he is able to transcend that notion, and to give out rather than to take in, he has become an individual and knows it. Until he does, he is cattle.

A man's awareness derives from fragile wave and molecular disturbance, remote from his idea of himself and subject to easy misinterpretation. He lives, really, an utterly solitary life. The stars are no more distant from his body than his dearest friend is from his awareness. But, instead of developing the attributes of the isolated organism which he finds himself to be, he throws as much of his personality as he possibly can in with the herd—and, of course, becomes liable to all the misfortunes of it. I refer here to psychological rather than physical misfortunes. In this degraded and degrading condition, man serves a term in his body and dies, never having looked into himself, never having grown or learned, and without any knowledge of the meaning he might have given to his subjective existence, which, so far as his real chance for knowing went, was all he had anyhow.

Most herd activities are intended to be ruled out by the brain and the personality. The great inhibiting organ that keeps trying to compel us to think does so because it is trying to keep us from acting like swine. But today we are living up to that birthright only in the narrow province of science. Outside that, we are hardly making a stab at using the brain for its intended purpose. The common American no longer bothers even to wonder why he is doing many of the things he does.

He goes to the Easter service because, long ago when he lived in the woods, he used to celebrate the arrival of spring with a little dancing on the grass and a lot of fornication. He likes gangster movies and murder mysteries because he, too, once belonged to a cluster of club-carrying brutes who knocked off people who got in their way. He kids, but in some occult way admires, the chromatic vortex on his wife's head which she has bought under the general description of "a hat," because he comes from a long line of barbarians who have had the habit of plastering every sort of material on women's faces and heads as a symbol of mere womanhood, and somehow the object on his wife's head gives him the pleasant sense of her womanliness. He turns earnestly to the astrology column of his newspaper and frowningly consults the next day's augury, because he has patronized witch doctors and soothsayers for thousands of years and it does not occur to him that the rubbish he reads no longer makes sense in the time and place where he resides. Martial music makes him warlike, because his ancestors drummed themselves into countless fights before him, and when there is war and martial music is scarce, as in the present one, he writes reproachful letters to the editors. He hunts for birds and animals that he does not need for food, because he was once a hunter. His suit, like his body, is a ragtag and bobtail of the habiliments of human beings for hundreds of years and much of it is very awkward and uncomfortable in his present way of life, but he will not give it up, because his clothes, like his soul, belong to a mob. When he tips his hat, he is doing it because men a thousand years ago used to wear iron visors over their pusses—and not for any other cause at all.

Hats, indeed, have a remarkable effect upon the common man. They have it, because headdress has always been a sign, with him, of special merit and personal unction. Hats are therefore magical, still. People putting on hats put on the qualities symbolized by the hats, or try to, or assume that they have done so. Thus a cardinal, getting a red hat, assumes that some of the magic of hatism has entered into him, and becomes, because of the red skimmer, either holier, or harder to know, or more oracular, or more venal and lascivious on the ground that the red hat gives him special hellroom.

Notice the effect of party hats upon guests. A pompous exponent of some recondite branch of jurisprudence, all belly and dignity, can change, by the magic of a paper hat, into what he and his fellow poops regard as a clown and a merry wag. The existence of the hat on his head means, to him, that certain pretensions have been temporarily abandoned and another set put in their place.

What the brass hat does to the brain of most common men is almost too painfully evident everywhere today to go into: there will be a section, here, on soldiering. The next most dangerous form of hat is the flat hat, or mortarboard, of the academician. This hat conveys title to all wisdom. It has been worn by the millions of mongrel jerks graduated from our universities in the last decades; it has done almost every one of them a lot of harm, and thus all society, by giving them an unwarranted illusion of knowledge and, so, of authority. Since most colleges teach nothing, not even the first steps in how to think or the rudimentary facts on how to acquire information, the flat hat on the pate of the American graduate is a hallmark of philosophical treason —and there are enough of them to shingle hell.

The fire hat makes the fireman into a chopping demon whose zeal is highly regarded by the mob but whose effectiveness in putting out fires is open, usually, to great question. This hat, however, is useful for hiding small valuables picked up on the premises where fires are being attacked. I have heard it said that all firemen are kleptomaniacs and I doubt this, but the hat may have in it some small part of that special magic or legerdemain. What the fez does to the noble of a Masonic order is another thing that fascinates and frightens me. It makes him, ordinarily a man of aplomb and conservatism, able to parade the streets in outlandish costumes, for one thing. It also gives him the magic power to jab electrical shocking devices betwixt the glutei maximi of pretty girls—a power he certainly did not have under his fedora.

The subjective effect of a busby is unknown to me, but I, and everybody else, understand the effect of a crown, which is a hat of a sort, or at least a headdress. Cowboy hats, Stetson, ten-gallon jobs, are especially strong medicine. I have seen runty Jewish Hollywood producers put on one of these hats and, after a look or two in the mirror, purchase the complete outfit including high-heeled boots, leave the studio, take to riding with ex-ranch hands, and become so proficient that within a few months they were chasing calves out of chutes with the punchers and roping and tying them unaided within a few seconds of the time in which the champions could do it. All this—the effect of a hat—hurling back, with the sheer formidability of a symbol, the effect of thirty consecutive generations of ghetto life and producing a character indistinguishable except for his height from the standard Zane Grey idol.

A monk's hood must subdue a man, though there's a black mass or two in it for him, but a nun's veil, first put on, must be as numbing as castration, which, in effect, it represents. And there are records of men going batty after their first few minutes in an Indian hat and commencing to throw hatchets at the neighbors. But hatism, one of the profound isms, goes unrecognized, though it throws much light on the magical powers man has shorn from himself and invested in the accouterments of gangs.

To prove that by the negative, there is Calvin Coolidge, who put on, at one time or another, more hats for the fetishists in common humanity than any other president and who not only looked but was unchanged, the baffling mystery of zero, in coonskin cap, war bonnet, fez, topper, Homburg, or boater. Even a sola topee would not have given warmth to him; he kept trying to find a personality in a hat, or even a camera personality; but a hat cannot be worn inside out and a small wind will blow it off. The hatists forget those truths.

Indeed, the symbol of the vital man, the rebel against stupidity, the artist in nature, the soul at peace with itself because of understanding and lustily at war with the world for the same reason, is the bareheaded man. The reverent man is also bareheaded, and the humble man; so, too, is God. Nobody has yet figured out a good enough hat for God. I would deduce that the institutions which proliferated the greatest number of hat styles for men were the farthest from reality and wise aim and thus the closest still to barbarism.

The exalted common man is slave of instinct, slave of the herd, slave of superstition, slave of magical gadgets, the embodiment of evil, and the testing ground of every mass folly the devil can invent. He is the organ of the accumulated smut and sneakery of ten thousand generations of weaseling souls, the spirit of unleavened earth, the genetic end-product of a long run of inferior and infernal adaptations, the survivor of all known forms of needless stupidity, bestiality, and knavery. His power to rise up and repeat his pattern endlessly is immense and it has been, so far, nearly futile. His most colossal achievement is his ability, in spite of the doltish millennia out of which he has grown like a fungus, to keep producing specimens of men who give the whole breed a possibly exaggerated cast of hopefulness.

Had this creature more intellect than base impulses, or even a tendency to examine his personality for the profit there might be in it, rather than to examine the pockets of his neighbor, he would have triumphed long ago. He has thrown away too many opportunities, in too many races, under too many forms of government, with too many sets of mores, for any reasonable judge to expect a swift evolution of him now. His numbers have always weighed every social balance prodigally in his favor. His champions have always been the sternest, keenest, and stoutest hearted in his species. But every time so far he has come an abject cropper. At this present moment he has produced a worse brodie than ever before, despite the advantage of increased objective knowledge, and he is engaged now in using the fruitful discoveries of the one set of men who were, for the first time ever, manifestly on a right track to smash himself and everything he has built and his ancestors before him.

This lofty creature, common man, within the space of the last decade, finds that he has made a piker of every savage who preceded him and of all their once avowedly terrible enterprises. How unimaginative and what a small-scale operation was the Inquisition when statistically compared with the works of the Gestapo and the G.P.U.! What a harmless little spear-and-hot-pitch pirate Attila was, when considered alongside Hitler! What piffling amateurs Himmler has made of the Borgias! While we Americans sat here on our confused shores and bickered over interest rates, common man everywhere else has contrived to top every past bestiality on his vicious record by its square. What Joshua did to Jericho yields to Rotterdam and Coventry; the sack of Rome was a circus compared to the sack of a city called Nanking. And even so, the business is only started.

But it is happening to you and me and the year is A.D. 1942 and the men who are running from common men are men called Albert Einstein and Thomas Mann. Brother, take a look!

There is still an elixir in mankind worth all this travail if it can be crystallized and put into universal service. I shall discuss it later on. But I must spend more time—much more—showing in such ways as I am able that we are further from the crystallization than we were, that the road to it is different from the roads we intend to take after this war, and that it is a damnably hard road. All others lead to hell, in the marginal flame of which we are living today. Certainly the road is not to believe we are living in an era of unusual enlightenment, or to believe that we are already superior and saved, or to believe that we have passed beyond instinctual behavior into a realm of a free and intelligent choice, or to believe a conditioning of certain reflexes will rescue man from his myths and misery, or to believe in the happy half of all the legends in time and reject the half that explains despair and how men arrive at defeat, or to try to define who we are wholly in objective terms, or to put our entire faith in a heel called "common man."

Common man built all the old cities and either knocked them down or let them go to ruin. He fought all the other wars for reasons which he was positive were the same as ours today. The pyramids are a monument to his failure. So is Chichen Itzá. So is Cologne. Every thought in the head of the most erudite man alive today, save for a very few that bear upon the nature and organization of bricks, has already bloomed in the brains of thousands of other men—bloomed, been written down, lain forgotten, enjoyed resurrection, and died again. Common man has at long last got himself so far out of gear with nature and his environment that he is beginning to see the shape of extinction, whether he recognizes it as such or not. According to the big law of living beings, he has about used up his opportunity. National death wishes have already seized on parts of him. The death demand of races is boiling in the same furnace. From there it is only one more step until man punishes his whole species for vanity with self-extermination.

CHAPTER IX

The New Order for Common Man

THE PSYCHOLOGICAL ACCIDENT WHICH HAS BEFALLEN THE
Germans will not be accepted by good and true Americans as a clue to
the hidden, hideous side of Uncle Sam's subconscious. But it can be
used as direct evidence to show those who will think of themselves,
experimentally, merely as people what happens even to twentieth century men who get in a collective jam.

For the purposes of the class lesson, a principle of natural law must
be explained. That is the law of *oppositeness*. By introducing the law
to your conscious brain, I am running the considerable risk of losing
your attention. But the insight to be gained is worth the concentration;
the law is not my idea, any more than the law of gravity; and this
homily is not for bums, anyway.

Most of what you have, and want, and are, depends, for its maintenance at present, upon your *ignorance* of the law of oppositeness in so
far as it applies to your instincts, tastes, yens, whims, wishes, and hopes
—both expressed and secret. The Constitution of the United States
takes the law into consideration, vaguely. The idea of a democracy is
an admission of the existence of the law. But if you understood the law
and obeyed it, you might, conceivably, be uninterested in having four
cars, a life insurance policy with double indemnity for accidents, a motorized lawn mower, or a college education. You might prefer, instead, to cultivate bees, learn Sanskrit, write obscure poetry in a language you had invented, or throw milk bottles at policemen. You
might also, of course, be a damned sight better adjusted to your life.

But you would not, in *any* event, merely be an incessant consumer of
whatever people happened to be manufacturing at the moment. You

117

would be hard to fool with a political speech or a sermon. Your understanding of the ways of common men would be enhanced, and your temper, though often stirred by new and surprising casual agents, would be easier to control and a source of energy rather than of perturbation. That is a good deal to offer. But I did not promise you would understand the law, even when I had done with describing it.

*   *   *

Consider the Chinese. He has a tranquillity that others have always envied. He is able to face death comfortably, and alone—without priests or relatives trampling prematurely arrived lilies. He is tolerant. He is so progressive that Western society has not yet caught up with all of his practical discoveries and inventions. He accomplishes much of that by understanding that *Newton's law of action and reaction applies, equally well, to subjective processes,* although he does not express his understanding in those terms.

Western society has not tried to catch up with that psychological discovery. For if people became handy in applying it, business would be hurt. The political "ins" would not be able to maintain themselves. Wars might be foreseen and fended against. Booms and panics would be leveled down to the passable achievement of getting along fairly well—which is all common man is capable of. There would be calm.

So much for the advertisement and so much for the warning to industrialists. Now for some bearings and observations.

*   *   *

The law of "opposites," everlastingly linked in pairs, forever at odds in the objective world, reconcilable only within a man, supposes that, for every course upon which feelings, instincts, imaginings, and thoughts are embarked there exists an equally real, opposite course. To the extent that a human being fails to choose a line between those courses, and follows one, more than another, inside himself, he suffers reaction within himself. His power of choice is limited, naturally, by his awareness of what courses he is following and how far he is pursuing them.

*   *   *

Love, as I have implied, sets up automatically the possibility of hate. To the degree that the person who loves recognizes his vulnerability to hate, he chooses a conscious set of guards and balances and uses psychological *energy* to maintain them at all times. In so far as marriage, for example, is presumed to protect love it represents a device to stave off an opposite: objectively by laws and policemen; subjectively, by vows and determinations. Fear makes courage possible. Somebody who has performed a "brave" act is somebody who has done something generally regarded as dangerous. If there were no danger in the act, it would not be regarded as brave. But fear is, in itself, an instinct designed simply to reveal the nearness of danger. So, it may be assumed that the "brave" person was afraid. If he was not afraid, in the given circumstance, due to any of an infinite number of combinations possible to his particular nature, his bravery cost him nothing and should, in all justice, have been conceded no value as a psychological quantum.

Fear (while we are thinking about it) has been so corrupted by cockeyed social standards and values that people, these days, are more likely to fear an unreal danger in, say, the field of manners (such as a social snub) than to fear its opposite: a *real* statistical danger (such as an automobile accident). A common, if ghastly, *system* for dealing with fear—and, indeed, with *any* instinct—is to make subjective life itself seem so worthless to the individual that he would prefer, unconsciously, to be dead rather than to continue a presumptively futile existence under the additional burden of a driving instinct. That, in itself, is another form of an opposite state—and, as I think you can see, explains the numb resignation with which so many millions march from modern cities to death. Life in their cities has little seeming worth to them, and the war instinct makes their whole continuum unbearable.

*   *   *

Aristotle's "golden mean," the ideal spiritual goal, represented a point of awareness at which all the overweening opposites had been accepted and understood. That is the only point at which the choice and achievement of a "golden mean" *can* be made. Similarly, the "philosopher's stone" of the Middle Ages was a symbolic expression of this same balance of personality at the center. Christ always spoke from that premise. The Beatitudes, for example, express the reconciliation of opposites in as many ways as he could think of, offhand. They are a sermon that still is never really heard in Western society. To the Chinese, the phrase "in Tao" represents the thought-out, felt-out knowledge of all the opposites a man can find inside himself—and his resultant centering of his ego, his consciousness, his total personality, upon a point that lies between them all.

Modern science calls this "mysticism," as it does (and always has) every proposition which it has not yet investigated and labeled, or has labeled without investigation. Indeed, in this connection, it might pertinently be stated that evidence of the credulity of scientists is, often, their skepticism.

*   *   *

We are dimly aware of inward opposites. We are vividly aware, of course, of the fact that external phenomena are bound up in opposites. There is Newton's law of action and reaction. Night and day, black and white, up and down, in and out, fair weather and foul, the action of gravity that brings down what goes up, the effect of molecular motion, or its slowing, which produces heat and cold—life and death, past and future, and so on to the limits of imaginable conditions.

Our proverbs take this oppositeness into consideration and perhaps half of them are, in essence, mere reminders of it: "Every cloud has a silver lining"; "Too many cooks spoil the broth"; and again, the opposite to *that:* "Many hands make light work"; "It is an ill wind that blows nobody good"; "All work and no play makes Jack a dull boy"; "Here today and gone tomorrow." Religious proverb is, again, a massive documentation of this same idea in its many forms—and as such represents an effort to get man's mind into the acceptance of opposites and a reconciliation of them, so that *he* can be in the center. The theme of death as resurrection is a symbol for the subjective opposites in life and death. Christ expressed in endless forms this idea, which fascinated him beyond all others. It was a great truth which had come to a few learned men in Palestine out of the Far East; it taught them that personal peace derives from subjective qualities of individuals, and that a detachment from absorption in objectivity, alone, could furnish a starting place on a road toward composure.

"To him that hath shall be given, and from him that hath not shall be taken away even that which he hath"—the pronunciamento out of which generations of ministers have made a perfervid and slack-witted mess—becomes lucid when it is considered as a statement of *subjective* opposites: he who has detachment and integrity shall be rewarded with its self-increasing fruits; he who lacks it, and is therefore concerned only with animal and fiscal affairs, shall lose the power of detachment, in the end, and have nothing.

The idea of being "born again" referred to a washing away of orientation merely toward the objective world and the institution of a new, introspective attitude.

*   *   *

What we call "oppositeness" today, even in the world we understand fairly well, is not analyzed. And oppositeness in the complete world of reality—the world in which a feeling is regarded as real, along with a nutmeg or a flatiron—is confused and undefined. Oppositeness is more than the positive as over and against the negative. More than the presence of an object or a quality as over and against its absence. Oppositeness includes—besides the negative—a converse, and also a contraposite. In all three of them there is a complementariness to the positive.

We do not talk, for example, about opposite colors, but about complementary colors. But we take the spectrum of white light and make it into a circle, showing a physical opposition of the primary and complementary colors. Their use in art and decoration, according to that opposition, pleases us because the complementary colors do not clash but harmonize, and we have the discrimination to see as much. In music, there are other realms of opposition, simple and mathematical—

and other harmonies which depend upon the complement of exact numbers of vibrations. Thus counterpoint is an opposite which we employ without much consciousness, and which can be measured by mathematics.

* * *

Again, there is man and woman. These have been regarded as the "opposite" sexes. Their opposite aspects, from the historical standpoint, are of infinite variety. Their *complementary* relationship is asserted in myriad rules, dogmas, ideals, and so on, and its functional achievement is regarded as the goal of all men and women paired in sex relationships. Today, however, it is unfashionable to say that men and women are opposite. Women, either misinterpreting the democratic thesis or adopting the extroversion of Western man at the expense of all female subjectivity, are vigorously engaged in trying to prove that they are not opposite to man, but either identical or "just as good." They are certainly not identical, even from the gross physical standpoint, and while an individual woman may be "just as good" at a given process hitherto performed by males, no statistician would regard single instances as proof of anything about the whole group of women. They are different from men, still. Often, even in industrial fields (much to the amazement of management), they have proved to be *better* than men. They are better at fine work in repetitive operation, for example. If management had paused to reflect that women, all through human evolution, have been constantly occupied with the repetitive manual skills—spinning, weaving, mending, pounding corn, washing clothes, and stringing beads—it might not have been so surprised at the efficiency of the feminine shift in the airplane works. But individual female achievements, on the one hand, or special mass female effectivenesses, on the other, do nothing to prove that men and women are the same outside of their different generative appurtenances. Industrial tables will not elucidate the sex differences. Social activity may not—since most of the props of our society are made to be used by both sexes. We must look elsewhere for contrasts.

Subjectively, we recognize that men have some "femininity" in them, and women some "masculinity." We see exhibitions of it, often enough, when a man is frustrated, or woman—and, finding his or her usual approach to a given situation ineffective, he or she automatically goes into the opposite state, trying to solve the frustration by methods vis-à-vis those which are normal. Let us examine this business.

Frustration produces *fear* of one sort or another: every frustration is a threat, real or implied, to the individual. A threat is danger. The age-old reaction of instinct to danger is fear. Fear must be turned into action. Action born of fear demands one of two opposite courses, always: either standing and fighting or running away. Now, a man or a woman can run away from this resultant of a frustration, whether it is material or psychic, and often, in the running, use up the physical and mental energy stimulated by the circumstance. But if the act of running away seems cowardly, even to the runner alone, there will be subjective consequences as well as physiological ones. These are called, or lead in the end to, fugue, neurosis, escapism, and so on.

But if the frustration, which led to fear and then anger, is in *itself* subjective rather than physical—if it arises in a debate or a squabble rather than in the course of a fist fight—and if the man or woman engaged in it finds that the ordinary attributes of his sex pattern are not adequate to overthrow his or her opponent—and if he elects, still, to stand and fight—each will, very often, assume the characteristics of the other in the remaining engagement.

Thus a man who is good and mad will be frightened out of his masculinity and suddenly start behaving in a womanish manner. His voice will rise to a treble; his points in argument will become irrational and "feminine"; he will turn himself into a consuming fury; when he reaches the slapping and hair-pulling stage, he may often, because of the Marquess of Queensberry, double his fists to force the issue; but he may merely slap—like a woman. Slapping, indeed, with gloves or bare hand, is the classical invitation-in-wrath of noble males too mad to act like men, who wish, when they calm down, so to act later, with guns and swords.

Women, on the other hand, in the same circumstances, go into a mediocre but palpable imitation of men. They become as if cold and intellectual, though thought has nothing to do with the change; they argue icily (manlike) with "facts" and "data" and "logic." Defeated in their natural province of feeling values, they undertake to make war from man's province of detached thought. The "reasons" of an angered woman become multitudinous and articulate; she argues, and insists as she does so on the justice and integrity of each of her points— even while she ignores all actual laws of logic and throws her words about ad hominem, begging the question, debating in total non sequitur, forgetting that post hoc is not essentially propter hoc, and so forth.

Thus angry man, who behaves like a shrew, a harpy, a valkyrie, a siren, a gorgon, a witch; thus angry woman, acting like a supreme court justice, a pontiff, a pope, a saint, a skeptic, a martyr.

*   *   *

That example of "going into an opposite" is only one of many which could be cited to illustrate the subjective "opposite qualities" (or complementary ones) of men and women. It implies not only their opposition to each other (in the schism evoked by duress), but it also shows the capability of each sex to produce within itself manifestations of the *opposite* sex, and provides as good an illustration as any of another aspect of "oppositeness" with which I need to deal here, for the purposes of preparing for a discussion of the Germans.

In each positive element, idea, article, condition, law, statement, and so on, is the germ of its opposite. Objectively, we understand this: there is no such actuality as "all white" or "all black." There is no "absolute zero" but only an approach to it, and no "absolute heat." Scientists, up until recently, tried to deal with nature as if it *were* absolute in every final form and sense. Nowadays, appreciating the relativity of all things, they hold no such attitude. The actual determination of one value apparently *precludes* the determination of any other value accurately. For a scientist, this is skittering very close indeed to mysticism, although to the psychologist-philosopher the implications of the existence of such a state of affairs have always been apparent, everywhere.

Only the speed of light is regarded as theoretically an absolute. But since the nature of every object changes even when it approaches that speed, the one absolute left to the physicists has a universally modifying effect rather than a freezing one. Further research into dimension and relativity is awaited with great interest as it is even now explaining much old truth in terms of the new language of mathematics. And the philosopher of the future, speculating upon the nature of man in cosmos, will certainly have to draw upon the conclusions of math, wholly, for his background, just as Aristotle drew upon the natural history of his day. If the speed of light is absolute, and I daresay it is, though I venture to add that the nature of light needs still more subtle investigation, and if all else is relative, then we have, indeed, a radiant confirmation of the thesis that each positive contains the germ of its opposite, excepting light, which has only the almost inconceivable opposite of utter darkness.

*   *   *

The Chinese Taoists have made a symbol for these paired opposites which permeate reality, tangible and subjective: the interlocked commas which form, together, a circle; it is used as a trade mark by the Northern Pacific Railroad. These are called the yang and the yin. One is white and the other is black. One represents light, good, positiveness, and so on. The dark one represents dark, of course—evil, negativism, and so on. In another sense the white one, the yang, represents man. The black one, woman, in whose black insides all men living are generated. The Northern Pacific leaves out the full picturization of the original symbol. In it, there is a black dot in the yang and a white one in the yin, representing the presence of the germ of the one in each of the others. And between the dots there is a bridge, both above and below, from one to the other, in three dimensions, which means, to the Taoist, that these qualities are bound together, constantly partake of each other, and change into each other—as I have shown they do in the illustration of the behavior of men and women in situations that seem to demand a broader style of action than that normally accessible to them.

Our American orientation toward the world of goods, of objectivity, of what we call "fact," is so intense that the average adult, while he may apperceive each proposition of oppositeness as it is made, will from habit reject the whole proposal, viz.: that all he is and does and knows or does not know is controlled by the law of paired opposites, and that each one of the opposites contains the germ of the other.

This categorical negation is "Western" thinking, and in part that aspect of it which the Oriental mind scoffs at and rejects. Americans are amused or annoyed with all manner of the manifestations of "oppositeness" in the Eastern mind; but they seldom admit the validity of any, let alone their practicality or reasonableness. A few will confess that there is some sense to the plan of paying your doctor while you are well and stopping his salary when you get sick. But Gandhi's theory of "passive resistance"—which I, too, regard as impractical—is not given understanding enough. It may be no good in the present circumstance—or it may be, depending on your point of view—but it should not be dismissed as the crotchet of an old fool. It is an expression of the principle by which China, again, has devoured and thereby destroyed every "conqueror" who came over her borders—up to the Jap.* The Allies in India have been playing for weeks of time. Gandhi

---

* It is an odd, *dated* thought—the realization that, a dozen short years ago, we could wonder if the Chinese might have to absorb (to conquer) the *Japs*. And now that they have been taught (in a sufficiently active minority) to conquer themselves in communism's name, we might wonder if the Chinese could eventually assimilate the Russians, save for the fact that they have no opportunity: a very few Russians (rather—their books, ideas, propaganda, promises) made a conquest of China without risking the genes of the Soviet itself. How odd it is, too, that so many Americans fear a similar trick may

is playing for the centuries. Who will be right? Can you say, for certain? You cannot, of course. Biological absorption is as much a victory in the long-range scheme of things as immediate physiological destruction. Our preoccupation with the external world of this moment makes long-range thinking unacceptable to us. But from the Indian standpoint, the Japs may well be the opposite germ of a growth into a new, horrid reality, a Japanese India—so that Gandhi's scheme, while it has precedent and realism behind it, may not be the right one for this hour.

An idea, purpose, motive, wish, dream, hope, fear or hate, existing in the *head* of an individual, involves the principle of opposites only in so far as the contents of that person's *head* are concerned. But as soon as any such quantum is set in motion, it also sets the laws of the opposites in motion, and they will impinge upon every person who is touched in any way by the act of the individual. That is equally true of groups, mobs, nations. So long, for instance, as a nation is preoccupied at home with its concept of, say, liberty, it will produce only domestic progress or regression in the categories of freedom of all sorts

---

be turned here by a little skullduggery and much talk! To do so, is to exhibit one of two possible psychological conditions. It is to display the unconscious sensation that the United States is so bankrupt morally, so impoverished intellectually, so near the abyss—that a handful of zealots with an obsolete fanaticism can overthrow the lot of us. Or else it is to reveal the unconscious selection of a lesser fear (however unreal, illogical and implausible) adopted to save the dreading individual from having to face a *different* fear—but one so real, so terrible, so near, he will substitute *any* smaller alarm to hide the source of what stirs him unendurably.

It was not until 1945 that I saw how Terror (with its attendant whipping boys, fugue, hysteria, rigidity, apathy and so on) would take form in this fair land—too late by years to enter in "Vipers" a lucid picture of the prickamice at bay.

Ah, well! Sorrow enough (and fun, too) for one book.

and slavery of all sorts—of responsibility among free men acting on their own choices or of irresponsibility of slave populations who have delegated their liberties to their masters. When, however, any such nation considers another—to seize it or to befriend it—the domestic preoccupation becomes action at home and effect abroad.

*   *   *

A "boss" is a master to the degree that he can control the persons he bosses. A congressman is a master, with delegated power to limit the liberties of the republic. So, too, a demagogue is a master, because his adherents sign away to his demagogic promises a certain large or small part of their independence, freedom of personal choice, and liberty of movement. All political freedom necessarily involves individual responsibility, or the alternative of delegated responsibility, which, while it deprives the individual of certain amounts of his freedom, returns certain emancipations from personal and social responsibility. The workings of this relationship of opposites are becoming alarmingly apparent to many people.

They have been evident in past generations. Our Constitution tried to provide for them and, assuming that the average voter would understand the major problems of his state, took great pains to enfranchise every voter. But the average voter understands little of his state, civilization, and society now—which has brought about his willingness to delegate his powers to almost anybody in return for a little local profit and an illusion of national management. He is beginning, perhaps, to *feel,* if not to understand, the consequences of that reckless granting of his own power. His birthright has been sold by millions, and millions have in return the inevitable mess of pottage. Here is oppositeness at work within a democratic society as it works in an individual.

If people are conscious of opposites, they plan on them as inevitable reactions to every primary cause. If they are not, the reactions fall upon them anyhow, and they are astonished, enraged, or frustrated. Abstract truth has no consequences when it is merely a thought. When it is enacted, which is to say imposed, it always has at least two consequences. In the same way, untruths produce consequences in action. We forget this, as inhabitants of a republic. We try, instead, to ignore, conceal, deny, and refute the inevitable consequences of our acts whenever those consequences are not germane to our immediate purposes.

Our responses, in all the fields of our endeavors, in all our written history, are thus *cyclical.* We embrace one absolute with firm conviction and put it in effect, only to be caught, sooner or later, in its opposite manifestation. We generally carom from that, back into the direct opposite which preceded the first maneuver. Sometimes we learn a little and make a certain temporary or even quasi-permanent compromise or reconciliation. We may, indeed, be on the threshold of many such reconciliations—but only if we understand the laws of nature which underlie all reconciliations and act according to those laws, rather than to our own written statutes.

We Americans have booms and depressions. We have unemployment in the midst of want. We have famine at the same time we plow under our edible crops. Our markets surge up and our markets sag down. We try the Republicans and then we try the Democrats. We fight for states' rights and then we try to waive them by setting up a strong, central government. We adopt pacifism and it gets us into a world war under circumstances which come close to bringing about our quick defeat. But we hasten to become militarist in order to assure a future of peace. We boast that we are Christian, rational, and possessed of organized law—and we demonstrate at home and abroad by our behavior in myriad forms, by our very vital statistics, that we are barbaric and irrational and that our law is a chaos.

Our society is manic-depressive. It has not yet been compelled by circumstance into a paranoid form of united action, but it may be.*

---

* Full many a hundred psychologist, psychiatrist and the like is busy, these days, explaining that we *are* (or are becoming) paranoid (or schizoid with paranoid tendencies) and citing in the evidence items as diverse as the increasing incidence of park vandalism and the

We have paid a great deal of lip service to liberty, but we have lost much of our liberty in the sense it was intended by the founding fathers; first, because our goods wants caused us to set up an industrial society in which interdependence is so extensive that personal freedom had to be sacrificed to maintain it; second, because we refused to continue to accept personal responsibility for the over-all conduct of that vastly intricate society.

Since the brain evolved on man's neck to give him individual freedom of choice—and since it thus compelled upon him the consequences of his choices—our process is not congruous to our nature. We are still trying to abolish the paired opposites, somehow. Every con-

---

rise of McCarthyism (which, let it be said here for the benefit of future editions, was a kind of demonic putsch led by a senatorial führer from the beer halls of Milwaukee).

Furthermore, what I have called "united action" and said here leads to all-out paranoia, is taking shape everywhere: in the enforced "conformity" mentioned in another footnote, in the general antipathy for "controversy," in the compulsiveness which has added "God" to our patriotic Pledge, in the fantastic rise of suspiciousness toward science and scientists—et al., ad naus.

The notion of an "America" in which people are obliged to "conform"—or are even pressured socially toward narrow and rigid ideas about politics, other nations, communists, what-not—was not quite imaginable (save to people like myself) when the lines referred to here were set down. To what, in God's name, the readers in 1943 would have asked, can all Americans *conform* and leave any real America at all?

They do not ask, now. The conformity lies, as Riesman and others have pointed out, along the sterile and destructive lines of negatives. Nowadays, we insist we know what we oppose (though we cannot actually define it) but we do not even pretend to know what we are *for*. In that circumstance, our only *greatness* has been liquidated— temporarily, let us hope.

gressman is busy with the effort—every economist—every sociologist. And the harder these mutts try, the sillier their words become, so that today's real ecclesiastic for the common man is the economist and he talks the piffle of the fifteenth century theologian, as I have said.

*　　*　　*

Another form of mass behavior was, of course, possible to us. That was not to struggle with and against the opposites, but to "go into" one of them. To take a national pattern, that is, directly at variance with the pattern in which we had been struggling and which had given us so much trouble in the form of depressions, unemployment, poverty, and so on. Instead of extolling the essential nobleness of common man and striving for his rights, in order to get, somehow, for one and all, the vast material comforts and blessings seemingly implicit in machinery, we might have taken the opposite position that common man was nothing, only the elite mattered, and *they* should take charge of the machines and dole out the fabricated goods. Common man, with a certain amount of historical democratic precedent lying around (ancient Greece, for example) and with the great present example of the material effectiveness of Britain and America, both at least attempted democracies, has been getting himself imbued everywhere with one or another interpretation of democratic idealism as a means to a greedy end as well as to practical ends. Obviously, if we had gone into the opposite of the enshrinement of the machine through the power of an elite class, we would have had a fight on our hands.

*　　*　　*

Germany did it.

*　　*　　*

If you think over what I have said about common man, in the way of criticism, not to say excoriation, you will realize that much of it sounds like Nazi pronunciamento. Perhaps you made that observation in your mind as you read, and if so, I am glad, for it was my intention that you should make it. The attack on the "pluto-democracies"— on their corruption, falseness, baseness, sefishness, arrogance, weakness, stupidity, inefficiency, wrongheadedness, lack of realism, and general incompetence—made by Hitler in *Mein Kampf* was well deserved and *almost* wholly justified.

By leaving out his interpretations of the faults he found, his theory of the reason for those faults, and his plans for what to do about the faults—by regarding, only, the *faults themselves* as described by Hitler —you will discover a great deal of valid indictment similar to some that I have set down in this book. That the basic causes of the observed effects existed in *every* human being and in *every* nation, Hitler did not have sense enough to note. But that mankind, in other countries as much as in his own, was making a failure of trying to live with machinery, Hitler saw plainly.

The mechanics of Hitler's mind—the mechanics which explained the rise of national socialism—are simple. Well aware of the protective identification of the individual with the clan, mob, herd, and nation—inasmuch as *his own* was complete—Hitler undertook, like every politician and every evangelist, to convert or emasculate all those who dissented from his premise, which, in his case, was to push Germany into the opposite of the democratic attitude. This he did.

He did it at a time when the people of Germany were glum and impotent after their defeat in the last war. He did it at a time when world depression had made Germany, the least favored nation of the 1920's and early 1930's, a land thoroughly impoverished and miserable—a land which had descended from the overweening attitude of arrogance into the equally overweening opposite of self-pity. Pity can lead one to embrace the devil. Self-pity can lead one (or one hundred million) to *become* the devil. (When the acts of your earnest, sacrificing "virtue" fail [1918], you try the opposite acts, naming them virtues and earnestly sacrificing to *their* mandates.) Pity, like its twin, intolerance, should be centered on reason or it will become intolerance. And self-pity will become revenge.

The Germany which Hitler decided to throw into an opposite of the postulates of surrounding Western mankind was ripe for the absolutist shift. The very use of the word "total" in reference to the process is an example of its oppositeness—the piling of *all* on *one side*. Germany had been compelled by treaty to try to make itself into a democracy: what it called the "Weimar Republic." But among Germans there was no tradition of democracy. Germans had not made a long struggle like that of the British toward the enfranchisement of the common man. Germany's popular struggle had been confined to the construction of an elaborate system of class privileges and prerogatives, administered by the courts and enforced by officers of the law. The people had not striven to get the vote—it had been handed to them—and the business of electing deputies to the Reichstag was unfamiliar and foreign. Their adherence to their caste rights was so ingrained, however, that Hitler, for all his totalitarian activity, was unable to abolish them publicly and universally until this, the spring of 1942, and even so the act occasioned a great demur in the heavily indoctrinated body politic.

Not only was a memory of long effort toward liberty absent in the folklore of the people, but the memory of an exactly opposite tradition was vivid: the tradition of militarism and of oligarchy in state affairs. This *was,* on the contrary, deep-seated.

Germany, of all the large Western nations, had most recently gathered itself together out of the basic material of modern nations: small, separate feudal clans, states, and colonies, loosely associated by language. That language association involves, of course, other deep, common elements of background. The Germans in all parts of the present nation—north and south, east and west—derived from similar sorts of battling baronic principalities, and they, in turn, from the barbaric peoples that had inhabited Mitteleuropa and the Scandinavian peninsula for several thousand years: Goths and Visigoths, Huns and Vandals, the progeny of all manner of Asiatic looters.

The ancestral types had enjoyed a long record for wanton descent upon alien civilization. They had always sacked and burned it, never taken home any of its culture, never added a biological leaven to a fading society, and so remained, throughout centuries, the agents of reasonless ruin—a Malthusian device of dubious value, a mere human chopper-upper. They heaved each other back and forth across the face of the continent, and they left in the genes of the Germans an especial instinct to wreck.

That must be so, according to all sensible inference, because the second chore undertaken by Hitler was to glorify the activity of annihilation by opposing it in the public mind to the namby-pamby, wishy-washy do-nothingism of democratic pacifism, a process possible only if the vandal archetype still throbbed and burned in German race memory. Hitler succeeded with such universal and instantaneous ease that it can be attributed *only* to a special German cult of the human urge to mayhem. It overthrew religion, science, and the modern sense of decency with a combustible rush. The 1930's in Mitteleuropa burgeoned with the trumpets, flags, feasts, slogans, costumes, legends, bonfires, and fur hats of Attila getting his gang together for another foray on Rome. Valkyries, Götterdämmerungs, and all the rest of the boiling blood-pot of primeval Rhenish man went whirling around in Mercedes-Benzes, and it is a great pity that we let these supervulgarians get onto the scientific method, just as it is a pity we let the Japs, because they were both bound to make worse hell faster with science than we did.

The first psychological trick Hitler had to play upon his mob was, of course, to stop the depressive melancholia, which was their form of a fugue from the frustrating reality of the fact that the French, English and Americans had, after a long and beastly stand in the mud, beaten the living tar out of the best Germania had to put into the trenches. This Hitler accomplished by a device so simple, so universal, and so much in the way of progress today that it is surprising common man has evolved far enough to avoid the use of it against every one of his frustrations. He seldom does avoid using it but, under the best democratic aegises, he has often tried to, and sometimes succeeded.

Hitler explained to the people that they *had not been beaten,* but betrayed. This is everyman's alibi—the foolish abuse of himself that keeps his eyes closed to truth, his brain unaware of blame, and his feet walking toward darkness. Because they *had* been beaten—and damn well beaten—by a somewhat, although not vastly, more honest and integrated group of nations, they liked to hear that they had not been beaten, but sold down the river. Why a person who makes a determined stand and loses fairly prefers to think he has been made a sucker of, I should not have to explain at any great length by now. It is the saving of face—of national ego—at the expense of all other values.

I have already said that man's ego—the importance he puts upon his limited awareness of who and what he is—has become all of man to man, so far as man himself is concerned. This unholy, starveling error is responsible for the trouble he has with himself. And there are national egos just as there are individual and mob egos. The flaws in these egos are noticeable to outsiders—but since one of their main purposes is the hiding of flaws, they are invisible to the participators in a joint ego. The Englishman's "superiority," projected from the mere fact of his English birth, is his ego, in this relationship. Our navy's ego has been expressed by the continuation of the big-battleship program in the face of all reason, need, lesson, and event. Ego is unsound, and so insane—but most men live largely by it; most, indeed, know nothing else. Few nations know anything else, either, except in flashes from individuals in them.

Hitler *rescued the German ego*—which was, as we have seen, bound up in the idea of arms, destruction, and invincibility, and which had been frustrated. He told them that, because of their *purity* and *integrity* of motive, they had been the innocent victims of—*the Jews!* The mechanism is that which I have described, whereby a man behaves like a woman. Because he used it, Hitler is really more of a Delilah than an Antichrist.

While the Germans were furiously (and victoriously) storming every fort in the west and the east, Hitler said, the Jews had gnawed down their house from within. This is the oldest dirty trick man knows —the trick of begging the question via the whipping boy—illogical, feline, dissembling, and vile. Hitler found a fall guy for the Germans and then persuaded them that their original premise of might making right had been sound, after all. Only, according to Hitler, it would now be necessary to match with cunning the cunning that had hitherto interfered with the processes of might. The Germans would have to be even cleverer and more tortuous of mind than the hypothesized fall guys had been. Might thus embraced the weakest of all implements: treachery.

To the glum and frustrated instincts of these people, this folly made sense. It takes a very detached man to admit he had got his arm chopped off because he was silly, or vain, or inordinately greedy. Men as groups have not yet evolved far enough *ever* to admit collective, contemporary viciousness. (Here again is the demonstration of the importance of individualism and individual disciplines toward individual freedoms of choice. Here, again, is the evidence of the meaninglessness of the horde—of the asininity of *enshrining* "common man" beyond blame. Here, too, is the reason people, believing in themselves as a bunch, believe in a quantum they cannot budge collectively and can tackle only man by man. Mobs have no conscience, only instinct, and mobs are unconvinceable. The North and the South, in America, are still fighting the Civil War, and each side still *"knows"* that the other was wrong.) Hitler supplied the key to mass instinctualism that opened the prison of German frustration and set it back on the red-hot rails of conquest.

Believing that they had not been licked in a fight, but betrayed by crooks at home, and believing afresh in the glorious principle of violence über alles, the descendants of the Teutons, Huns, Goths, and who not, picked up with an emotional roar where they had been clipped off. Even fairly reasonable people, once they had accepted the idea that cunning men had betrayed them, were ready for the next step: Hitler's embrace of cunning as a public tool, of the great lie, of treachery, deceit, diplomatic perfidy, and the wretched rest of the Nazi technique.

Americans profess not to understand why Germans "stood for" this sort of manifest corruption—though there has always been enough of it to be seen in American politics to frighten anybody. But any American, if he thinks, will realize that the acceptance of *one* false basic integer in a mathematical formula makes the whole proposition false. Psychologically, also, that is true. The fact is that the Germans, by and large, *did* accept—even welcome—the fundamental alibi. The rest was automatic, in their case. They went hooting back to paganism; every laboratory, every factory turned to war work with gusto. It was easy, from that point on, to steal the money and the raw materials not already present in the Reich.

We, the rest of the world, allowed the process to expand for the reasons cited by Hitler and for others. We were too greedy ourselves to give up greed at home in order to arrest even its dangerous aspects abroad. We were preoccupied with domestic problems and could make no headway with them because we were attacking them on an economic instead of a human basis. Some people in England, France, and America found that large quick money profits could be made by trade with Germany despite the fact that all German trade was based on swindle and would eventually ruin every trader. Other people saw a measure of justice in various Hitlerian claims and calumnies and felt that there was a considerable portion of "right" on the German side. There was—but there is some "right" in the behavior of cannibals; trust in it has stewed many a missionary. Still other men, rich capitalists afraid of the bolshevization of Russia and its underground spread in other nations, judged that Hitler would keep his promise and attack Russia, which, indeed, he has done. Whether or not the Hitler rant against "revolution" could have saved the world from any is no longer a question; it never was—actually; two million Germans, or more, have whooped into lethal Russian guns to make it seem meaningful; their real purpose, always, was only to maintain Hitlerism. Those capitalists who are still alive are doing business, now, with Stalin, and hoping for survival, which the Russians hope for also, and which may conceivably be managed. Finally, many democratic men accepted the debased German invention of a fall guy—the Jew— and therein found another quantum of "rightness" which set them spiritually, if not alongside the Nazis, at least not against them.

The use of anti-Semitism by Hitler at this time is an astonishing evidence of the principle of opposites in the workings of man's soul.

There is a reason behind it which even the Jews do not understand. And yet, by every social and economic measurement to which man is accustomed, there is no sense whatever in anti-Semitism. The statements and figures upon which Hitler bases his monstrous accusation are simply crap. The Jews did not betray Germany before or during or after the war, any more than the Gentiles. Germany was whipped and it had to surrender when its one hundred per cent Aryan navy turned red and refused to sail. Such was the immediate occasion. The Jews in Germany gave just as many lives in the war, per capita, as the Protestants or Catholics. They gave as much money. They were neither richer nor poorer than the others. They maintained the fatherland, along with every common man, right up until it collapsed. Afterward, within the fatherland, so many of them persevered in civilized activities that even Hitler had to "create" thousands of them "Aryans" to maintain his state—and of those he lost, many brilliant ones are making a deficit for Nazism in their laboratories which will tell sorely against the cause of the Herrenvolk in the end. If they had been allowed to stay decently in Germany, as Germans, they would be experimenting and planning for the Reich, even today.

There is this same anti-Semitism in America. I hear the swirl and mutter of it around me in restaurants, at clubs, on the beach, in Washington, in New York, and here at home. No basis exists for the statements that accompany it in *any measurable fact*. "The Jews," people say, "own the radio, the movies, the theaters, the publishing companies, the newspapers, the clothing business, and the banks. They are just one big family, banded together against the rest of humanity, and they are getting control of the media of articulation so that they can control us. They have depraved every art form. They are doing it simply to break down our moral character and make us easy to enslave. Either we will have to destroy them, or they will ruin us."

The garbage goes in somewhat that vein. It has been shown, time and again, that the widespread impression of what Jews own in Amer-

ica is idiotic. They own two or three large banks, among hundreds—
a number out of proportion to their ratio in the whole population.
Banks—Gentile banks—own the movies. There are more Gentiles
than Jews in the movie business. Their race bears no relation to the
quality or the moral viewpoint of the pictures which they produce.
America was a whoring, rum-swilling, vulgar nation from the start.
Protestantism, Catholicism, and Victorianism combined to give it a
veneered notion that it was a land of purity, sweetness, and light—
but it never was; and the Jews who profit by the venality and pruri-
ence of our folk are no more numerous in proper ratio than the micks,
wops, and so on, who do the same. There were some Jewish gangsters
in the Volstead era—but there were shanty Irish rum barons, and Si-
cilians and Italians, out of all proportion to their incidence here. Jews
own a good many theaters because what we call "the theaters" occur
in New York, and New York is where the majority of America's Jews
live. Jews own half a dozen conspicuous newspapers, including the
New York *Times,* which is regarded by Gentiles as the best newspaper
in the world, and Gentiles *own all the rest.* The Hearst papers, the
Scripps-Howard papers, the McCormick-Patterson papers, the papers
owned by John Knight, alone, represent chains that fantastically out-
weigh all the papers owned by Jews—and in those chains are many
papers which are a blight on decency and sanity: strictly Gentile
dirty work, prejudice, and corruption. The Jews own a big piece of the
radio, which also centers in New York. They own some of the clothing business—but only a fraction of the whole.

There isn't *any* sense in the accusation that Jews belong to some
sort of international cabal which plans to control the world. A person
might as reasonably believe that a lama in Tibet decides everything
for everybody. "Zion" is an idea of the same silly order of magnitude.
The Jews do "stick together," locally, to some small extent—and so
do the Catholics and so do the Methodists—and so would you if you
belonged to a group that had been persecuted for two thousand years
by everybody. But there are Jews in every nation, and they are loyal
to that nation as are the rest of the people in it, and Jews within a na-

tion struggle one against the other as hard as the other people and in the same way. There are myriads of poor, vulgar Jews in a few big cities; their collective behavior is not nice to look at—but there are the same steaming slews of wops and micks, and they behave the same way or even worse. In Oklahoma, or in Georgia, are wildernesses of people who, for sheer miserliness of soul and hog-trough behavior, have never been approached by any Jews there is a record of. Life is measurelessly finer in the Bronx than on Tobacco Road.

The "factual case against the Jews," upon investigation, crumbles away so completely that a man who was anti-Semitic (if he had intelligence—an impossibility, however, since being anti-Semitic precludes the attribute) would have to change his opinion *at once,* when confronted with the data. Anti-Semites have been shown the facts, of course, but they persist in their attitude. Indeed, after thoroughly investigating the facts and the sources of the facts, they go on repeating the then proven lies of their original false position. This is, of course, a suicide of all reason by the deliberate self-deceiver and represents the birth of a treacherous man—a man who, having seen the truth and recognized it, adheres nevertheless to a dishonesty.

Why?

That is the question which, for the last ten years, has racked the mind of every Jew—German, American, English, Spanish, Austrian, Russian, and probably Chinese, if any of them still know they are Jewish.

One reason is simple. The so-called "case against the Jew" is the case against humanity. The fault of the Jew is the fault of mankind. But it happens that, in every large nation, there exists a minority of Jews who have carefully maintained their separate identity. To ascribe to them the faults of common man—and to them solely—furnishes a convenient alibi for common man, whose doting vanity has now got him in such shape that he can bear neither to continue as he is nor to look at *himself* for the reasons of his course. The psychology is primitive and therefore, in modern man, infantile. It is the psychology of the school child who says, "Jimmy put me up to it" or "Tony dared me." Even the teacher is sometimes taken in by that specious formula. And it is easier for everybody, Americans included, to say, "The Jews corrupted us" or "The Jews wouldn't play according to the rules so we had to cheat, also," than it is to say what is true: we Americans have always been the slickest bunch of cheaters in the history of time, and furthermore, proud of it!

That much of anti-Semitism is understood by at least a minority of intelligent Americans who are not Jewish and who do not propose to let in the horror of antidemocratic national policy by allowing a gaggle of men with slime instead of gray matter to blame the Jews for the stink that simmers visibly out of their own dirty mouths. The little red schoolhouse should have taken care of this whole business—but the little red schoolhouse has become the national privy.

However, that is only part of the ferocious rot. Anti-Semitism has stained the centuries. There must have been, once, a reason for it, a point of origin. And there was—long ago. The Jews, sadly enough, have their religion to blame for their now senseless predicament. The Old Testament described punishments that will be passed on to the "fathers and sons, unto the third and the fourth generation." They are suffering such punishment, now. Our written law says that no son can be held for the crimes of his father. Society, actually, gives the son of a criminal father no such break. He is generally avoided or demeaned. In the matter of group and race behavior, the process is magnified in violence and extended in time. Thousand-year-old hates still spell out battle cries heard on the fields of Europe today. Preposterous— insane—another sample of that against which the individual lives to fight—but true, none the less; a blind freight of unrecognized instinct.

It was effective, if obvious, of Hitler to select the Jews as his whipping people: there they were still partially identifiable and somewhat clannish—with a history of having been scourged for centuries without retaliation. But it was also ironic. For, by the choice, the Nazis began making themselves into the Jews of the future, and in exactly the same way the Jews begot their spitefully preserved tragedy. To the extent that the Nazis are successful in perpetrating and maintaining their arrogant pride of "race" they, too, will pay off through the centuries; for *that* was the crime-against-man of ancient Israel.

Man will stand for, and sometimes even appreciate, the superior achievements of individuals. He will absorb conquerors. He will throw them off. He will even accept slavery quiescently for a while. But he will not stand the subjective arrogance of a herd. His instincts tell them that there is no superiority of herds and that all men are, as men, basically alike, for better and for worse. Pride goeth before a prat-fall and a haughty spirit before the hotfoot. The arrogance of the English got them the peculiarly perverted hate of the Japs; the Japs will get *our* detestation.

The Jews, beyond all men until the Nazis, carried that particular vanity to its outermost excess—the segregation of themselves from the rest of humanity, into a "superrace." Their vainglorious beginnings are traceable in the Old Testament. Under Joshua, and others, they rolled over the Near East, burning cities, leveling them, sowing salt in the ruins, carrying away the woman for concubines, and putting the males to death. If you will take the trouble to read the Talmud, you will find that the orthodox Jews had a code (which *they* practice no more than we do the villainous codes of *our* Old Testament) whereby there was even a separate morality for Jews. It was necessary for them to be honest and decent only with each other. All the rest of man-kind was cold turkey, to be preyed upon, cheated, lied to, swindled, and knocked on the head. No punishment for gutting a goy. Ten points and a gold star, rather—as in Mohammedanism.*

---

* This, in its literal sense, is an error. I have since read the Talmud and realize my impression came from a published *discussion* of it— the work, beyond any doubt, of an anti-Semite. However, in the psychological sense, the sense that Jews considered themselves the master race, the "chosen people"—and in the historical sense that the Twelve Tribes dealt ferociously with their Gentile neighbors—the assertion holds valid.

One needs not to read the Talmud, a just and wonderful book, but

These wiper-outers of three millennia ago or more were, in their turn, conquered and dissipated. But they clung to their orthodoxy, or parts of it, wherever they went for a long time. They remained "The Chosen People" and their orthodox religion insisted that the day of judgment would eventually arrive when Jehovah would appear and hang up all their enemies so that Jews could spit upon them while they squirmed in torment. Such religious patterns are more or less universal—the product of man's instinctual investiture of his creeds with his own inner nature, whether it is good and altruistic or frustrated and vengeful. Read the Bible. Moreover, because they felt themselves to be superior and select, the Jews refused to *breed* with other men.

That was the insult supreme.

When a Jewish girl married a nice, hard-working Frenchman in, say, the time of Louis XII, her family crossed her name off the books, rent its garments, and poured ashes on its head. When the eld-

---

only the Old Testament, to learn these things. Indeed, the Bible itself is a long, seldom-broken account of sado-masochistic reflexes in various tormented, arrogant people. Barbaric people, to be sure; yet its uncounted murders, massacres, tortures, crucifixions and the like form the acknowledged *basis* of our Western society!

It is a wonder we never notice what *that* means—a wonder, just for instance, at such an instant as this, when there happens to be a brouhaha over children's comic books, so-called. Without the sado-masochistic foundation of Western personality, the little apes could never *have* such appetites! One hesitates to call the Bible a comic; but it is, surely as man breathes, the first and greatest *horror* book of all and nothing the kiddies see in the pulps can touch it.

We do not—not yet, at least—have any national habit—when we are confronted with human horror at home—of looking sharply at the base of our culture. Such a look is more than most men have the guts, brains, knowledge, honesty and—may I add?—the *inner serenity*—to dare.

est son, a bright young physician recently graduated in Padua, ran away with the Rhenish miller's daughter, the same thing happened and the lamentation was even worse. This excessive and ostentatious practice of superiority was unbearable to the neighbors. They threw the Jews into ghettos, took their money, tormented them, raped their good-looking women, and generally raised hell with them. The Jews, in millions of cases reduced to nothing except their belief in their essential superiority, clung to that all the harder—and were kicked the more—and thus became professionally a martyred class for a thousand and more years. In the period, having to work harder to live than their fellows, they naturally survived to some extent through the genes of the most crafty, the fastest thinking, and the slyest. Thus there may have developed in them, a little more than in other men, a strain of intelligence and guile which made effective traders of them. At any rate, they became effective, also, as scientists and doctors and musicians and teachers. Possibly their average I.Q. was never any higher than the human norm; but certainly they managed to produce a somewhat higher ratio of effective brains on the level near the top. *At* the top, again, all men, according to Hooton, are equal.

The smartness of Jews,* to the extent that it was real, or the mere

---

* Norbert Wiener, in his autobiography, gives currency to a possible explanation of this shadowy seeming of superiority and it seems to me that Dr. Wiener's idea deserves thoughtful consideration. All during the Dark Ages, he points out, the bright sons of the Roman Catholics were educated to be priests, while the studious daughters were made nuns. These, vowing a kind of self-castration, remained sterile. Down the same centuries (and to-day, too) rabbis (though also picked from among the gifted children) produced (and still produce) sizeable families. Thus, perhaps, Wiener suggests, the predominant church of the medieval world destroyed its own best genes systematically—while the religion of the Jews tended to favor genetic maintenance.

It is an idea nobody can argue. The thing happened. It continues to

reputation for it, if it was not, annoyed the never-bright multitudes. It gave no discernible trouble to smart Gentiles, that I have found a record of. But the subjective quantum became extraordinarily conspicuous because of the self-pronounced superiority of the Jews and their actual unwillingness to mix themselves biologically with the rest of the species. For those two crimes, above all others, they were condemned and officially held down. Out of those acts came a great and terrible prejudice. A thoroughly reasonable, self-protective prejudice, in a sense, and in its long-vanished time. For if ever there does appear upon this planet a tightly knit minority of really superior people, it will be the end of all the rest of mankind—and mankind knows it, not having come through a billion-odd years of evolutionary struggle for nothing.

Had the Jews been humble, they would have avoided their suffering. But they were bound to suffer, century after century, so long as they refused to marry other people, as indeed even the humblest Catholics have. And a people that calls itself "chosen" can scarcely be credited with humility. The original device of self-styling themselves the top people on earth was to compensate, doubtless, for those feelings of guilt-born inferiority which are inevitable among all conquering men. It is a futile, dangerous device. Christ railed at the Jews for it, until he lost all popularity with them, and he has enjoyed none among them since. He was the enemy of business, of banking, of interest—and mortgage-brokers, of the ladies' guild and the self-important tax assessor, and the people didn't like it then any better than they do now. The Jews crucified Christ, their greatest hero, and are almost

happen. Ireland is dying because of it. If I were a Roman Catholic, that fact, alone, would set me thinking all the rest of my days. For it is one of the most hideous statements ever made. It discloses, by inference, the price that churches must pay to keep masses of people in instinctual thralldom by the expedient of taking charge of the sex instinct. That, in turn, goes to the heart—or near it—of What is the Matter with Us All.

the only people to have done such a thing. (We Americans have skimmed close to it on occasion; we shot Lincoln; and, of course, the Nazis have crucified all heroes.) That single act was an expression of the wrongness of the behavior of Jews two thousand years ago.

It has nothing to do with the behavior of most Jews today.

Indeed, very little of the substance in this explanation pertains to *any* Jew alive today. Orthodoxy, even in its mild and later forms, is perishing. Jews marry Gentiles by thousands. It is no longer possible to tell them from other men by the way they look or talk—and it probably has not been possible for centuries. Jews shudder when they hear the word "chosen people" because it gives them, now, no sense of vanity but only a frightful awareness of the retribution man has charged against their assumption, long ago, of that title. If, overnight, all the people on earth could forget that there had been "Jews" in their various nations, it would be impossible to pick out, by any criteria, who had once been one sort (Jewish) and who had been another (Gentiles). There is no longer any way to determine the matter, if there ever was one, and if there are hooked noses on more Jews, there are still hooked noses on plenty of bishops.

Unfortunately, the consciousness of Jewishness cannot be eliminated overnight, either from Gentiles or from Jews. It represents a memory —a memory of a race of people, once conquerors, once authors of the idea of superiority, once the terror of the Near East, and afterward for two thousand years and more so recklessly determined to stick to the notion of superiority that they reviled the rest of man—no matter what penalty they had to pay for doing it. Such is the cost of every "Herrenvolk" idea. Contemporary Jews—innocent of any blame whatever, but still attacked at every turn by the long, harsh, reasonless, race memories of man—are born and live and die in the fantastic and irrelevant predicament of merely being Jewish.

It is little wonder that, no matter how they try to escape the fabulous rage of the memory, no matter how often and how meritoriously they protest the utter injustice of it, no matter what they change their name to or whom they marry, a difference often clings to them. The

Anti-Semite—dull, unperceptive, and uncomprehending—*compels* that difference by his savage tradition of revenge. He makes believe that the old, instinctually valid accusations of the Jews are still real and current. He supports his lickspittle racial document with popeyed fabrications. He persecutes with words and innuendo and blackball where he no longer has gall enough to do it with blows—substituting mental barbarism for physical attack because he resents the colossal indignity that the whole business is now bringing upon his own head. Indignity—since it is unworthy of him, having lost all relation even to the basest of his instincts.

The Jew gravely seeks some means to endure this. As long as it continues, he will not be quite the same as the others. Either he will have to defend himself by direct counterattack of it, or by exemplary and sadly proud conduct—or else he will have to hide away from it, or try to forget it by living as much as he can only with other Jews. That is his last ordeal for the old sins of his forebears; a neurosis— both personal and collective—imposed upon himself and the rest of his kind by the dastardliness of common men who go on for stupid generations practicing revenge when the cause of it has vanished, practicing it because it gives them pleasure, because it diverts their sensibilities from their own vast nastiness—and so appears, for little instants, to lighten the crushing burden of *their* inferiorities.

Out of such scant traces of pre-Christian Judaism as he could uncover, and out of this pitiful neurosis, Hitler made *his* case against the Jews. Onto it, when he had got the fire going again, he heaped all the wickedness of man.

Then he swallowed the fire. Or, perhaps, it swallowed him.*

---

* American anti-Semitism, these days, is twisting about in search of similar stratagems. Communism is widely regarded as "Jew-dominated," in spite of what amount to Soviet pogroms.

Science, though under popular suspicion, has not yet (to my knowledge) been attested by the yahoos as "Jewish"—albeit a great many scientists are Jews (and, incidentally, very, very few Catholics).

He led the German people, the good with the bad, the bright with the ignorant, the Protestants and Catholics and the tree worshipers, on toward a new Jericho.

Here is the marvel and the joke! Here is the cosmic laugh—the cruel fun for the ages! Hitler made the Germans over into the living image of the long-dead Jews. As Joshua, the man who could plaster the sun and the moon against the sky, created he the superman, the Herrenvolk. Of course, Nietzsche and Spengler and a few other decrepit half-wits, together with some brilliant morons like Haushofer, helped Hitler into the furnace. Bismarck had run over the ground, and so had Wilhelm. But Hitler got going when the world was wondering if it could seduce itself again successfully, and he went all-out, which neither Bismarck nor Wilhelm had dared attempt.

I suggest, then, that the American rabble rouser of the near future could take this implied platform as the "front" for a red-white-and-blue totalitarianism and, under the banner of, "Down with Jewish-Communist-Science" transfix fitful millions exactly as Hitler did.

Indeed, if any Executioner of Freedom ever does exhibit that device, he should be stopped in his tracks and not allowed—like some other menacing buffoons—to grow big for even a little time. Our muddled millions have reached so panicky a pass (and have so little will to put the charge where it belongs—on themselves) that the binding together of such awesome symbols might snatch away their last restraint.

I give this recipe for national doom, not as a prophesy but, simply, so the nature of the ingredients (and the result of eating the pudding) may be known clearly and well ahead of the possible event. It would be quite easy for an expert malefactor to make science seem "Jewish." But we, like the Soviets, must depend on science and *scientists* until we discover who is to triumph, or how to live together—and after that, *forever.*

Soviet Russia, let us note, gives scientists all-out *support*—while we have begun their persecution. What could be more mad?

The Germans, it seems, were the chosen people, and not the Jews. The Jews, indeed, were the scum of the earth and first on the extirpation list. The jubilant and resurrected Herrenvolk extirpated them. All other men, according to Hitler, were muck and could be cheated and rooked at will—a page out of the Talmud. Cheating a non-Nazi stepped you up in party favoritism—a little something from the Koran. Conquer Europe, Hitler said, with the sword, and the rest of the world with shekels—another precept of the Jew of antiquity.

The great huzzoo was on—murder, rape, pillage, arson, mass bombing, anything you could think of, so long as it presented the Herrenvolk in the light of horsepower superiority and other human beings in the gutter. Kick them, beat them, torture them, kill them, and in the end they will knuckle under. Only, they didn't—a fact which the Jews discovered and which is even now puzzling the Germans, who have been cooking up parts of this grisly plot for about three-quarters of a century. The conquered people did not like their masters, no matter how agonizingly their masters tortured them. The outlying, somnolent, pluto-democratic sons of corruption began to look across the sea and snort with indignation. The British did not quit, even when Mr. Goering's bombs had got them to within a couple of weeks of quitting—and their intention was to stay with the bombs till the last minute of the last hour of the last week before they quit—an intention which, again, puzzled the Wilhelmstrasse. The dreadful Bolshevist donkeys, too, would not retreat even when they were hip-deep in the blood of their brothers, fathers, wives, aunts, sisters, friends, and strangers—a fact which caused an anthropoid murmur of consternation to run through the steel ranks of the supermen. Nobody quit. And nobody will. The Germans have for some time had the practice, like those foolish and long-dead Jews, of quitting when there is still something left. But the common people, the non-Herrenvolk, did not see it that way. They still do not.

Moreover, Hitler has run his ferocious arrogance far beyond the boundaries of his Promised Land, this time. When he and his people are defeated, they will have to give up forever, in consequence, the idea of their superiority; if they do not give it up, they will have to live in the ghettos of the world for two thousand years, kicked and spat upon, mistrusted and reviled—and the resurrection of an old pattern, proved hideous by the history of the Jews, will be the reason for their doomful future.* Because they, too, have committed the unpardonable

---

* As I noted in Chapter I, I failed in 1942 to foresee how soon we Americans would bury in our unconscious minds the guilty behavior of the Germans. But the psychodynamics of that process were clear to me before the end of the War. Here is what I wrote about it in my syndicated newspaper column in April, 1945:

". . . we, the people, will undertake (in our usual way) to erase from our minds any real memories of this war. The peacemakers, the hopers, the selfish, the stupid and the silly will start a 'combined operation' of wishful thinking. Then, by and by, nobody will believe that World War II was as hideous as it really was: the skeptics of the 1950's and the 1960's will explain that there was a good deal of credulity in the war years plus a good deal of lying about atrocities together with a lot of invented propaganda; and the statesmen and the businessmen will get together—ex-enemy with ex-ally—to make the immemorial decision that they were pretty good fellows, after all. . . . In those distant days it will finally be agreed that the Germans and Japs didn't make the war, but only the Nazis and only a few of them and only a handful of Jap war lords.

"By that time, the conscience of humanity will be getting pretty clean (in its own, always-prejudiced estimation) and that will be the day when somebody, somewhere, really gets his shoulder—and the shoulders of several scores of millions of the same sort of people— under the exciting job of starting World War III.

"The process is most familiar to every detached student of mankind —even if it is also sad. It's an almost inevitable process, too, because if the people of the world did go on remembering the truth about to-day's war, it would slowly dawn on each of them that, even as individuals, they share to some degree the blame.

sin against the races of men. They have said they were better. They enwhore but do not marry. For that they are done. The meek—not the arrogant—shall eventually inherit the earth, and this is why.

This is one of the great laws of the paired opposites; this is the inner meaning of democracy; this is why each man must live his life for common men—even when they are busy with some new variety of

---

"For, not only those who live by the sword, *but also those who let other people live by the sword,* are liable to die by the sword, as the fresh graves of a multitude of Americans show forth. That, however, points to a heavy human responsibility which the new generation will endeavor once more to shrug off. Each new one succeeds, too."

The italics above have been added to make plain my prescience in 1945 about what presently became an American refusal to stand up for freedom when the Soviet conquistadores insisted upon an *un*free Atomic Age. We have let the Soviets "live by the sword" for ten years since the above was written and we are now, indeed, in peril of dying ourselves by the sword named Hydrogen Isotope. This is how we repressed the guilts of the last war and so failed to perceive the guilty laxness which so soon led to our present dilemma.

The German repression of German guilt was even more swift and awesome. I have often thought that the unconscious effects of Christian symbology may partly explain the postwar German capacity for shrugging off blame. The thesis deserves exploration. For, after all, Hitler was everywhere in Germany held to be a savior and a messiah. His melodramatic suicide in the midst of his flaming empire is regarded by many Germans as the result not of ironic justice but of treachery. To them, Hitler was "crucified"—and, perhaps, they unconsciously extract from the parallel a comparable sense of "atonement" and "forgiveness": Hitler died in agony—"for their sins"—which are thereby expunged. Some such unconscious warp of logic may go far to explain the shameless irresponsibility of German multitudes today.

fallible and detestable epoch: that which the Germans reviled and persecuted they became.

Hitler and the stilted bigwigs with no necks and no backs to their heads, who invented all the monstrous "sciences" of the new order by consulting their instincts, using steel-filing-cabinet methods to catalogue them, and so justifying them according to the credulous dogma of many non-German scientists—Hitler and this insufferable welter of poltroons who collected minutiae about other men and so found the ways to precede the Wehrmacht with swarms of brain-locusts that devoured because few recognized them and even they did not know how to exterminate them—Hitler and this ghastly bunch of educated maggots, motorized morons, Goths in gas masks, Teutons in tanks, dive-bombing Vandals, and Nibelungs with adding machines created together, according to a law they did not have the penetration or even the will (which is the same as the wish) to understand, this bloody boomerang, and upon it they rode into battle to extend the Lebensraum, little knowing how the thing would sooner or later ineluctably crash back into the Heimland they already had.

Because they were ignorant of the cosmic statutes under which they operated, their very operation became autonomous. Thus the nation, like the angry man or woman I have described, fell *into* every imaginable opposite of the surrounding "enemy" peoples, without realizing it was doing so and without even wondering why.

Take a look:

Great men, specialized cerebral powerhouses of all sorts, had not been able to deliver the magic goods of humanity-in-chains. Bismarck, Wilhelm, Hindenburg, and the other high-ranking generals had only split open millions of German bodies. What then? Then try a *little* man, a man far from great. Apotheosize the pipsqueak—the man unsullied by education, travel, and experience—the lowest grade of everyman—the clown and comic, with his disgusting vanity and his every thought a pure product of his reptilian instinct. Hitler, in short. The giant brains had fizzled. Science had not brought into Germanic being the foul dream of decades of scream and shuttle in Mitteleuropa.

Science and education were getting the inspiration nowhere. Turn then, Germans, to nonscience. Burn the books! Down with Heidelberg! Shoot the Ph.D.'s! Up with might, cruelty, intimidation, the physical pressure of a million thumbscrews! Down with brother love! Down with psychology that teaches these matters are not voluntary but autonomous! Up, the ravening prickamouse! Heil, Housepainter!

If the thing had ended there, some detached members of outlying society might have grasped its enormity and its peril. But it went on in excesses of itself. The urge toward oppositeness was so intense that outlying society began to laugh, when it should have been getting ready to die.

Down with old anthems! Make the national song a eulogy to a pimp. Make a "Minister of Enlightenment" out of another Nibelung, twisted in body and mind, possessed of such flaming prejudices as light only the way to hell—blazes of dark fire! Goebbels! For the marshal, the military front man, the fellow with the medals, take the greatest travesty of the figure in the nation: take an apostrophe of Germanism, the swinish human porker, the fat boy with the dimples, the man who has been in college but who goes about in shorts and a leather vest with a dirk in a scabbard, the piggy eyes and the great belly, erudite puer aeternis full of infantilism and highly polished, the dope fiend, moreover, as an added measure of self-castigation for the whole Volk! Where Germany had its iciest dignity, where Germany had attained, through negativism, its most positive archetype—the thin, raw Prussian with his monocle and his indexed cruelty—put, by all means, Hermann Goering. From the old generals take the oldest one, returned by the senile circuit to the childishness of his people. Bow out Hindenburg with a frightened little smirk. Put in Ludendorff, who has gone back to druids, stone festivals, and Odin!

On and on the process carried the paranoid nation. It made apparent sense because it represented a great psychological rebellion; it made actual sense, too, because these new archetypes, unearthed from universal instincts and from the special branches of learning appurtenant to Mitteleuropa, were as valid for Germans as the rational and

Christian premises of Western man. Either is sterile without the other; either is dangerous without parallel recognition of the other because it is only half a man—but the Germans didn't know it, the Britons didn't, or the French, or the citizens of Oklahoma. This turning inside out, and the German welcoming of it, was incomprehensible to democratic men, and so they laughed at it. The only alternative for them would have been to be afraid—for that, too, is instinctual; the savage (even as you and I) either fears or ridicules what he does not understand. We ridiculed, because we were too busy to be afraid. It was economically cheaper to laugh than to fear—at first.

I will leave it to some other person, at some future time, to make a full report upon the unconscious zeal with which the Germans turned wrong-side-out all those principles and tenets of so-called civilized man which they had superficially adopted by the end of the first quarter of this century. There can be no doubt of the fact that they did so, and no doubt of the reason for it. The mechanics of the individual personality are superimposed on the group and intensified by the numbers of the group. These mechanics operate under many laws, and one of them is this psychological parallel to Newton's. The behavior of modern German society furnishes an exquisite example of the theorem and all its imaginable corollaries, in action.

Why in hell American "psychologists," who ought to be as eager as all other scientists to discover fundamental laws, reject or ignore this one is hard to understand. They, of course, like the Germans, are entrenched in *their* half-consciousness and want nothing valid to be recognized in all the firmament excepting only if *they* discover it and give a nomenclature to it. These one-track metaphysicians are not even interested in the thousands of years of honest and therefore scientific experiment and reflection of men in China or Tibet or India or Palestine. The ancient thinkers, one can hear Columbia doctors argue, didn't know Ohm's law. So how the devil could they have known *anything* of importance? And if the village yogin could perform mental and physical acts inexplicable to the Columbia University sachems, then the sachems were "mass hypnotized," or their recording instruments weren't working right, or the chap was a trickster: Pavlov is never wrong. We could abide these maestros even if they realize that instincts, too, come from the conditioning of all living throughout all time. But not when they try to tack the spirit of man to a sheet of beaverboard in a graph of two lines, one red, one blue, the stupid jerks!

The spectacle of primitive-medieval man engaged in the physical sciences on a high plane, but simultaneously attempting to support a subjective dogma on the levels of his forebears, is another one for the ages and has produced the flat-hatted microcosm of neo-poops. These men try either to compress all the truths of man's personality into the results of a few kindergarten observations or to shoo them into churchly intellectual systems which are already as badly ruined as Thebes.

Let them investigate on new planes. Let them investigate the opposites. Let them study, say, human hatred. Then they will stop the eternal newspaper utterance about hatred in connection with our enemies, the Germans, which is regarded by every manner of scientist, college president, statesman, and religious smoothbrain as some sort of spiggot that can be turned on and off at will, rather than as an eternal quantity in man's instinct, the opposite of love, and something to reckon with for the next million years. Let these giant multiquacks study Americans in the light of what they really do and what goes on inside their helicoid personalities. Let them study the crowds at football games, gossip, virgins' dreams, subjective attitudes toward urination, the Ku-Klux Klan, women's pages, Homeric laughter, the followers of Huey Long, bawdyhouse monologues, wallpaper choices, evil, why the social findings of our great foundations rot in files, the man at the wheel and what it means to him, dialogues in elevators and trolley cars, industrial boredom, and all such closely related matters.

Let them study *man*.

This brings us to the scientists.

CHAPTER X

Uncommon Men

THE SPECTACLE OF A GREAT PHYSICIST, ASTRO-CUM-NUCLEAR, who was also a leading apologist-for-God-according-to-the-Congregationalists,* was one of the merriest to be seen in the past two dec-

---

* This referred, of course, to the late Dr. Robert A. Millikan, then President of California Institute of Technology.

One notes, with something of a sigh, how the "universe" now "changes" almost annually. When Millikan sought a "creating God," what happy days they were—the good, old, days of Jeans-and-Eddington. For a while, after that, the expanding universe people had the thing in hand and we were rushing apart on galaxies that ran as trains to noplace—with the gloomy prospect (in some billions of years) of being Left Alone in Space—us, and our trifling Milky Way.

Right now, Hoyle and some bright Britishers have presented the "constant-if-inexplicable-creation-of-hydrogen universe" and things look cozier. Maybe, after all, God *is* perpetually re-creating the expanding, vanishing Cosmos!

Years of study of these matters—or perhaps just years—have given me a certain sanguinity about astronomers. I am still amused that so many people are compulsively ridden with a need to "find" an "eternal" universe: the fact perfectly illustrates how it is mankind invents every, little separate "god" according to his knowledge of himself (and his ignorance) at the moment. So, for me, this perpetually rear-

156

ades, for those who take their merriment out of Imminent Despair. The intellectual predicament of the personage had him at odds with his own cloud chambers. It made necessary, he seemed to feel, the confinement of all observed phenomena to the frame described by St. Paul —and not just that, but to the Congregationalist definition of the St. Paul border. This brick-like nuance led, among other things, to a debate upon whether the universe was winding up or whether it was running down. Posses of learned men scrabbled over the planet setting balloons into the stratosphere and peering through smoked glass at eclipses in order forever to settle this matter; all sorts of manifestations of God were boiled in test tubes and ground up with pestles in the hope or the fear that what had started some two billions of years ago was or was not building up to an awful letdown some five or ten billions of years hence. The enterprise of these mahatmas and their discussions per se were of considerable classical moment, and even of conceivable future practical use to, it might be suggested, some sweating tycoon who could get control of the stock in a corporation that had harnessed the cosmic or solar radiation thus uncovered and wire it to every home, where it would be utilized for the cooking of waffles, the operation of electrical clippers, and the mechanical reversion of unsalted butter to sweet cream.

The most engrossing point of the boggle, which rapidly became international, was not the elucidation of the structure of atoms which accompanied it, or even the amount of commerce that might be derived from the data, but the impulse which compelled an extraordinary erudite Congregationalist to hypothesize ecclesiastical "verities" upon a purely secular investigation. Had this wizard examined his Bible

---

ranged and re-solved conundrum of space-time-energy has that humorous value.

But as to the data and the astronomical pronunciamentoes, I am inclined to think that nobody, exactly nobody, in this century, the next, or the next millennium, will learn enough about it to make a firm quotation on a True God.

with the acuity he applied to electromagnetism, he would have found several psychological needlings toward truth-at-the-cost-of-any-dogma. Evidently, he had never done so. Instead, he went about brandishing screeds of mathematical formulae to reassure nervous preachers—who did not understand a symbol in them—that God was still putting the universe together, using particles which shot along at hundreds of millions of volts, and that the claim of certain equally learned atheists and agnostics to the effect that these demonstrated rays represented schism, was devil-talk. At about this same time, many brother theurgists tossed books out of their observatories to reassure the fundamentalist plebiscite, and some of these works seemed naïvely honest, but all contained, perhaps, another unidentified motive: a phobia against latter-day inquisitions. A few poetically minded freebooters followed the dispute from end to end, among them myself, but nobody besides me, so far as I am aware, bothered to view with alarm the human poser behind the galaxies of math and apostrophic harangue.

A quietus of sorts came over the thing, I recall, when the devil worshipers managed to refute some of the more technically canonical claims of the holy men and thereby drove them back to their cryology, spectroheliographology, glass giants, cyclotrons, transformers, electron tubes, Wilson chambers, magnets, Geiger counters, least squares, relativity, shears, and library paste, in the presumptive attempt to find out some new information which could be construed into proof that God the electrochemist is every man's next-door neighbor, and a Congregationalist also.

But humanity at large was impassive in the presence of the man who thought such proof was necessary beyond all other truth; humanity took him for a mighty savant; even the erudite agnostics bothered to argue with him endlessly on his own grounds of predeterminism. As much as any of billions, this debate showed forth the depth of penetration of instinctual behavior even into the modern scientific mind—and the passion which went into the refutation of physical-conclusions-à-la-Congregationalism was as illuminating as the

Congregationalist passion, for it showed, often, not so much a desire
to arrive at truth as a desire to persecute dogmatists for the hell of
it, and it was conducted with as much sanctity of agnostic essentialism
on its side as there was documented faith on the other. Passionate ir-
religiousness is, in itself, a religion, because it is a passion and must so
be treated.

But except for a few good belly-laughs implicit to several ten- and
twenty-page equations, there was no adjustment among scientists even
on an unconscious level. The stark and staring evidence that modern
man at his very best is still the child of instinct and compulsion, of
medievalism and fire-dancing, escaped notice by the victims in both
camps. Now, of course, these geniuses are engaged in a great world
war, come about because they and their fellow men have not yet recognized that breach and spanned it. The equipment in Cambridge,
Chicago, Pasadena, and San Francisco is studying human destruction—
a meaty principle itself—and will possibly set precedents whereby we,
or our children, or theirs, will manage someday so many large explosions that all the machines will be broken and we can start anew,
worshiping trees and pirouetting around the tribal blaze. It may be,
of course, that instinct itself will prevail in a new form and the academicians will set aside their gadgets in order to think awhile about
themselves; or perhaps reason, passing into a realm of integrity unheard-of in the West, but still acting via the snarled conduits of the
laboratories, will hit upon the sore cause in the individual, and start
the new lines of research necessary for survival and progress. Those
are thin possibilities, in view of the spectacle of scientists presently at
work.*

---

*The above paragraph has set many persons agog owing to the
fact that it contains a clear forehint of atomic bombs. The "equipment
in Cambridge, Chicago, Pasadena and San Francisco" did, indeed,
"set precedents" whereby the "large explosions" were managed.

Now, it was no trick at all, in 1941, to predict atomic bombs:
the only question was the date of their contriving. Indeed, I had writ-

* * *

Further to illustrate (a) these absurdities of science; (b) education; (c) leadership; (d) "abstract idealism," whatever that is; (e) the canyons which lie between who we are and who we think we are, and what we do and what we think we are doing; (f) the gulf between the classical and the applied; (g) the ignominious condition of man as contradistinguished from his available possibilities; and (h) sundry other relevant and associated concepts—I have elected briefly to survey our doctors of medicine.

These gentlemen consider themselves scientists and are so regarded by society. Yet, in their attempts to deal "scientifically" with people, they have uncovered a world of material which does not fit *their* preconception of the human pattern. Medical doctors are, moreover, familiar objects to the layman, and as such more understandable than mathematicians, so they will make a less imponderable example for the average reader.

There occurs in *Tristram Shandy* a character by the name of Dr. Slop, whose shambling peregrinations through that remarkable book provide an earnest picture of the medical hypocrisies of his time. The

---

ten, in 1940, a fantasy about uranium bombs so accurate it was later to get me into some embarrassed trouble with Military Intelligence, which could not imagine *I* could imagine so much without illicit access to secret information.

G2 *ought*, of course, to have known that in 1914, immediately after Albert Einstein announced his theory about energy and mass, Herbert George Wells wrote a novel about atomic bombs.

What, to my mind, seems interesting in the paragraph above, is my hopefulness—admittedly "thin"—that the scientists might soon turn to the study of *man* for an answer to the horrid problems of our era. But the spectacle of humanity nowadays—along with the present occupations of science—makes it plain my thin hope was rank optimism. In that basic sense, "Generation of Vipers" is less a vivid portrayal of things to come than a sort of astute "Pollyanna."

glittering paraphernalia of the modern medico, his sterile technique (what a valuable description!), and his manifest extension, in theory at least, of the human span of life quiet most contemporary suspicions that would otherwise arise anent his cousinship with the fumbling Slop. The shrewdness, courage, nobility, skill, and integrity of some doctors upon some occasions does not concern us here. In attempting to learn what is wrong with us, we have very little business, at this hour, to consider what is right. And I propose to show that, while there may be nothing slovenly about the family medico's clinic, he is still, as a rule, Slop in his head and heart—a superb instance of the contributions of science to sophistry, by oversight, neglect, avoidance, and a basic untrustworthiness that is scarcely bearable.

The doctor—the modern doctor—your doctor, upon whom you call in all crises which appear to you to have a protoplasmic origin —is an extremely well-educated person in the accepted sense of the phrase. He has mastered the fundamentals of chemistry, biology, physics, anatomy, and the derived skills of prescribing drugs, sewing, drilling, sawing, cutting, anesthetizing, bandaging, and so on. He occasionally frowns over the fact—known to him and mentioned in an earlier part of this book—that half the patients who appeal to him are suffering from ills, both real and imagined, which cannot be cured by drugs or surgery because they arise from such causes as grandmother-detestation or failure to make the girl down the street. Thus, while he knows in his heart, if he is even a mediocre doctor, that half his clients demand other remedies, he goes on, as a rule, dosing and snipping until they are likely to totter about the world as mere toxic remnants of persons.

Now, this is a very grotesque indictment. To murder a man is bad; to drive him permanently insane is still worse, for you murder him every day so long as he lives. Our willfully arrogant Slops have murdered millions. They have also packed the lunatic asylums with other millions who are in a suspended death to which they fled in order to escape our society, with the full connivance, as a rule, of some person or other who calls himself a physician. Doctors have, no doubt, temporarily saved more human lives, at least in recent decades, than they have collaborated in quickly destroying, but to grant them any accolade on that basis is nonsensical. The half of sick humanity with which they only pretend to cope is a rebuke in the form of living monsters, first, because doctors do consciously pretend to deal with the problem and, second, because they seldom either investigate or cry out against the causes of this enormity of misery and never willingly memorialize the proletariat in re what they know.

Of all human beings, stuffed with science and outwardly dedicated to truth, who have an opportunity to study individual man at first hand, these gentlemen come by the largest, the most frequent, and by far the most revealing chances. But they are, as a class, embarked upon the exploitation of what they discover, or its concealment in prisons for the cuckoo, or a delegation of its treatment to a body of rare sages and magnaquacks whom the doctors do not understand and whom they class—all equally—as psychiatrists; or else, above everything else, they are engaged in trying by joint clamor to protect their medieval perquisites from investigation and change.

Let us start with the beginning of this nonsense. A scrutiny of it is germane to this book. Indeed, for the reader who looks toward science for salvation it is required reading. Science is all right, that is, but the scientists are far from all right. Until they are, how can science come to anything but more human folly? Very well. Half the hospital beds of our land are taken by "mental" cases, and about half of those who apply to the medical profession for physical attention are ailing, according to the latest advices, of neuroses. In consequence, and purely as an experiment, *you* can assume that half the time *you* visit your doctor, *you* are there because of a problem in your psyche and not your intestines. From this you must necessarily deduce, if your doctor gives you a pill instead of advice or orders a basal metabolism test instead of a teleological row with your aunt, that he is fooling you half the time, and quite probably himself.

Now, it is hotly denied by laymen and only grudgingly admitted by physicians, in spite of the appalling body of factual proof, that a pathological condition can occur in your body, which springs neither from germs and viruses nor from protoplasmic mechanics, but from a subjective attitude or the lack of one. The full extent to which you can mar your skin and bog your blood stream by action inside your head is not known. But certainly you, as a human being, are able by subjective means to contrive, under divers circumstances, fever, rashes, fits, swellings, immobilizations, pseudo pregnancies, abortions, vomitings, chills, sweats, atrophies, hypertensions, low blood pressure, loss of appetite, malfunction of glands, various cardiac disturbances, migraine, catarrh, constipation, diarrhea, numbness, hypersensitivity, ulcers of the stomach and gut, hallucinations, bed-wetting, morbid compulsions, the precondition which leads to the contraction of colds as well as tuberculosis and all other contagions and infections, spontaneous external bleeding, spasms, contractions, convulsions, flatulence, paralysis, adhesions, ankylosis, all forms of mania, gleet, galling, impotence, satyriasis, belching, acute indigestion, chronic debility, blindness, deafness, loss of the sense of smell, abnormal appetite, hiccups, and just about everything else in the medical lexicon with the conceivable exception of worms.

There is no use for the reader to ram his doctor-taught medical biases against that list. All such states have been not merely diagnosed many times as of psychological rather than physical origin, but they have been cured many times by purely psychological methods without the aid of any drug or instrument. These facts in no way set aside the possibility that a man's body can be sick or diseased without the causal involvement of his mind. They merely state that in multitudes of modern instances it is primarily the mind and soul that have hurt the body. In different societies and other ages, neurotic illness was probably different, and the nature of much lunacy also—which someone should investigate and report on.

This is not, however, a brief for Christian Science, which holds that all ailment is the product of metaphysical error and no doctor is ever needed, but only somebody to read a book. To the sick layman, the situation may present a level of quandary beyond his depth. Indeed, it generally must, and the doctor is the logical person from whom to solicit treatment.

But half the doctors in the world are not psychiatrists and the medical men do not send half their patients to psychoanalysts. A capable doctor will confess to an intimate colleague, or even on occasion to a layman, that he *should* provide psychic and not clinical care for half his patients. To that statement he may add the thought that he needs such care himself, and has no time for it, and the information that it is about as difficult for a medical doctor to persuade the ordinary college graduate, or you, to go even to an able psychiatrist as it was for Christ to sell anybody in the money on the notion of giving it to the poor and getting about the more important business of truth-seeking. Good psychiatrists, never good enough for *all* their human patients, engage solely in the business of aiding persons toward seeking truth about themselves.

Since society is founded upon lies, and since all men are, in countless ways, exponents of the most groveling forms of intellectual and moral crookedness, the psychoanalytical method is slow, mentally painful to the deluded patient, at least at first, and likely, instead of rendering him whole, to spring him upon his startled fellows in the overweaning and enlightened possession of some corner or giblet of eternal truth which, isolated in a still unclear mind and hatched autonomous in a still prejudiced company of persons, makes his behavior seem so bizarre that his friends avoid him, and he is liable to become disappointed not only with psychiatry but with himself all over again and develop a new set of stigmata.

That sort of behavior, common in the patients of psychiatrists, has done much to discredit the psychological approach to human suffering. It is unfortunate. The incompleteness of knowledge in all branches of science has had the same tendency. Thus, recently, for instance, it was a common postulate among all reasonable men save a few that machines heavier than air could never fly, although manifestly birds did and they were heavier than air. Galileo himself made no headway in trying to convince the courts that his discoveries were correct; his proof was not complete and palpable enough for the apes in black robes who judged him. Psychology, which, for some reason, is called "psychiatry" when it is used in connection with human misery and mental disease, will, of course, survive its apparent failures and the gaps in its practical knowledge. Great men with great truths have seldom had much support from their associates, and such is the case here. It is more spectacularly the case, indeed, than ever before, because a man will grudgingly yield a point sometimes on the movement of heavenly bodies, but he will be immortally god-damned if he will yield a point about the movement of his own bowels. Here is the new frontier, of course—the theme, again, of my book.

In experimentally assuming that when you are sick you have, half the time, trouble with your psyche rather than your system, I know I am making myself liable to all manner of shabby lampoon. You will engage me at once by arguing from the general to the particular and pointing out the case of a friend who, cured of a hideous eczema by a psychiatrist, next took to sleeping with his sister and boasting about it in public. None of the relationships between eczema and incest in the case are clear to you, though they might be to me if I had all the known facts, and I could reasonably rebut the whole bedridden business by showing how a second and even wilier psychoanalyst might get the lusty clown off his sister or, at the very least, stop him from boasting about it.

By using the second person in the foregoing, I have, of course, endeavored to suggest a suspicion of yourself—to give you a doubt. I am aware that the statistical method cannot be enjoined reasonably upon the individual. It should be borne in mind by him but never sedulously accepted. I am also aware that psychology is at present an incomplete science; in fact, these chapters are no more than an invitation to extend its frontiers.

But I believe that Freud, because he was the first, will be recognized someday as one of man's greatest pioneers, and that Jung, because he understands the work of his predecessors and has added much to it, is by far the most knowing of them all—the largest contributor

to wisdom of this era. I am extensively indebted to Jung for my observations here.* I have attempted to apply his principles, discovered,

---

* The work of Freud and Jung has, of course, become more widely
understood since these words were set down. In a prior footnote I
mentioned Toynbee's indebtedness to Jung. The medical profession,
with its new field of "psychosomatics" has embraced much Freudian
knowledge; and a growing number of first-rate medical schools include psychoanalysis in their curricula.

One stumbling block to a spread of the new Intelligence is the
puritanism of the academy. University psychologists generally avoid
psychodynamics owing, beyond doubt, to prissy fear of the powerful
part played in personality by the drives of sex. Many psychology professors, furthermore, unconsciously dread the new science: it inevitably deflates pomposity and pretense.

A further difficulty lies in the fact that, since Freudian and Jungian
concepts concern the unconscious mind along with symbols and processes of a nonverbal nature, they are not amenable to direct, intellectual perception. The logic of psychodynamics, though as sound as
thermodynamic logic, differs from pre-Freudian and pre-Jungian notions of "mental logic." A certain amount of direct analytical *experience* is essential for an understanding of dynamic psychology; intellectual comprehension cannot precede such individual ways to insight. That "experience" is not accessible to a mind in unconscious,
rigid opposition to unfamiliar formulations, however logical and scientific. Far too many professors who consider themselves "scientists"
have just such a prejudice of which they cannot let themselves be made
aware.

As one who has had "experience" both in Freudian and Jungian
analysis, I often think of that when psychological "scientists" dispute
psychodynamic ideas on the categorical grounds of their scientific "discipline." Indeed, I occasionally feel that when a scientist relies on his
"discipline" (essentially the noblest method for gaining knowledge) it
has become, in his particular case, an end in itself and no longer a

rediscovered, and interpreted from old knowledge, to some new matters, along with certain principles uncovered and described by Freud and Adler. Unfortunately, Jung is an obscure and somewhat clumsy writer. His books and papers, written in German, English, and French, have not all been published in America. Of his writings in English many have concerned small branches of his investigation, and of his translations many have been made by persons who had only a hazy idea of what he was discussing. The divergence of opinion among those three leading psychologists, although not so considerable in the main as it has appeared or so argumentative as it was merely various, has led the medical profession into a charivari of ribald cheering. Most doctors hate (therefore fear) psychology because it tends to make monkeys out of their solemn necromancy and to do them out of business. Few doctors have had the sense and enterprise to investigate psychology beyond James, which they recollect vaguely from premedical schooling, and behaviorism, which is not so much psychology as neurology; and doctors, like plumbers and popes, hate to admit that they are running around the earth with their pants down.

So, while Freud was both respected and ridiculed by most scientists but largely forgotten as far as possible and as fast, and while Adler was accepted by a coterie for his studies of inferiority and superiority,

---

means. Instead of being able to apply his scientific method in *any* category and to *any* logic, he has become stuck by discipline at the point of what is already known. He is in consequence unable even to conceive of the possibility of knowledge that is broader, other, or different.

The result is not science but "scientism"—authority set above free inquiry; and, while almost any sane scientist will admit that science has much truth to learn, almost every other scientist will behave intellectually as if nobody had a right to question the finality of his concepts in his special field.

That is silly—and only psychodynamics adequately explains how it can happen to pretty good minds.

which offended traditional man less than Freud's studies of his sexuality, Jung was not widely read and hardly understood at all. In his own seminars he managed to convey his ideas more effectively than in his books and treatises.

The late Archibald McIntyre Strong taught me most of what I know about Jung's psychology, and that teaching has made Jung's books, lectures, and monographs comprehensible to me. I cannot say that my own ideas of human psychology are Jung's, Freud's, Adler's, or anybody's, but theirs only in so far as I apperceive what they have learned. Beyond that, they are my own interpretation.

But in reference to Jung I cannot refrain from pointing out that some few of his explorations and discoveries have so impressed the medical and academic psychologists that they include him always among the three leading scientists in the field of human personality and behavior, even though as a rule they seldom recall anything more about him than his description of introversion and extroversion. Professors and medical men have taken a convenient but meaningless and altogether reprehensible way of classifying the three great psychological scientists: to Freud, they attribute discovery of the subconscious mind; to Adler, inferiority; to Jung, introversion. Freud's studies of libido, of the death wish, of symbolism, are less well remembered and appreciated. Jung's contributions to those subjects are almost unknown.

Almost unknown, too, are Jung's studies of the female principle in the male personality—its functions and effects, together with the parallel phenomena in women; his greatest work, perhaps, which had to do with instinct and the archetypes; his analysis of the functions of the personality or "mind" of the individual; his subsequent demonstration and description of subjective functions which lie largely outside the range of language as it is used subjectively; his encyclopedic compilation of data to show the mechanisms by which conscious personality has sought to integrate itself in every form of society and every time of man; and his demonstration of the nature of individual personality as a whole, which is derived from those several analyses and many others. These colossal studies exist today in a kind of library limbo, waiting, like others, for the man or the times to reopen the books and give the science to the people.

Whether the renaissance which might follow such activity is around the corner or a thousand years away at the end of a murky train of more medievalism is not, I suppose, of much importance to Jung— and Freud and Adler are dead. Perhaps Jung has felt that he did his utmost in assembling the truths and has no energy to promote them. More probably he feels that in nature man and truth and time are all related, and that his discoveries will be put to use when men are prepared to use them or have sufficient need to know about them, and that there is no merit in trying to hurry the hour. That is the history of most discovered knowledge, and as usual the men who call themselves scientists do the most to hinder, ridicule, conceal, and outlaw each fresh principle.

(To quarry these various strains of productive insight into individual man and to use even a careful, small selection of the recovered chemicals for a haphazard litmus test of man in general, as I am doing, is certainly presumptuous. And a writer in my position must warn against the application of the statistical principle to the individual, even while he is engaged in the business of trying to con the individual into a critique of himself, by discussing men in general. That is only one of many seeming paradoxes which I ask my reader to try to reconcile—another opposite—in the middle of which I sit with my typewriter.)

Doctors do not know very much about psychology—or care— though our Western padishahs have about licked materiology, and you and I are suffering and perishing largely from psychological causes, not only in hospitals but on battlefields. Scientists and teachers will have none of it. Statesmen and politicians have not yet heard about it. All of them still depend upon unlettered instinct—which Hitler calls intuition—in a world where lopsided sanity has made the instruction of instinct a pragmatic imperative.

In the days of the village and the small town, the family doctor had what learning there was, and some "intuition" also, as well as a considerable insight which he came by in the daily discovery that men were nothing like what they seemed to themselves or told each other they were. Thus the family or country doctor was able to deal in mental hygiene with a skill which, though indifferent, irregular, and untrained, nevertheless had a sound basis. Such a doctor, having been brought the Methodist church soprano in a state of hiccups, and knowing from common talk that the damsel was enjoying two styles of l'extase in the organ loft, might find a way to cure her distress which involved practical counsel rather than medication.

This function, which put the physician in loco parentis, added a paternal magic to the magic he already possessed as the tribal witch doctor and medicine man. It borrowed, too, from the priestly magic and made him a confessor, which he had to be, anyhow, to find out about what in hell was wrong with people. Thus there centered around him a host of herd archetypes besides the main one which was rightfully his, and the erecting of great cities filled with strangers was not allowed by the medical profession to change these magical benefits, because they were flattering, lucrative, and occasionally still helped him do his work.

However, as cities grew, the doctor "treated" fewer people about whom he knew the gossip. He knew the background of almost none. Enlightened strangers brought him lumps because they were afraid that they might be cancers. But people who consulted city doctors for illnesses of the flesh which originated in their conduct, or their inhibitions to conduct, seldom delved into causal situations—particularly in view of the fact that the suffering for which they were trying to get aid was, itself, a disguised attempt to hide the causes or to escape their consequences. Individuals are terribly alike and they are also, on scrutiny, terrifyingly different. Much of their difference lies in what has gone on in space and time long before they were born, or long before they were at any given point, and is, thus, abstruse and inaccessible in its own right.

The city specialists, untrained in instinctual processes and unable in an hour of history-taking to learn much background, practice healing on the mentally or emotionally deranged with even less assurance than the country doctor. They are, as the honest ones will confess, lucky when they get a patient who has a physical disease or condition which they can recognize and for which they know a fairly effective cure or palliative.

Nevertheless, most of them still take everything that comes along and have a sporting go at treating it.

You and I are the ones who come along and our mentor is Dr. Slop. The higher the standards of his medical school the better a "scientist" he is likely to be. That is to say, he will not treat scabies as insect bites, likely. But he will almost certainly undertake to deal at elaborate and costly length with your high blood pressure, even though he may suspect that it has come on you from being the exasperated and uncomplaining employee of a martinet for twenty years. Your boss is killing you or, more accurately, your refusal to quit him or your fear to—but your doctor will behave as if it were your heart and arteries. There will be diets and vitamin injections, electrocardiograms and baths, sedatives to take t.i.d., and specialists to consult, prohibitions in re tobacco and alcohol—but none about your boss, because the doctor doesn't reckon him into the picture. To do so would not merely cut off your income and hence the doctor's fee; it would be an entering wedge whereby the problem of bosses would become a problem for doctors.

In my own lifetime, the medical profession has condemned itself time without number by its own practice and in damning itself it has proved the case for psychology. Medicine is a profession, like the other sciences, in which *fads* in thinking are very likely to determine procedure and to obscure fact for long periods of time. This business is again a mental genuflection to social patterns rather than to sense, and it has contained many contradictions which, by now, I am sure the reader is getting to expect and to understand.

I can recall, for instance, the national sweep of Fletcherism—a medical principle which involved the chewing of food to impalpability and the subsequent permitting of it to trickle down the throat, an act of ingestion presumed to accomplish miracles for the jaw-grinding dolt. Some while later experiment proved that the amount of chewing applied upon beef, at least, had little to do with the speed of its digestion and, indeed, retarded it. People were urged to bolt their beef in gobbets. The fresh-air school had everybody down with pneumonia; now Haldane comes along to show that fresh air gets to us even through cement walls and bricks—nobody, evidently, having studied air as a gas and houses as porous, before entering into the fresh-air campaigns. There was a fad for cutting out tonsils, one for taking out wombs, and at least one each for removing breasts, adenoids, glands, and other vital objects. There was a bran and salad fad that must have given colitis to a tenth of the populace and is still raging. There was the remarkable Dr. Hay, not acknowledged as a full wizard by the brethren, I admit, but a gentleman who got an uncommon number of the people engaged in the technically impossible attempt to eat their proteins and starches separately. Right now there is a vitamin fad. There was a fruit juice fad that got people trots. Diathermy is coming in. People were thrust into the sunshine for incredible periods; then it was discovered that too much sunshine was as onerous to the body as too little. There was the colonic stasis fad, and if all that was preached by the nawabs during it was true, every man jack among us would have silted up to the navel years ago. In the days of that one, the citizens were living on physics and having their guts washed weekly, cleaner than Oom's. There are at least fifteen different fads which stem from the sinuses, and there has even been a fad in birth control that set millions of men trying to regulate their woo by the menses of their women with the help of adjustable cardboard charts. There were doctors who said the incidence of cancer was due to the use of aluminum cooking utensils, and *that* got to be a fad. There was a fad for mercurochrome and there still is, though one of the voivodes cultured tetanus in a solution of the stuff. There was a great to-do over maggots for pussy wounds, and airplanes went whizzing about with sterile larvae in their cargo hatches for a while, though I have heard little about this affair lately. Coolidge, the tireless experimenter, sat in a roomful of chlorine for his cold, when *that* was a fad; all treatments for colds, in fact, excepting possibly rest, narcosis, and psychiatry, are wholly fads, because nobody yet can regularly hit a cold on the nose at all. Mineral waters at spas are a fad of immemorial record, and every spa had some to drink and some to immerse yourself in, and all the baths merely make you wet and nearly all the potions just make you loose. There have been, in my time, fads for getting rid of adipose, including the use of formidable drugs, and people have been killed by these fads, driven insane, and otherwise ruined for life, but the nostrums are still sold, when all the while the whole world of man knows that to grow thinner you need only eat less and take more exercise and if you cannot do that, it's generally your head, not your pod, that needs attention. There are fads directed upon infancy, such as a banana diet, though, in my time, bananas were once thought almost poisonous (despite the fact that healthy natives by the million ate them in hands every day), and there are fads for adolescence, such as running around the gym track, and fads for old age, such as quiet and early retiring—or night life and a young outlook. A hundred old wives' remedies for the menopausal afflictions have yielded, in fact, to a hormone, but the advertised remedies for the condition still fill pages. There are fads for tooth care galore, and none of them ever reach the teeth any more than a suppository does. At this other end of the tract, there are fads for piles. At this end, too, rose the mightiest fads of all, the irrigation crazes, and the amount of silly material that has been passed through the human sphincter, in the last twenty years, is exceeded only by the absurd ideas which have run from the human larynx. You can look back and recall, I daresay, a dozen now exploded physiological activities into which your doctor has plunged you—and you can laugh heartily at yourself, if you have a mouth left to laugh with.

These sciamachies demonstrate implacably that the doctors haven't much idea what they are doing. There are even grimmer fads—nifties that seep around in the trade—maiming and slaying their tens of thousands, but those are professional secrets and only the piled dead, who cannot speak, indict the happy-go-lucky practitioners of them.

The curious fact of faith, revealed in the cures sometimes occasioned by this pitiless piffle, is never examined. But a moment's thought will demonstrate its presence, the good of it and the danger. Since half the human beings who apply to a doctor for care arrive in the waiting room with a psychological cause for their physical complaint, it is necessary only to convince them that the treatment is going to succeed for it to do so. Of course, such conviction, being an inner event, must be as deeply driven into the personality of the victim as is the prior conviction, which has given rise to the symptom. And that is where the magic, which has accrued to the doctor through no effort of his own, makes itself effective. Each patient is likely to be preinclined to the belief that what the doctor does will cure what he has, for otherwise he would hardly visit the man. The patient's attitude, mood, prejudice, or superstition is enlarged by every possible method. I cite some of them for you below:

The doctor makes you wait, implying that he is busy and hence red hot. His office is usually a cozy spot with plenty of *National Geographics* lying about, and maybe *Harper's Bazaar* if he goes in for carriage trade. But you are given a glimpse, almost certainly, of a white room crammed with extremely intricate and ominous-looking gadgets. The fact that these are mostly just pincers, with a few knives thrown in, does not occur to you. There are, also, books. A doctor always displays his library, and the witless client, in pain and funk, is automatically led to believe the sirdar has read every line of every volume, though the high shelves probably contain bound backs, and certainly few living doctors have actually perused a quarter of the linage in their collections. Ninety per cent of their total useful medical knowledge could be printed in the number of volumes a man can carry in a book-strap. You sit there. This man, you know, is a "good" doctor. A friend has told you. There are not—somewhat as in the case of economists—any "bad" doctors; at least, if you had heard that this one was bad you would not be sitting there—looking at photographs of the pagoda-water-temples of the Aguiki—with your neuralgia.

This is preconditioning—part of the cure. You believe this particular malarky can help you. And, if you believe it, by golly, it may be he can. Your neuralgia comes from the fact that you married a finale hopper, or flapper, who, through the years, has turned into a fountain of carbolic acid. What with wincing, shuddering, dodging, fending, grimacing, arguing, hollering, and generally turning your viscera into vinegar, your blood into lemon juice, your dung into slime, your hair into nothing, and your skin into the sort of dank leather that covers an old baboon's behind, you have got neuralgia. Your neuralgia persists and increases because there is a law against strangling this bitch. It gets to be jumping neuralgia when she finds out that you have hired a secretary with a face that is not a flour-and-water paste topography. You are stuck with this commonplace situation and you cannot get out of it, so, if you happen to have a twinge—and even wild animals get twinges—and if you happen to find that the twinge gets you some pity, silence, emancipation, a chance to read a book, or merely a louder caterwaul which impresses even the neighbors as uncommonly mean under the circumstances, you enlarge the twinge. It gets out of hand. You go to the best man in the city for the affliction—Slop—and you are sure, by the time you get into his presence, that he can fix you.

He sizes you up, decides you have been under strain, listens to brave, spaced intimations that your wife is a geyser of lewisite, and gives you some barbiturate in a pink elixir. You thank him gratefully. A charge of twenty dollars for this act will enhance the magic of the man in your estimation. You will take the medicine and it will cure your neuralgia. Two weeks later, at the club, you will tell the boys you haven't had a twinge in ten days. Then they will run for Slop with their varicosis, catarrh, night sweats and the like.

Your trouble has left you. You were not, remember, one man in a thousand but, from the statistical incidence of complaints of that general type, five hundred men in a thousand. The medical average of "faith healing" is not one hundred per cent, of course, but if the witch men manage to cure the main symptom of one neurotic in five, you are now a hundred men in a thousand. This explains the apparent success of quacks and of fads, of fools and old wives, of osteopaths and chiropractors, of Christian Science, and partly, of Lourdes.

The trouble with it is, of course, that your neuralgia has been separated from you, but no such radical procedure has been applied to the basic affliction: your wife. You now have two alternatives: a recurrence of the neuralgia or another malady. With such horizons widening before you, your inner nature will determine your choice—not consciously—but determine it, nevertheless. Pain in the belly? Why not try a mild ulcer? Persistent cough? Work it into chronic bronchitis —or even t.b. Get a rest from Gloria and see the world. Anyhow, somebody else.

Psychologists know this. Doctors know it—or should. Common men sometimes know it. A quarter of the medical fees paid, at a conservative estimate, a quarter of the clinical and nursing work done, and a quarter or more of the remedies prescribed and bought are services to the spirit, and, as such, passing abatements only. And this is but one of scores of major human wastes which spring from identical causes. Witch-doctoring and quackery, mummery and nonsense, robbery, withal a Niagara of nonsense, a mountain of mulcting, a swindle and a scandal, and if your grocer did a tenth as much to you you would have him in the clink, even though we will agree that grocers, as a class, are a collection of choice thieves and liars too.*

---

* Inquiry into the shortcomings of medical men has now become the chief hobby of magazine editors. In view of that, I suspect, if I were writing "Vipers" over, I would somewhat come to the defense of doctors—at least by attacking those who make unenlightened forays upon them.

Alert medical schools, furthermore, are currently introducing into the curriculum courses in Psychosomatic Medicine and graduate train-

Your doctor has little protective interest in your health; and he has a cash motive for it to get bad. He is probably not concerned with medicine at all as an applied preventive science. He does his free work and makes his charity rounds. These sops make him, often, a criminal accessory after the fact. His lifelong contribution to public health is, as a rule, to avoid it like the plague, which it so often is. You assume that "doctors" are in charge of the welfare of your community and so they are—but they are not the doctors you patronize. You assume that some sort of local medical association keeps tab on general health and it may, or may not, but usually it dodges what it calls "issues," "controversial matters," and "political angles." Thus, the baby you lost with "croup" was murdered by your family physician because he knew there was diphtheria around which the health services weren't quarantining properly and so was the only citizen who could have protected your baby. The smug rat didn't, and the baby died.

"Conditions" are an eye-rolling sorrow to your doctor; slums are a sadness about which he does precious little. His professional ethics stop his mouth and God alone knows where his conscience is. He

---

ing in Psychoanalysis. Men like O. Spurgeon English are leading the profession out of the bedside manner and into the couchside. It is therefore to be seen that increasing numbers of people who have the wisdom and the courage to acknowledge they are mentally ill, will be able to get assistance of a useful sort.

But the far, far vaster numbers who imagine themselves in perfect mental health but who actually require immediate succor by men in white bearing straight jackets, will not be much benefitted. The theory that what a few M.D.'s are painfully learning now will soon percolate through the body politic is not especially sound. What doctors knew *yesterday* has not yet touched the minds of those who patronize the equal-numbered quacks, who believe in astrology, who attribute sickness to broken mirrors or night air, who burn candles to keep well, and so on.

could, if he has kept his eyes and ears open and knows his science, indict a hundred people in your city for acts so despicable and crimes against man so revolting that you, if you understood the truth, would be ready to go out and slay. But public opinion permits even the doctors to practice medicine and not health, so that all their science is, in that sense, mythology and malpractice. In most instances, common man is to blame for his troubles; in this one that is not true, except in so far as doctors are common men—pompous and foolish.

The famed Oath of Hippocrates, somberly pronounced by each medical student upon his graduation, does, indeed, contain the promise that the swearer will do his best for the patients who call him. Outside of that, it is a sordid claptrap, the kind of thing one would expect lodge brothers to swear to, which promises that doctors will help other doctors at all times, pass the art of medicine along in the fraternity, perform no abortions, seduce no patients, and keep mum about what, these days, needs more airing than the linen of a secondary luetic. The sense of this affidavit (and the sense of the rest of academic "tradition," which has robbed science of most of the scant wisdom it came by so hard) is that medicine, like buggery, shall be a private business. Originally, it may have been meant only as a pledge that the doctor will not take advantage of his information to gossip, but the effect of a cabal is in the business, a shrinking-violet attitude, a pants-wetting nice-Nellie-ism, behind which modern doctors hide from the scorching scorn of their own education. The thing suggests, along with the rest of their shabby and antiquated asininities, that they have taken from their Oath a meaning which lets doctors collectively keep their lips locked while their patients die lingeringly, and at great expense, rather than en masse and at once.

Of course, they do not know anything real about Hippocrates, or even if he existed; if he did, it was two thousand and more years ago and science is supposed, these days, to be lighting the world. Certainly the doctors have not undone any part of the secrecy and cliquery, mumness and medievalism of their attitudes toward medicine; they take full responsibility for knowing about it, but none for doing anything about what they know. Let me illustrate.

In Miami, which I can see out of my window, the welfare of common men is at a fantastically low ebb compared to what the doctors, who live in my block, could do for it with medical science. Some of these physicians occasionally raise a mild cry at the poxy paradise, but their fellows hastily shush them and they take care not to be quoted in the press—lest denunciation be regarded as *advertisement!* Moreover, any criticism is rebutted by a horde of ignorant or purchasable M.D.'s.

This is a modern city with all the props and pride of such; it has a considerable beauty, as beauty goes in municipalities; and it has spent lavishly to proclaim itself a center of good health—a resort, a place of hygiene, cure, and well-being. Nothing could be farther from the truth. The paradox has come about partly through the stupidity of the people, but even more because of the medieval attitude of the doctors, who are too weak of mind to attack quacks and too deeply immured in their dynastic rituals of brotherhood to explain any truth to anybody but each other. Miami is a singularly good example of the kind of world our scientists are content, and even eager, to live in.

Here, in less than a square mile, are packed forty thousand Negroes, who live in wooden shanties, airless and crowded, along alleys scraped in coral so rutted that children have drowned in their puddles; thousands of them lack sewer access or even proper outdoor toilets; their sludge stands and stinks, alongside their dead animals, in their dooryards. Two or three nurses, two policemen at a time, one small clinic, and a few black doctors take what care they can of this Hadean goatyard where the vaporous breath of multitudes of the ill exudes in a thick, sweaty porridge of contagion and there is no ventilation. The tuberculosis rate is four times the bad white normal in the area. The venereal rate is well above fifty per cent. Out of this compact and seething cesspool has come one plague, at least, of dengue fever, which infected three hundred thousand white Floridians. The steamy environs wriggle with fleas, flies, lice, rats, and all other vermin; low-grade typhus is endemic here; typhoid occurs, dysentery—and the surface wells from which thousands must get their only water are polluted, condemned, and none the less in use. The commoner diseases have never been counted, quarantine is not possible, and poliomyelitis has stalked pickaninnies down their decrepit, slotlike streets within the last year. The agonies are inexpressible. And yet these people are the serving class, the cooks, waiters, butlers, pantrymen and dishwashers of the fine homes and the resplendent hotels! By day they emerge from their fetid province and spread abroad to work; by night they are crammed back and walled in, because this is The South. There have been rich men's babies who got gonorrhea from the attentions of nurses hired out of this hell, and all manner of other sickness, blight, pox, and affection. The day yellow fever or cholera or the plague is inadvertently imported here, this natural culture medium will hurry it through the blood of the blacks, like the dengue, and so convey it to the proud owners of the castles, manors, palaces, and great hotels.

Somewhat to the north lies the malaria belt that stretches into Georgia, and this deadening disease is in the veins of many people. Tourists, stopping in Florida's inns and camps, have caught it and taken it back to their homes. There is no law that compels men to pasteurize milk here; undulant fever has stricken hundreds of the best citizens and the worst with its aching debility that lasts for a year, or two, or five, and cannot always be assuaged once it is caught. Buboes like grapes and plums hang on the cattle udders and their bacteria may be in our ice cream or in our hamburger, and perhaps yours by export. Impetigo is common enough among our children to be called "Florida sores"; there is some hookworm here still, especially among school youngsters; the main channel through our boasted Biscayne Bay has been condemned for fishing and for swimming but the people go on eating the fish and bathing there. Down our turgid, tide-repressed river comes the thick scum of countless canals and there are pathogenic amoebas in the viscera of whole communities of people living along them. We are trying to care for this infestious purgatory by hos-

pital facilities geared to a city with less than a quarter of our population and the wards of the one hospital are so crammed, vomitous, and
revolting that the head of a great medical association has pronounced
them pre-Civil War—but they are not changed. Politicians have
planned and fumbled plans for a new hospital these many years—but
this city needs six, and a purge besides.

Such sewers as have been dug beneath the boom-laid streets empty
into the bay that separates Miami from Miami Beach and the accumulation of noxious silt in the once pellucid waters of the bay is such
that it has become a thin, green-brown potage. Offal floats whole
along the elegant sea walls of the rich from private dump-holes and
from boats, and the squalid smell is stepped up to a greater pungency
with each passing year. This bayful of human debris and street wash,
moreover, together with its flotsam garbage and its gagging jetsam,
rides into the ocean on each outgoing tide and the purple water of the
Gulf Stream, filthily dyed, carries it north where the trade wind sometimes brings it ashore on famous Miami Beach—upon sand once kept
so clean by nature you could have eaten it without harm.

Federal health inspectors have retched and cursed and warned and
made reports for years about it all, but very few of their recommen-
dations have yet been faithfully put into effect by the people of Miami; and the doctors have hardly raised their voices, even when the
want of a ten-cent basin for bichloride solution in the hospital has lost
them babies through contagious diarrhea. These men, instead, have
toiled in this squirming and intolerable city for a generation, often
with great personal profit; they, above all, have the knowledge and
therefore the power to bring about the Augean job of reformation.
But for every one who faintly tries, the eyes of fifty roll up saintily in
their heads; they clasp their hands and walk on sadly.

This city spends, as a rule, one quarter of the per capita funds regarded by the federal health department as minimal for its most desperate needs. This year it may shave that budget by a fifth and not
one doctor's voice that I have heard of has yet been raised against the

starveling, murderous nonsense! This is America. This is 1941 and 1942 and 1943. This is all the fruit the tree of medical science can bring itself to bear.*

Phooie!

The profession, as it is called, is too ethical, too clannish, too self-important, too mystical and insworn, too purse-proud and conniving and complacent and sick in its head, to practice health. Dr. Slop is smothering in his own privy. I do not think especially much of socialized medicine. But I think a good deal of professional integrity and zeal and responsibility. And I think the doctors better come out of their monasteries to give man the benefits of what they have discovered, or else we better burn the doctors, teach medicine to some moral men, and call them by a new name so that we can get well. This city I see from my window, this dim, dripping, diseased inferno, is as good an answer to any scientist as can be found on the earth. Take a look, Slop. Take a look, everybody.

The doctors are giving us damned little healing.

And I am tired of the books they write to show us what fine fellows, what heroes, travelers, raconteurs, and connoisseurs of chablis they are. For my doctor, I want a connoisseur of feces. It is time and past time we writers undertook to compose treatises about the doctors. With them, as with the generals, it is not enough to be brave in the face of death; they must be bright, also, which is the rarer thing. Most of them are far from bright.

I daresay you have not had as much opportunity as I to pry back-

---

* For the benefit of tourists—with civic pride and even a slight lump in the throat—I am able to report that this dreadful picture has been wiped clear. Today, Greater Miami has excellent hospitals, a fine public health record and a growing medical school. Indeed, as I drove this morning to the modern office building where I work (surrounded by conditioned air and zebra skins) I was obliged to detour: the streets of Coral Gables were ripped up. Greater Miami is even getting sewers!

stage in the medical fraternity. A man needs veins flushed with liquid helium for that adventure, because these fellows have a system for deceiving us and doing away with us under circumstances of great suffering that is enough to turn your hair white. If they are incompetents and know it, they are apt to roar and chortle at the discomfiture and death they have caused by whacking out the wrong organs and giving the wrong drugs. If they are able, they particularly treasure a host of gruesome stories about their inept associates, who, they will assure you with a shrug, have no more right to open up a human peritoneum than they have to undertake the government of India. But they never even think of stopping the meddlesome assassins.

So-and-so, they tell you, with a blast of copraphagous ribaldry, operated this morning for appendicitis and discovered he was dealing with a case of pneumonia! The man who just walked by, they will chortle, sneezed while groping in some poor woman's entrails yesterday and cut in two her common bile duct. This lethal mishap seems to be, for some reason I have not yet got on to, an excessively hilarious one. Old Bodkin, they chuckle, has had a patient in this morning for the fifth radical slitting of a face infection; the patient is barely conscious, suffering the tortures of the condemned, and manifestly moribund, but Bodkin, true to surgery as a bombed admiral to a battleship, has not yet tried the sulfonamides. Very funny.

Because of my long, intimate, and varied association with these burgraves of biology, I could regale you with such anecdotes indefinitely. The three I have just listed came under my direct observation and, quite aside from the harm they did my friends, and the somewhat unnerving effect they had upon my private confidence in doctors, they appeared to me to constitute, with the body of material I have left unwritten, a most considerable indictment of the personalities of the men in medical practice. Their hilarity over each particular précis of their own folly seems malapropos to a mere layman, even though he be living and well at the time. A casual mental hygienist, such as are most psychiatrists, might regard the mirth as Homeric and a compensatory reflex for the strain and ardor of the surgical performance. I am, myself, not unsympathetic with that opposite and integrating brand of personal spasm which is known as "gallows humor," as any reader of mine might guess. But the doctors have both worn out the device by using it too much and lost themselves in it.

It is one thing, so to speak, for a medical student to nip the ear from a cadaver and put it in the pocket of a friend; the discovery and withdrawal of the ear at, say, a banquet in a night club may be a somewhat juvenile occasion for laughing yourself weak; but it is surely another thing to snip living organs, accidentally, out of the bellies of previously viable human beings and to regard that deed, also, as a potential store of risibility against long winter nights. In doing that the doctors have got themselves into a position anent life which is not congruent to their alleged ideals, or they have degraded their respect for mankind to a degree that resembles the attitude of a fascist, or else they have—which I think most likely—taken so seriously their magical prerogatives that they believe themselves no longer as other men, but holier, like priests, and beyond contamination because they have abolished contamination with words, like the atheists.

The last possibility represents, of course, a deep immersion in superstition by a whole profession—the very one which claims to have no superstitions whatever—a claim, incidentally, most frivolous and perilous for any modern man to make. These fusty witch men, I feel sure, claw the air, pinch their windpipes, slap their thighs, and hoot over the needless demises of you and me because of an arrogance which stems from the even less palmy days of medical art, when a man was allowed to bleed you to death because he was as much an ignoramus as you, and from a still more remote era, in which an oscillating savage with feathers in his hair had the tribal right to hand you a clay pot of poison not so much to cure you as to discourage the devils in you and, incidentally, to see if you could survive it. During those primitive days the treatment of the devils in a man sometimes had a sound, subjective basis, even if the physical procedure was dubious. In these modern days there is no soundness of the medical approach to the devils either in patients—or in doctors.

The Oath is a symbol of it all, a treasured continuum of the mixture of reason and taboo, logic and bugaboo, which pervades the medical world. Besides the social irresponsibility of the profession, and its monkish ability to transmute its horrors into laughter around the cloister tables, there are many more external evidences which prove my contention.

There is, for instance, the same colossal barricade between science and instinct that is to be found in the other learned activities of contemporary man. Physicians, like physicists, can be Congregationalists if they please, or even Catholics. Against the latter form of orthodoxy some Protestant M.D.'s are continually muttering, but they have not managed to stop the social interference of that huge, and in some ways wonderful, sarcophagus of man's soul.

In order that you may understand this clearly, and incidentally see once again why I deem your era to be as medieval as any, I beg you to make a brief and solemn visitation with me.

The time of this junket is today. The place is a hospital in a great American metropolis. (It is not Miami, though the stigma of Miami is universal in America. Indeed, the many accusations brought against Miami, here and elsewhere, will doubtless cause the boosters to improve nothing, but, rather, to hunt in the reports of other cities for yet more somber statistics, and they will find them—here for this and there for that—and so, smugly, retort that nothing need be done because there are others worse off—a form of reasoning so invidious and so ubiquitous that, alone, it may be enough to destroy democracy.) This is a northern city, with factories, a fresh-water port, schools, universities, art institutes, concerts, foundations, skyscrapers, a medical college—the whole gaudy panoply of modern enlightenment. The hospital belongs to the city and provides relatively good care for its indigent inhabitants.

In the room which we have entered, on a bed, splitting the night with screams, is a woman wearing a Gates gown. Across her bulging abdomen flick the constrictions of labor. Around her neck is a thin, gold chain with a cross upon it. Her hair is lank with sweat. The ghastliness of pain has stripped her eyes of all other sensibility. She has been lying here, squeezing and squealing, for thirty hours, unable to expel the dumb kicking content of her womb. Now, the machinery mobilized around her indicates that her strength is spent and she must either be relieved of her birthless burden or be killed by it. The intern, the nurse, the house physician are waiting—the nurse white with a sharing of horror which she cannot repress—but the two men nonchalant because this matter is routine. One looks at a watch and makes a joke. The other shrugs apathetically. From the bed, the woman bubbles and trills with intensified pain and underneath the sound is the low gather of despair. With a sudden sanity composed wholly from a swimming, urgent awareness of her danger, she looks at the men and the woman with entreaty. The nurse, thinking of the technological battery at her elbow, says, "Can't we just—?" And the physician says, "No. It might—"

They wait.

There is a voice in the corridor, sonorous and petulant, and a rubber-heeled tread. Into the room without a knock, dressed in the proper vestments for the occasion, comes a priest. His eyes are banal. They turn toward the ululating woman and harden in repugnance. The nurse hurriedly produces a tray upon which is a glass syringe and a pan of boiled water. Over the water, the priest makes a prayer. The woman turns her face away and mumbo-jumbo fills the room with the same, old, wicked incantation. The sleepy priest holds up his two fingers, waves them, and inadvertently dabbles the water. The physician flinches, but time, not bacterial probabilities, is the factor, so he does not demur.

The woman's gown is raised. Her blue belly, shuddering and writhing, and the black stain of her shaved mons are exposed for the holy man. He approaches with the filled syringe. She screams. A monstrous contortion bends her double. The grimy hand of the churchman brings the impure instrument in contact with the flesh, where blood gurgles as if the slash in it were made by a sword. The syringe is intruded. The bulb is squeezed. The words are spoken. The unborn child has been baptized according to the ecclesiastical canons. Blood vomits from the bottom of the woman onto the hand of the priest, which he withdraws quickly. The air is impregnated with her voice. Now it stops, and only the memory of it infests the chamber. The priest looks resignedly at the physician to see if a further unction is needed. Hard are the perquisites of righteousness, his eyes say testily; to get up in the middle of the night and sanctify abominations!

The doctor has at last gone to work.

Such is baptism in utero*—an extremely ordinary event, a churchly rule for those of its faith, licensed by our great and small metropolises, smiled upon by government and medicine—whereof the instance I have shown here is by no means the most horrid or disgusting, but rather a typical one, shorn of many grotesqueries I could describe with equal truth.

Here, again, is science, awe-stricken and self-debased in the pres-

---

*A number of Roman Catholics have written to me in shocked denial of the above. They stated they never heard of such a rite and defied me to prove it was practised.

The archives of any big-city hospital where "old country" Polish Catholics reside will show the truth of the claim. My correspondents, ignorant of what happens under the big, black cloak of their own Faith, reveal a commonplace hypocrisy of the Roman Church—and of other churches: dogma is graded according to credulity even within a single sect, and what is imposed on some is kept secret from others.

Confronted with the barbarian fact, my correspondents generally visit a priest and then indignantly reply to the effect that the women "asked for baptism in utero."

Now, I am not a man who believes the world should be—or even can be—purified or enlightened by force or even by law. I feel the only road to improvement is the raising of awareness—education, in short. But I do believe it is time public steps were taken to educate even old-country Polish-Americans above the level of trust in such grim hugger-mugger as this holy ritual.

ence of one special brand of codified godism. In the scene, it mattered
not whether the healers were of the same faith; they were bystanders
by law. This is your society—this is the modern age.

Or is it a scene from hell—or one from the opaque heart of the
Dark Ages?

Here is chastity and purity; here, a quintessential function of a
sworn celibate. If you do not know this business is going on about
you, whose fault is it? Yours, for not forcing your way into the dim,
endless dungeons of medicine's secret places? Or is it the fault of science, which is a daily witness and might be expected to report this and
a thousand other similar truths, because it *is* science? Ask your family
doctor. Unless he is both brave and honest, you will see grow on his
lips a padlock forged millennia before the scientific principle was
fixed in the mores of men.

Here is another vein of base metal for research. Having uncovered a little of it, I forbear to go on with the pick of reality and the
shovel of truth. I ask you only to reflect upon the consequences of
such enterprises to the outlook of the persons who get involved in
them. That is all I ask, but that I entreat.

The doctors are condemned as a whole, again, by their infuriated
defiance of a public tendency toward health insurance and toward any
step that may be called the socialization of medicine. If this defiance
were accompanied by a practicable plan, agreeable to all, whereby the
mordant and the miserable of this republic could get themselves a fair
measure of mere physical care, the emotion could be interpreted as an
urge to restrain man from foolishness and guide him into wisdom.
Such is not the case. With a few notable distinctions, the medicos have
merely bellowed wrathfully at progress, and there is in the sound of
their voices too much of the tone of a baby bereaved of its candy. The
exceptions, moreover, irrespective of the merits of their various plans,
have been persecuted exactly as all other heretics have been persecuted, except only for physical torture, which, to hear some doctors
talk, is none too good for them. Because they have tried to solve the
clinical dilemmas of groups, rather than poor or paying individuals,

they have been thrown out of societies, castigated by name in the news-papers, refused the fraternal and scientific rights of the profession, and in some instances driven beyond poverty to suicide, which is the handy modern equivalent of the rack, and a more hideous one if you happen to be stretched by it.

All this stentorian rigmarole tends to demonstrate that the physicians are not engaged in trying to preserve a truth, since they do not offer any in rebuttal, but to protect a prerogative which has lost its social value in the face of current reality. While, on the one hand, they use every conceivable innuendo to convince us they are the purest scientists, on the other, they politic, scribble, and scheme to maintain what can only be their magical powers. They never deal with the problem of each individual and his ailments, or all and *theirs,* in these activities, but only with mystical assessments of their own worth as secret personal counselors with alleged superintuition and a fictitious claim to knowledge of the private patient's bents and foibles.

It would upset this gentry severely to have to regard its institutions and its traditions from the standpoint of reality; that is, to have to adjust professional superstitions to scientific facts. But they are going to have the deed forced upon them by public pressure, if the public outlasts the immediate present. For the schism in medicine is plainer to the people than any of the other, equally abyssal chasms which divide what we really know from what we pretend. In medicine, it causes people physical pain which they see is needless, and this is an age that has surpassed all other ages, not only in pleasure-seeking but in pain-avoidance. Even that might have been otherwise if the doctors had practiced healing.

Instincts are *moral:* to each there is an opposite—a price for denial, and a price for excess also. That is an established aspect of nature. A science which tries to create a province outside morality wherein to reason or experiment is self-confuted, because such regions exist only in the vainest imaginings of man's ego. And a group of men who attempt to think like gods but to deny their devilishness and who, at the same time, turn away from the humanity of which they are an inextricable portion and which they have sworn to serve are predestined, sooner or later, to find themselves slaves of humanity, turning their formulae and their machines toward the total destruction of their own works. Such an event is not an irony in an amoral universe, but the result of an ethic, which I have called The Law.

Conscious morality, the individual's choices made from a centered understanding of all the opposites—great and little, instinctual and reasoned, of the brain and of the heart, physical and psychic—is the transcendent function of a man. It is his route toward every value, inner and objective, as surely as the route of a river lies along the curved affect in space we call gravity.

The scientists have not yet discovered this, for the most part, but only here and there intimations of it—as suggestive, but also as incomplete, as the phrases in Wordsworth's "Ode."

Here is a résumé of the critique of the so-called *medical* science, which derives from the pattern of sanctity-in-pigeonhole:

Half man's physical ills come from his psyche, but most doctors, aware or not of the origin, keep dosing man with pills alone. That is sophistry. Preventive medicine, or "public health," scientifically half the battle against sickness, is spurned by the doctors on the grounds that they belong to a secret society, and the lodge brothers find in it neither glamorous magic nor great profit. That is anything but art, and certainly not healing. That part of the "family doctor's" sorcery which had validity was the psychological part—the intimate knowing of the personality and background of each patient—but the most important doctors today—the famous and ingenious city specialists, who neither know nor want to know about the personalities of their patients (and sometimes, even, never say a word to them)—are the most avid of all in the lodge clamor for the retention of magic privilege. These men do not wish to exercise it, but will not have it conveyed even by name over to "psychology" where it belongs. That is hypocrisy.

As long as the doctors insist upon taking full command of their science, its schools, its place in society, and its administration, they should be made to bear the consequences of their decisions. Indirectly, they will be. Those decisions, rooted in archaic notions and attitudes, are slowly costing them their command. If society itself takes charge, they will, indeed, be socialized, and quickly too, just as the physicists have been federalized in war, and physics has become, for an uncertain while, gunnery.

If the doctors are willing, they can scientifically redivide their science, parcel it out correctly, and so, by satisfying the logical needs of the people, retain their dominion. They will have, then, to publicize, promulgate, and man preventive medicine with as much endeavor as they do private bonesetting and pill-rolling. A hundred American Miamis are even now silently compelling that. They will have to catch up, as a group, with the psychological sciences, which only a few of them partially understand today; and because half the people have an erythema multiforme that is the symptom of a frustration rather than an ipso facto rash, they will have to add a couple of years to their special quadrennium for this new learning, or turn out a half of themselves psychiatrists.

From that necessity they can ultimately relieve themselves by so enlarging their present limited efforts at public education as to ensure in the end *a society with better individual integration arising from a general knowledge of psychological truth and law.* Such a project may easily take a couple of thousand years, but the medicos have been on the theme of Hippocrates for longer than that, and all of us are ready for a change. Today, indeed, is not too soon to start. The movement could be inaugurated, of course, by *any* branch of learning or by *any* determined society of persons—or the government could undertake it.

Who does it is unimportant. I merely suggest the opportunity to the doctors, because most of them are dandy fellows, though they have been puffed up about their enlightenment for much too long.

While they are engaged in the reform they might as well take cognizance of the additional fact that much of their lodge mumbo-jumbo has already been penetrated by hoi polloi. An eloquent bacteriologist here and a celebrated urologist there—grown loquacious in old age—

have been giving the thing away in chunks. Medical columnists are hastening this fumigatory process. Too many people, for example, understand that "erythema multiforme" means "many-shaped red blotches," which they will have already diagnosed before they presented themselves for study; the pompous nonsense of translating a plain spectacle into mere Latin will not have the intended effect of impressing the patient. It is time to undo much of the clumsy, obsolete Latin and Greek organism of medicine—just as it is time to abandon the disgraceful self-righteousness of that part of medical "ethics" intended to protect only the patient but used everywhere to protect the *doctor* from having to behave like a scientific human being.

I suppose the doctors have never thought of wielding their power consciously, as they do unconsciously. I imagine it has never occurred to any of them that they could compel almost instantly as much social progress as they now retard. But I often reflect that the doctors, if they wished to, could achieve a number of obviously necessary forward steps by simply going on a strike. Such an idea, of course, is a violation of the orders posted in the temple about 500 B.C. But it is illuminating. A frantic public would knuckle to the striking doctors quicker, by a thousand times, than, say, to striking priests or ironmongers. The people live so much closer to pain than to ideals or humanitarianism that the truth of the hypothesis is readily admissible. But if the doctors ever do come to striking, I will wager it will be to maintain their medieval warranty under the law, which lets them dose and lop and charge exactly as they see fit.* The likelihood of a strike by this guild is small, because the members could never agree on whether to sit down, picket, or genuflect.

Feeling no illness at this moment that an aspirin cannot cure, I can

---

* Consider, in this respect, how doctors recently and in great numbers have gone into tantrums, turned to lobbying, and set up a salary "check-off" of a labor-union sort—to oppose (as "socialized medicine") almost every reasonable effort of the layman to insure his medical care and its costs.

afford this excursion which, God knows, is justified. But when the next cramp seizes me, or I translate a melancholy into boils, even I will recapture some of my faith in the magic and telephone in the most imploring tones for Slop. Such is the grip in which they have us all. But until then I will be in a condition to make war against these clutchings of the past. With luck, I may even outlive Slop. If I do, I will certainly decorate his grave.

CHAPTER XI

Common Women

MOM* IS THE END PRODUCT OF SHE.

She is Cinderella, the creature I discussed earlier, the shining-haired, the starry-eyed, the ruby-lipped virgo aeternis, of which there is presumably one, and only one, or a one-and-only for each male, whose dream is fixed upon her deflowerment and subsequent perpetual pos-

---

* You are now about to read (or re-read) one of the most renowned (or notorious) passages in modern English Letters.

This chapter has put the word "momism" indelibly in our language; it has broken a path through sacred preserves into which all manner of amateur critics (along with the stateliest psychiatrists and the United States Armed Services) have since proceeded, pouring out articles, monographs, bulletins, research reports and shelves of books showing how right I was to speak as I did of a certain, prevalent sub-species of middle-class American woman; and the chapter has typed me apparently forever as a woman hater—indeed, as the all-out, all-time, high-scoring world champion misogynist.

It is this last I regret. The fact that legions of individuals, and finally the Army, followed me in condemnation of that special type of American mother I called "mom" merely affirms my work: the Oedipus complex had become a social fiat and a dominant neurosis in our land. It was past time somebody said so. As a way of life, it is shameful in grownups of both sexes; as a national cult, it is a catastrophe.

session. This act is a sacrament in all churches and a civil affair in our society. The collective aspects of marriage are thus largely compressed into the rituals and social perquisites of one day. Unless some element of mayhem or intention of divorce subsequently obtrudes, a sort of privacy engulfs the union and all further developments are deemed to

---

But, since I love women more than most men, I believe I love them more deeply and knowingly, and since I respect motherhood whenever and wherever it is worthy of respect, I find it somewhat distressing to be forever tagged as Woman's Nemesis. The fact is that only moms— or incipient moms—could imagine, after a close reading of this very chapter, that I had any other sensation for *real* women than love. Quite a few thousand ladies perceived that fact and so wrote to me. But millions, who thought they read otherwise—or who never read the text but took rumor of my diatribe as Gospel (in mom's fashion) —have given me a false name.

To such females, womanhood is more sacrosanct by a thousand times than the Virgin Mary to popes—and motherhood, that degree raised to astronomic power. They have eaten the legend about themselves and believe it; they live it; they require fealty of us all.

From them, I received dozens of scurrilous, savage, illiterate, vulgar and obscene epistles, letters which but made my point that much clearer—to me. But I have had hundreds of *times* as many communications from moms who confessed, from the sons and daughters of moms who suddenly saw whence their sickly dependencies came, and from multitudes of the learned, the celebrated, the world's leaders, who said in effect: *Thanks.*

So, for individuals, the message has often been of value. But insofar as its effect on this great nation is concerned (about which possibility people sometimes enquire), my risky effort to sever the psychic umbilicus by which millions of moms hold millions of grown American men and women in diseased serfdom, *achieved nothing.*

Mom still commands. Mom's more than ever in charge. Hardly five Americans in a hundred know today that mom and her bogus author-

be the business of each separate pair, including the transition of Cinderella into mom, which, if it occasions any shock, only adds to the huge, invisible burthen every man carries with him into eternity. It is the weight of this bundle which, incidentally, squeezes out of him the wish for death, his last positive biological resource.

---

ity have ever been questioned—by me, or by anybody else. The nation can no longer say it contains many great, free, dreaming men. We are deep in the predicted nightmare now and mom sits on its decaying throne—who bore us, who will soon, most likely, wrap civilization in mom's final, tender garment: a shroud.

Today, as the news photos abundantly make plain, mom composes the majority of Senator McCarthy's shock troops—paying blind tribute to a blind authoritarianism like her own. Mom reaches out from her shrieking hordes, cries, "I touched him!" and faints away. The tragic Senator stalks smiling to the podium and leads the litany of panic, the rituals of logic perverted, the induced madness of those the gods have marked for destruction. "McCarthyism," the rule of unreason, is one with momism: a noble end aborted by sick-minded means, a righteous intent—in terrorism fouled and tyranny foundered.

Today, too, there is mom and her mass affaire with Liberace. . . .

Tomorrow, she will shriek around and dote upon some other Hero, as sick, or as fatuous.

Today, while decent men struggle for seats in government with the hope of saving our Republic, mom makes a condition of their election the legalizing of Bingo. What will she want tomorrow when the world needs saving even more urgently?

We must understand mom before we lose touch with understanding itself.

I showed her as she is—ridiculous, vain, vicious, a little mad. She is her own fault first of all and she is dangerous. But she is also everybody's fault. When we and our culture and our religions agreed to hold woman the inferior sex, cursed, unclean and sinful—we made her mom. And when we agreed upon the American Ideal Woman,

Mom is an American creation. Her elaboration was necessary because she was launched as Cinderella. Past generations of men have accorded to their mothers, as a rule, only such honors as they earned by meritorious action in their individual daily lives. Filial *duty* was recognized by many sorts of civilizations and loyalty to it has been highly regarded among most peoples. But I cannot think, offhand, of any civilization except ours in which an entire division of living men has been used, during wartime, or at any time, to spell out the word "mom" on a drill field, or to perform any equivalent act.

The adoration of motherhood has even been made the basis of a religious cult, but the mother so worshiped achieved maternity without change in her virgin status—a distinction worthy of contemplation in itself—and she thus in no way resembled mom.

Hitherto, in fact, man has shown a considerable qui vive to the dangers which arise from momism and freely perceived that his "old wives" were often vixens, dragons, and Xanthippes. Classical literature makes a constant point of it. Shakespeare dwelt on it. Man has also kept before his mind an awareness that, even in the most lambent mother love, there is always a chance some extraneous current will

---

the Dream Girl of National Adolescence, the Queen of Bedpan Week, the Pin-up, the Glamour Puss—we insulted women and disenfranchised millions from love. We thus made mom. The hen-harpy is but the Cinderella chick come home to roost: the taloned, cackling residue of burnt-out puberty in a land that has no use for mature men or women.

Mom is a human calamity. She is also, like every calamity, a cause for sorrow, a reproach, a warning siren and a terrible appeal for amends.

While she exists, she will exploit the little "sacredness" we have given motherhood as a cheap-holy compensation for our degradation of woman: she will remain irresponsible and unreasoning—for what we have believed of her is reckless and untrue. She will act the tyrant—because she is a slave. God pity her—and us all!

blow up a change, and the thing will become a consuming furnace. The spectacle of the female devouring her young in the firm belief that it is for their own good is too old in man's legends to be overlooked by any but the most flimsily constructed society.

Freud has made a fierce and wondrous catalogue of examples of mother-love-in-action which traces its origin to an incestuous perversion of a normal instinct. That description is, of course, sound. Unfortunately, Americans, who are the most prissy people on earth, have been unable to benefit from Freud's wisdom because they can *prove* that they do not, by and large, sleep with their mothers. That is their interpretation of Freud. Moreover, no matter how many times they repeat the Scriptures, they cannot get the true sense of the passage about lusting in one's heart—especially when they are mothers thinking about their sons, or vice versa.

Meanwhile, megaloid momworship has got completely out of hand. Our land, subjectively mapped, would have more silver cords and apron strings crisscrossing it than railroads and telephone wires. Mom is everywhere and everything and damned near everybody, and from her depends all the rest of the U. S. Disguised as good old mom, dear old mom, sweet old mom, your loving mom, and so on, she is the bride at every funeral and the corpse at every wedding. Men live for her and die for her, dote upon her and whisper her name as they pass away, and I believe she has now achieved, in the hierarchy of miscellaneous articles, a spot next to the Bible and the Flag, being reckoned part of both in a way. She may therefore soon be granted by the House of Representatives the especial supreme and extraordinary right of sitting on top of both when she chooses, which, God knows, she does. At any rate, if no such bill is under consideration, the presentation of one would cause little debate among the solons. These sages take cracks at their native land and make jokes about Holy Writ, but nobody among them—no great man or brave—from the first day of the first congressional meeting to the present ever stood in our halls of state and pronounced the one indubitably most-needed American verity: "Gentlemen, mom is a jerk."

Mom is something new in the world of men. Hitherto, mom has been so busy raising a large family, keeping house, doing the chores, and fabricating everything in every home except the floor and the walls that she was rarely a problem to her family or to her equally busy friends, and never one to herself. Usually, until very recently, mom folded up and died of hard work somewhere in the middle of her life. Old ladies were scarce and those who managed to get old did so by making remarkable inner adjustments and by virtue of a fabulous horniness of body, so that they lent to old age not only dignity but metal.

Nowadays, with nothing to do, and all the tens of thousands of men I wrote about in a preceding chapter to maintain her, every clattering prickamette in the republic survives for an incredible number of years, to stamp and jibber in the midst of man, a noisy neuter by natural default or a scientific gelding sustained by science, all tongue and teat and razzmatazz. The machine has deprived her of social usefulness; time has stripped away her biological possibilities and poured her hide full of liquid soap; and man has sealed his own soul beneath the clamorous cordillera by handing her the checkbook and going to work in the service of her caprices.

These caprices are of a menopausal nature at best—hot flashes, rage, infantilism, weeping, sentimentality, peculiar appetite, and all the ragged reticule of tricks, wooings, wiles, suborned fornications, slobby onanisms, indulgences, crotchets, superstitions, phlegms, debilities, vapors, butterflies-in-the-belly, plaints, connivings, cries, malingerings, deceptions, visions, hallucinations, needlings and wheedlings, which pop out of every personality in the act of abandoning itself and humanity. At worst—*i.e.,* the finis—this salaginous mess tapers off into senility, which is man's caricature of himself by reversed ontogeny. But behind this vast aurora of pitiable weakness is mom, the brass-breasted Baal, or mom, the thin and enfeebled martyr whose very urine, nevertheless, will etch glass.

Satan, we are told, finds work for idle hands to do. There is no mistaking the accuracy of this proverb. Millions of men have heaped up riches and made a conquest of idleness so as to discover what it is that Satan puts them up to. Not one has failed to find out. But never before has a great nation of brave and dreaming men absent-mindedly created a huge class of idle, middle-aged women. Satan himself has been taxed to dig up enterprises enough for them. But the field is so rich, so profligate, so perfectly to his taste, that his first effort, obviously, has been to make it self-enlarging and self-perpetuating. This he has done by whispering into the ears of girls that the only way they can cushion the shock destined to follow the rude disillusionment over the fact that they are not really Cinderella is to institute mom-worship. Since he had already infested both male and female with the love of worldly goods, a single step accomplished the entire triumph: he taught the gals to teach their men that dowry went the other way, that it was a weekly contribution, and that any male worthy of a Cinderella would have to work like a piston after getting one, so as to be worthy, also, of all the moms in the world.

The road to hell is spiral, a mere bend in the strait and narrow, but a persistent one. This was the given torque, and most men are up to their necks in it now. The devil whispered. The pretty girl then blindfolded her man so he would not see that she was turning from a butterfly into a caterpillar. She told him, too, that although caterpillars ate every damned leaf in sight, they were moms, hence sacred. Finally, having him sightless and whirling, she snitched his checkbook. Man was a party to the deception because he wanted to be fooled about Cinderella, because he was glad to have a convenient explanation of mom, and also because there burned within him a dim ideal which had to do with proper behavior, getting along, and, especially, making his mark. Mom had already shaken him out of that notion of being a surveyor in the Andes which had bloomed in him when he was nine years old, so there was nothing left to do, anyway, but to take a stockroom job in the hairpin factory and try to work up to the vice-presidency. Thus the women of America raped the men, not sexually, unfortunately, but morally, since neuters come hard by morals.

I pass over the obvious reference to the deadliness of the female of the species, excepting only to note that perhaps, having a creative physical part in the universe, she falls more easily than man into the contraposite role of spiritual saboteur.

Mom got herself out of the nursery and the kitchen. She then got out of the house. She did not get out of the church, but, instead, got the stern stuff out of *it,* padded the guild room, and moved in more solidly than ever before. No longer either hesitant or reverent, because there was no cause for either attitude after her purge, she swung the church by the tail as she swung everything else. In a preliminary test of strength, she also got herself the vote and, although politics never interested her (unless she was exceptionally naïve, a hairy foghorn, or a size forty scorpion), the damage she forthwith did to society was so enormous and so rapid that even the best men lost track of things. Mom's first gracious presence at the ballot-box was roughly concomitant with the start toward a new all-time low in political scurviness, hoodlumism, gangsterism, labor strife, monopolistic thuggery, moral degeneration, civic corruption, smuggling, bribery, theft, murder, homosexuality, drunkenness, financial depression, chaos and war. Note that.

The degenerating era, however, marked new highs in the production of junk. Note that, also.

Mom, however, is a great little guy. Pulling pants onto her by these words, let us look at mom.

She is a middle-aged puffin with an eye like a hawk that has just seen a rabbit twitch far below. She is about twenty-five pounds overweight, with no sprint, but sharp heels and a hard backhand which she does not regard as a foul but a womanly defense. In a thousand of her there is not sex appeal enough to budge a hermit ten paces off a rock ledge. She none the less spends several hundred dollars a year on permanents and transformations, pomades, cleansers, rouges, lipsticks, and the like—and fools nobody except herself. If a man kisses her with any earnestness, it is time for mom to feel for her pocketbook, and this occasionally does happen.

She smokes thirty cigarettes a day, chews gum, and consumes tons of bonbons and petits fours. The shortening in the latter, stripped from pigs, sheep and cattle, shortens mom. She plays bridge with the stupid voracity of a hammerhead shark, which cannot see what it is trying to gobble but never stops snapping its jaws and roiling the waves with its tail. She drinks moderately, which is to say, two or three cocktails before dinner every night and a brandy and a couple of highballs afterward. She doesn't count the two cocktails she takes before lunch when she lunches out, which is every day she can. On Saturday nights, at the club or in the juke joint, she loses count of her drinks and is liable to get a little tiddly, which is to say, shot or blind. But it is her man who worries about where to acquire the money while she worries only about how to spend it, so he has the ulcers and colitis and she has the guts of a bear; she can get pretty stiff before she topples.

Her sports are all spectator sports.

She was graduated from high school or a "finishing" school or even a college in her distant past and made up for the unhappiness of compulsory education by sloughing all that she learned so completely that she could not pass the final examinations of a fifth grader. She reads the fiction in three women's magazines each month and occasionally skims through an article, which usually angers her so that she gets other moms to skim through it, and then they have a session on the subject over a canister of spiked coffee in order to damn the magazine, the editors, the author, and the silly girls who run about these days. She reads two or three motion-picture fan magazines also, and goes to the movies about two nights a week. If a picture does not coincide precisely with her attitude of the moment, she converses through all of it and so whiles away the time. She does not appear to be lecherous toward the moving photographs as men do, but that is because she is a realist and a little shy on imagination. However, if she gets to Hollywood and encounters the flesh-and-blood article known as a male star, she and her sister moms will run forward in a mob, wearing a joint expression that must make God rue his invention of bisexuality, and tear the man's clothes from his body, yea, verily, down to his B.V.D.'s.

Mom is organization-minded. Organizations, she has happily discovered, are intimidating to all men, not just to mere men. They frighten politicians to sniveling servility and they terrify pastors; they bother bank presidents and they pulverize school boards. Mom has many such organizations, the real purpose of which is to compel an abject compliance of her environs to her personal desires. With these associations and committees she has double parking ignored, for example. With them she drives out of the town and the state, if possible, all young harlots and all proprietors of places where "questionable" young women (though why they are called that—being of all women the least in question) could possibly foregather, not because she competes with such creatures but because she contrasts so unfavorably with them. With her clubs (a solid term!) she causes bus lines to run where they are convenient for her rather than for workers, plants flowers in sordid spots that would do better with sanitation, snaps independent men out of office and replaces them with clammy castrates, throws prodigious fairs and parties for charity and gives the proceeds, usually about eight dollars, to the janitor to buy the committee some beer for its headache on the morning after, and builds clubhouses for the entertainment of soldiers where she succeeds in persuading thousands of them that they are momsick and would rather talk to her than take Betty into the shrubs. All this, of course, is considered social service, charity, care of the poor, civic reform, patriotism, and self-sacrifice.

As an interesting sidelight, clubs afford mom an infinite opportunity for nosing into other people's business. Nosing is not a mere psychological ornament of her; it is a basic necessity. Only by nosing can she uncover all incipient revolutions against her dominion and so warn and assemble her co-cannibals.

Knowing nothing about medicine, art, science, religion, law, sanitation, civics, hygiene, psychology, morals, history, geography, poetry, literature, or any other topic except the all-consuming one of mom-ism, she seldom has any especial interest in *what*, exactly, she is doing as a member of any of these endless organizations, so long as it is *something*.

I, who grew up as a "motherless" minister's son and hence was smothered in multimomism for a decade and a half, had an unusual opportunity to observe the phenomenon at zero range. Also, as a man stirring about in the cesspool of my society, I have been foolhardy enough to try, on occasion, to steer moms into useful work. For ex-ample, owing to the fact that there was no pasteurization law in Miami and hundreds of people were flecking the pavement with tubercular sputum, while scores, including my own wife, lay sick and miserable with undulant fever, I got a gaggle of these creatures behind a move toward a pasteurization law, only to find, within a few weeks, that there was a large, alarmed, and earnest committee at work in my wake to *prevent* the passage of any such law. This falange, fanned by the milk dealers, who would not even deliver the stuff if they could get their money without, had undone even that one small crusade because it had uncovered a quack doctor, unknown and unheard-of, who had printed the incandescent notion that cancer, the big boogie of the moms, was caused by the pasteurization of milk!

In the paragraph above I have given, I know, the golden tip for which any moms able to read this volume have been searching all the long way. I had no mother: therefore, all my bitterness and—espe-cially—this cruel and wanton attack of moms for which, they will doubtless think, I should be shot or locked up. Well, let them make the most of that. All mothers are not such a ravening purulence as they, and mine was not. Mine, I can show, felt much as I do about the thundering third sex, as do all good women, of whom there are still a few. But I have researched the moms, to the beady brains behind their beady eyes and to the stones in the center of their fat hearts. I am immune to their devotion because I have already had enough. Learn-ing the hard way, I have found out that it is that same devotion which,

at the altar, splits the lamb from his nave to his chaps. And none of
the moms, at least, will believe that I am a lamb. Let them mark time
on that.

In churches, the true purpose of organized momhood is to unseat
bishops, snatch the frocks off prelates, change rectors just for variety,
cross-jet community gossip, take the customary organizational kudos
out of the pot each for each, bestow and receive titles, and short-circuit
one another.

Mom also has patriotism. If a war comes, this may even turn into a
genuine feeling and the departure of her son may be her means to
grace in old age. Often, however, the going of her son is only an occasion for more show. She has, in that case, no deep respect for him.
What he has permitted her to do to him has rendered him unworthy
of consideration—and she has shown him none since puberty. She does
not miss him—only his varletry—but over that she can weep inter-
minably. I have seen the unmistakable evidence in a blue star mom of
envy of a gold star mom: and I have a firsthand account by a woman
of unimpeachable integrity, of the doings of a shipload of these super-
moms-of-the-gold-star, en route at government expense to France to
visit the graves of their sons, which I forbear to set down here, because
it is a document of such naked awfulness that, by publishing it, I
would be inciting to riot, and the printed thing might even rouse the
dead soldiers and set them tramping like Dunsany's idol all the way
from Flanders to hunt and haunt their archenemy progenitrices—who
loved them—to death.

But, peace or war, the moms have another kind of patriotism that,
in the department of the human spirit, is identical to commercialized
vice, because it captures a good thing and doles it out for the coin of
unctuous pride—at the expense of deceased ancestors rather than
young female offspring. By becoming a Daughter of this historic war
or that, a woman makes herself into a sort of madam who fills the coffers of her ego with the prestige that has accrued to the doings of others. A frantic emptiness of those coffers provides the impulse for the

act. There are, of course, other means of filling them, but they are difficult, and mom never does anything that is difficult—either the moving of a piano or the breaking of a nasty habit.

Some legionnaires accept, in a similar way, accolade due their associates only. But legionnaires learned a little wisdom, since they still can function in ways that have some resemblance to normality. Furthermore, competition with the legions from the new war will probably make veritable sages out of thousands.

But mom never meets competition. Like Hitler, she betrays the people who would give her a battle before she brings up her troops. Her whole personal life, so far as outward expression is concerned, is, in consequence, a mopping-up action. Traitors are shot, yellow stars are slapped on those beneath notice, the good-looking men and boys are rounded up and beaten or sucked into pliability, a new slave population continually goes to work at making more munitions for momism, and mom herself sticks up her head, or maybe the periscope of the woman next door, to find some new region that needs taking over. This technique pervades all she does.

In the matter of her affiliation of herself with the Daughters of some war the Hitler analogue especially holds, because these sororities of the sword often constitute her Party—her shirtism. Ancestor worship, like all other forms of religion, contained an instinctual reason and developed rituals thought to be germane to the reason. People sedulously followed those rituals, which were basically intended to remind them that they, too, were going to be ancestors someday and would have to labor for personal merit in order to be worthy of veneration. But mom's reverence for her bold forebears lacks even a ritualistic significance, and so instructs her in nothing. She is peremptory about historical truth, mandates, custom, fact, and point. She brushes aside the ideals and concepts for which her forebears perished fighting, as if they were the crumbs of melba toast. Instead, she attributes to the noble dead her own immediate and selfish attitudes. She "knows full well what they would have thought and done," and in that whole-cloth trumpery she goes busting on her way.

Thus the long-vanished warriors who liberated this land from one George in order to make another its first president guide mom divinely as she barges along the badgering boulevard of her life, relaying fiats from the grave on birth control, rayon, vitamins, the power trust, and a hundred other items of which the dead had no knowledge. To some degree most people, these days, are guilty of this absurd procedure. There has been more nonsense printed lately detailing what Jefferson would say about matters he never dreamed of than a sensible man can endure. (I do not have any idea, for instance, and I am sure nobody has any idea, what Jefferson would think about the giddy bungle of interstate truck commerce; but people, columnists especially, will tell you.)

Mom, however, does not merely quote Thomas Jefferson on modern topics: she *is* Thomas Jefferson. This removes her twice from sanity. Mom wraps herself in the mantle of every canny man and coward who has drilled with a musket on this continent and reproduced a line that zigzagged down to mom. In that cloak, together with the other miters, rings, scepters, and power symbols which she has swiped, she has become the American pope.

People are feebly aware of this situation and it has been pointed out at one time or another that the phrase "Mother knows best" has practically worn out the staircase to private hell. Most decriers of matriarchy, however, are men of middle age, like me.

Young men whose natures are attuned to a female image with more feelings than mom possesses and different purposes from those of our synthetic archetype of Cinderella-the-go-getter bounce anxiously away from their first few brutal contacts with modern young women, frightened to find their shining hair is vulcanized, their agate eyes are embedded in cement, and their ruby lips casehardened into pliers for the bending males like wire. These young men, fresh-startled by learning that She is a chrome-plated afreet, but not able to discern that the condition is mom's unconscious preparation of somebody's sister for a place in the gynecocracy—are, again, presented with a soft and shimmering resting place, the bosom of mom.

Perseus was carefully *not* told that the Gorgons had blonde back hair and faces on the other side, like Janus, which, instead of turning him to stone, would have produced orgasms in him. Thus informed he would have failed to slay Medusa and bring back her head. He might have been congealed—but he might not. Our young men are screened from a knowledge of this duality also, but they are told only about the blonde side. When they glimpse the other, and find their blood running cold and their limbs becoming like concrete, they carom off, instanter, to mom. Consequently, no Gorgons are ever clearly seen, let alone slain, in our society. Mom dishes out her sweetness to all fugitives, and it turns them not to stone, but to slime.

"Her boy," having been "protected" by her love, and carefully, even shudderingly, shielded from his logical development through his barbaric period, or childhood (so that he has either to become a barbarian as a man or else to spend most of his energy denying the barbarism that howls in his brain—an autonomous remnant of the youth he was forbidden), is cushioned against any major step in his progress toward maturity. Mom steals from the generation of women behind her (which she has, as a still further defense, also sterilized of integrity and courage) that part of her boy's personality which should have become the love of a female contemporary. Mom transmutes it into sentimentality for herself.

The process has given rise to the mother-problem, and the mother-in-law problem, and mom has occasionally been caught tipping the bat, but she has contrived even then to make the thing an American joke in order to hide what it really is—as invidious a spiritual parasitism as any in the book. With her captive son or sons in a state of automatic adoration of herself (and just enough dubiety of their wives to keep them limp or querulous at home), mom has ushered in the new form of American marriage: eternal ricochet. The oppositeness of the sexes provides enough of that without mom's doubling of the dose and loading of the dice, but mom does it—for mom. Her policy of protection, from the beginning, was not love of her boy but of herself, and as she found returns coming in from the disoriented young boy in smiles, pats, presents, praise, kisses, and all manner of childish representations of the real business, she moved on to possession.

Possession of the physical person of a man is slavery; possession of the spirit of a man is slavery also, because his body obeys his spirit and his spirit obeys its possessor. Mom's boy will be allowed to have his psychobiological struggle with dad: to reach the day when he stands, emotionally, toe-to-toe with his father and wins the slugging-out. That contest is as unavoidable as the ripening of an apple. It may last only a second—in which a young man says, "I will," and an older man says, "You will not," and the younger man does. And it is a struggle no youth can engage in, but only a youth who has reached full manhood. But if it occurs prematurely, as under mom's ruinous aegis it usually does, it leads to more serfdom for the boy. He is too young for independence.

Thus the sixteen-year-old who tells his indignant dad that he, not dad, is going to have the car that night and takes it—while mom looks on, dewy-eyed and anxious—has sold his soul to mom and made himself into a lifelong sucking-egg. His father, already well up the creek, loses in this process the stick with which he had been trying to paddle. It is here that mom has thrust her oar into the very guts of man—and while she has made him think she is operating a gondola through the tunnels of love, and even believes it herself, she is actually taking tickets for the one-way ferry ride across the Styx.

As men grow older, they tend to become more like women, and vice versa. Even physically, their characteristics swap; men's voices rise, their breasts grow, and their chins recede; women develop bass voices and mustaches. This is another complementary, or opposite, turn of nature. It is meant to reconcile sexuality and provide a fountainhead of wisdom uncompromised by it, in the persons of those individuals who are hardy enough and lucky enough to survive to old age in a natural environment. But survival, as I have said, no longer depends on any sort of natural selection, excepting a great basic one which our

brains are intended to deal with, and which, if allowed to go brain-
lessly on, will have to reduce our species to savagery in order to get
back to a level on which instinct itself can rule effectively.

The mealy look of men today is the result of momism and so is the
pinched and baffled fury in the eyes of womankind. I said a while
ago that I had been a motherless minister's son and implied that I had
been mauled by every type of mom produced in this nation. I pointed
out that the situation was one on which the moms would try to fix their
pincers. I did not bother to prod at any misgivings they might feel
about what the rude minister's boy, trained in snoopery by the example of the moms, might have found out about the matriarchy and its
motivations through hanging around sewing clubrooms, hiding in
heavy draperies, and holing up in choir lofts. Rather, I let any moms
and adherents of momism who may be reading this slug along in the
happy belief that, whether or not *I* knew it, they had got me off base.

Now, really.

Some of the doting ones, ready to write off all I have said if I will
only make up and shove myself back into the groove for them, are
now about to be clipped—but good. For, by a second contumelious
revelation, I have caught onto all of middle-aged, middle-class,
earth-owning Mrs. America that I happened to miss in the portieres.
Hold your seats, ladies. I have been a *clerk* in a *department store*. Not
merely that, but I have been a clerk behind the dress goods remnant
counter. And not only that, but I have served and observed the matriarchy from the vantage point during *sales*. If there is a woman still
on her feet and not laughing, nab her, because that will mark her as a
ringleader in this horrid business.

Much of the psychological material which got me studying this matter of moms came into my possession as I watched the flowerhatted
goddesses battle over fabric. I have seen the rich and the poor, the
well-dressed and the shabby, the educated and the unlettered, tear into
the stacked remnants day after day, shoving and harassing, trampling
each other's feet, knocking hats, coiffures and glasses awry, cackling,
screaming, bellowing, and giving the elbow, without any differential

of behavior no matter how you sliced them. I have watched them deliberately drive quiet clerks out of their heads and their jobs and heard them whoop over the success of the stratagem. I have seen them cheat and steal and lie and rage and whip and harry and stampede—not just a few times but week after week, and not just a few women but thousands and thousands and thousands, from everywhere. I know the magnitude of their rationalizing ability down to the last pale tint and I know the blackguard rapacity of them down to the last pennyworth.

I have, as a matter of confidential fact, twice beheld the extraordinary spectacle occasioned by two different pairs of rich and world-famous women who managed, in the morass the moms make of the remnant counter by ten o'clock each morning, to get hold of opposite ends of the same three and a half yards of Liberty crepe or dotted swiss and who found out that the object under scrutiny was also being considered by another. This I hold to be the Supreme Evidence.

In both cases both women were "merely looking," but immediately they sensed possible antagonism for what *might* be a purchase (though the statistics ran about five thousand to one against *that*) they began to struggle with the state most insufferable to momism: competition.

First, perhaps, a lifting of a lorgnette; then a cold stare; next, a reproachful glance at the clerk, and a refined but snappy little jerk designed to yank free the far end of the goods. Riposte: a fierce clutch and a facial response in kind. Next, the buttery attempt—the so-called "social" smile—like a valentine laced around an ice pick, and a few words, "I *beg* your pardon—but I—er—am *looking* at—this remnant." The wise clerk will now begin to search for the floorwalker and, in general, canvass his resources. (I should say, of course, that while I have seen only four renowned women engaged in this contretemps I have seen dozens of less distinguished moms hit the same jackpot.) The upper-class rejoinder to the foregoing gambit is, of course, "I'm quite sorry, but *I* happened to notice that *I* selected *this* piece quite some time before *you* picked up the *end* of it." At this point a hard yank is, of course, optional. But usually there come two simultaneous jerks which loosen hair, knock both hats askew, and set the costume jewelry clattering. The women now start toward each other, down the remnant, hand over hand. Bystanders are buffeted. All dress goods that cover the rope of cloth are flung about. The dialogue takes a turn to "I'll have to ask you to be good enough to let go of *my* material!" It rises in register to a near-scream. Upper lips begin to sweat. Chests heave. Elbows swing up to the ready.

Both women are now yelling at once and the tonal quality is like the sound of fingernails drawn along slates. They punctuate their words with loud cries of "Manager!" and begin to jostle each other. Peripheral moms, punched by accident in the aggression, now take up with each other a contagion of brawls and bickerings. The principles, meanwhile, have met knuckle to knuckle in the middle of the fabric and are yowling in each other's faces. Toward this the floorwalker or section manager moves cautiously. The thing has an almost invariable denouement. One woman stalks out of the store and closes her account by mail, only to open it within a matter of days. The other triumphantly purchases the draggled cloth, charges it, signs for it, bears it away, and has the truck pick it up the following afternoon.

I have been a clerk. Clerks are wallpaper to mom, and it has never occurred to her that she needs to hide her spurting soul from them. Clerks see moms in the raw—with their husbands, sons, daughters, nieces, nephews, gigolos, and companion viragoes. That anybody such as I, an articulate man with a memory like a tombstone, should be standing behind a counter conducting an inadvertent espionage on the moms has never entered their brawling brains. But there I was— and I was there, too, in the church, and at the manse. And I have hung around hospitals a lot—and insane asylums.

It can be pointed out—and has, indeed, been pointed out before, though not, so far as I know, by any chap who has had such diverse and intimate contacts with the moms as I—that they are taking over the male functions and interpreting those functions in female terms. When the mothers built up their pyramid of perquisite and required reverence in order to get at the checkbook, and so took over the schools (into which they have put gelding moms), churches, stores, and mass production (which included, of course, the railroads, boats, and airplanes and, through advertising, the radio and the magazines), they donned the breeches of Uncle Sam. To this inversion I shall refer again. Note it.

I have explained how the moms turned Cinderellaism to their advantage and I have explained that women possess some eighty per cent of the nation's money (the crystal form of its energy) and I need only allude, I think, to the statistical reviews which show that the women are the spenders, wherefore the controlling consumers of nearly all we make with our machines. The steel puddler in Pittsburgh may not think of himself as a feminine tool, but he is really only getting a Chevrolet ready for mom to drive through a garden wall. I should round out this picture of America existing for mom with one or two more details, such as annual increase in the depth of padding in vehicles over the past thirty years due to the fact that a fat rump is more easily irritated than a lean one, and the final essential detail of mom's main subjective preoccupation, which is listening to the radio. The radio is mom's soul; a detail, indeed.*

---

* In place of, "radio," of course, the alert reader will now automatically substitute "TV." He (or she) may do this, currently, with some such question as, "Is TV truly as dreadful as was radio?" Time will erase the optimistic doubt.

For a few years, and until mom's commerce saturated it entirely, radio made a feeble effort to undo some of our prodigious self-subversion. TV, being a new medium, still does as much—with furtive attempts to expose mom or Cinderella in a soap opera, with big exhibits of big men doing big things at the nation's Capitol, with courtroom trials, educational movie shorts, and such.

But give mom time.

She will not rest until every electronic moment has been bought to sell suds and every bought program censored to the last decibel and

It is also a book in itself, and one I would prefer to have my reader write after he has learned a little of the art of catching overtones as a trained ear, such as mine, catches them. But there must be a note on it.

The radio has made sentimentality the twentieth century Plymouth Rock. As a discipline, I have forced myself to sit a whole morning listening to the soap operas, along with twenty million moms who were busy sweeping dust under carpets while planning to drown their progeny in honey or bash in their heads. This filthy and indecent abomination, this trash with which, until lately, only moron servant girls could dull their credulous minds in the tawdry privacy of their cubicles, is now the national saga. Team after team of feeble-minded Annies and Davids crawl from the loudspeaker into the front rooms of America. The characters are impossible, their adventures would make a saint spew, their morals are lower than those of ghouls, their habits are uncleanly, their humor is the substance that starts whole races grinding bayonets, they have no manners, no sense, no goals, no worthy ambitions, no hope, no faith, no information, no values related to reality, and no estimate of truth. They merely sob and snicker—as they cheat each other.

Babies die every hour on the hour to jerk so many hundred gallons of tears. Cinderella kidnaps the Prince and then mortgages the palace to hire herself a gigolo. The most oafish cluck the radio executives can find, with a voice like a damp pillow—a mother-lover of the most degraded sort—is given to America as the ideal young husband. His wife, with a tin voice and a heart of corrosive sublimate, alternately stands at his side to abet some spiritual swindle or leaves him with a rival for as much time as is needed to titillate mom without scaring her.

The radio is mom's final tool, for it stamps everybody who listens

syllable according to her self-adulation—along with that (to the degree the mom-indoctrinated pops are permitted access to the dials) of her de-sexed, de-souled, de-cerebrated mate.

with the matriarchal brand—its superstitions, prejudices, devotional rules, taboos, musts, and all other qualifications needful to its maintenance. Just as Goebbels has revealed what can be done with such a mass-stamping of the public psyche in his nation, so our land is a living representation of the same fact worked out in matriarchal sentimentality, goo, slop, hidden cruelty, and the foreshadow of national death.

That alone is sinister enough, but the process is still more vicious, because it fills in every crack and cranny of mom's time and mind—and pop's also, since he has long ago yielded the dial-privilege to his female; so that a whole nation of people lives in eternal fugue and never has to deal for one second with itself or its own problems. Any interior sign of worry, wonder, speculation, anxiety, apprehension—or even a stirring of an enfeebled will to plan sanely—can be annihilated by an electrical click whereby the populace puts itself in the place, the untenable place—of somebody called Myrt, for Christ's sake—and never has even to try to *be* itself alone in the presence of this real world.

This is Nirvana at last. It is also entropy. For here the spirit of man, absorbed, disoriented, confused, identified with ten thousand spurious personalities and motives, has utterly lost itself. By this means is man altogether lost. The radio, in very truth, sells soap. We could confine it to music, intelligent discourse, and news—all other uses being dangerous—but mom will not let us. Rather than study herself and her environment with the necessary honesty, she will fight for this poisoned syrup to the last. Rather than take up her democratic responsibility in this mighty and tottering republic, she will bring it crashing down simply to maintain to the final rumble of ruin her personal feudalism. Once, sentimentalism was piecework, or cost the price of a movie or a book; now it is mass produced and not merely free, but almost compulsory.

I give you mom. I give you the destroying mother. I give you her justice—from which we have never removed the eye bandage. I give you the angel—and point to the sword in her hand. I give you death

—the hundred million deaths that are muttered under Yggdrasill's ash. I give you Medusa and Stheno and Euryale. I give you the harpies and the witches, and the Fates. I give you the woman in pants, and the new religion: she-popery. I give you Pandora. I give you Proserpine, the Queen of Hell. The five-and-ten-cent-store Lilith, the mother of Cain, the black widow who is poisonous and eats her mate, and I designate at the bottom of your program the grand finale of all the soap operas: the mother of America's Cinderella.

We must face the dynasty of the dames at once, deprive them of our pocketbooks when they waste the substance in them, and take back our dreams which, without the perfidious materialism of mom, were shaping up a new and braver world. We must drive roads to Rio and to Moscow and stop spending all our strength in the manufacture of girdles: it is time that mom's sag became known to the desperate public; we must plunge into our psyches and find out there, each for each, scientifically, about immortality and miracles. To do such deeds, we will first have to make the conquest of momism, which grew up from male default.

Our society is too much an institution built to appease the rapacity of loving mothers. If that condition is an ineluctable experiment of nature, then we are the victims of a failure. But I do not think it is. Even while the regiments spell out "mom" on the parade grounds, I think mom's grip can be broken by private integrity. Even though, indeed, it is the moms who have made this war.

For, when the young men come back from the war, what then will they feel concerning mom and her works?*

---

* The young men never did come back from the war.

They came back—but the war went on.

This, mom decided was intolerable, and millions supported that repugnance. When some of the boys went forth anew to fight, the moms and the mom-pinioned pops soon tore the government apart to get a truce that brought not one day of peace.

So the young men and the moms and pops decided that they had not been fighting for freedom, after all, or against tyrants, after all.

They decided they had been fighting, all that while, for security. They had fought, not to save liberty, but for hot dogs, the corner drugstore, the right to throw pop bottles at the umpire—and the girl next door, mom briefly disguised as Cinderella.

They have it all, now.

Except Security.

For that, too, they accepted a counterfeit: secrecy. But not one secret remained undiscovered by the enemy. (The measures of security are—so predictably!—specious.)

Years passed. The young men and the moms and the pops grow ever more fervent in their trust of security-through-secrecy. The ship of state settles slowly and they bail with sieves, saying, "See? We float still."

The enemy explodes uranium, plutonium, hydrogen; still they absurdly cry, "Keep these things forever an American secret—for security's sweet sake. Peace, peace, peace!"

A great victory—for momish "thinking." For "love." The boys are indeed—home.

But where's man's freedom?

CHAPTER XII

Businessmen

THE MALE IS AN ATTACHMENT OF THE FEMALE IN OUR CIVILIZA-
tion. This we have seen through our survey of money, manufactories,
transportation, art, mores, and instinct. He does most of what he
does—eighty per cent, statistically—to supply whatever women have
defined as their necessities, comforts, and luxuries. In this light, he needs
some studying. He is able, still, to hide himself away with a modicum of inner dignity, or self-respect, in the classical enterprises of men
—those of the skilled professional, the statesman, the warrior, and the
academician. But the "practical" turn of the female instinct is toward
the goods, not processes, and she has relegated those classical functions
of man to the second degree. They bore her because she hadn't learned
enough to understand them. She can get what she wants without learning. Only in crises, where a surgeon, a lawyer, a diplomat, a general,
or a professor can increase her goods or protect her person does the average woman pay any attention (hence, tribute) to those men engaged in what are primarily men's businesses. She is usually far more
interested in the actual purveyor of the goods. It must therefore be
deduced that the leading personage in our female-worshiping civilization will prove to be the businessman. This, of course, he is—or was,
at least, until the recent crisis threatened the whole shebang.

There exists in man an orientation toward goods not much less
consuming than woman's anyway and, in addition, the femaleness
within him, put there to keep women from being wholly inscrutable

to him, has furnished a bridge for the transfer of all female materialism into his psyche. The ribbon across that bridge was cut the day he was persuaded to abandon the natural (mathematical) fifty-fifty arrangement he had with women—a day that began with Eve, probably, and has since whittled man away to the short end of the eighty-twenty arrangement currently in effect.

I do not know how much time you spend in reflection upon the quickness of material change that has befallen man, but I suggest that you spend a good deal. The blessings of science have come in about five generations mostly—and the bulk in the last two. So we are rank beginners at solving new problems which may have accrued to us through the gift. A cosmic bystander would not expect either Marx or the fascists to knock off instanter a perfect Q.E.D. for the problems which manifestly *have* accrued. Certainly the businessmen didn't attempt to solve any of these major concerns, or even anticipate them. With a mad halloo, they roared in by millions for a killing that had been within the reach only of dozens until Watt, Ampère, and the rest.

The American businessman, the tweedy, corpulent, horn-rimmed dollar-chaser (whom Europe would have understood even less if it had learned that he chased dollars to appease women), was a melting-pot job and the metal of him was that of pot metal—which is white metal—the nearest thing in imitation iron to slag. In another book I pointed out that our melting pot is also the cesspool. The American retort into which the various precious ingredients were put for refinement was, at the same time, the common sewer into which is poured much garbage and offal.

Think, for a moment, about the "stock" of this nation, not in the common-school-history manner, but in its opposite, as we are thinking about most matters here. At first, our shores were reached by many who were trying to escape religious persecution; this willingness to uproot their homes for an idea showed spiritual hardihood. But these were soon outnumbered by persons who came to make their way, seek fortunes, escape penalties of the law, and so on. Batches of assorted criminals were dumped on our littoral—some mere political exiles, others thieves, gamblers, minor scoundrels, the incurably indigent, the chronic riffraff of several nations.

When the eighteenth century ended, and man power was needed for the exploitation of the West, the sole test of a man's suitability for citizenship in this lofty and intricate republic became, in the case of millions, his ability to swing a pick. With these day laborers—as the legend of gold-paved streets spread to Prague, Copenhagen, Oslo, Minsk, Omsk, Constantinople, Naples, Vienna, Dresden, Toulon, and Hong Kong—came other millions, on their own, not muscle imports, but persons who wanted gold even if they had to dig it out of the gutters. Some headway has been made in instructing them, and their descendants, about democracy; but we should not forget that, while they paid loud lip service to our ideals at Ellis Island, they came here in the first place to *get*.

One reason for the fearsome default of democratic government is to be found in these persons and their descendants, who now must number half the populace, and their identification still with their basic reason for being here. Happily for them, it coincided neatly with the rise of materialistic momism. This is not an argument for a Herrenvolk, but for a greater attention to the common people and an insistence upon instruction in the true reasons for such ideals as have been given constitutional hellroom here. The D.A.R.'s, Elks, Masons, legionnaires, and everybody, pretty much, come from this mixed breed of fortune hunters and share, without thinking about it, the large and crazy idea that America is a place where you can get a million dollars for nothing. They feel cheated if it falls short of that rather arbitrary sum.

The businessman is moved by this same insane expectation. In his mind it lies close beside the idea that any boy can grow up to be president, a species of pseudo truth seemingly proved by numerous incumbents. He identifies the universal possibility of millionaire-ism with that other red schoolhouse gem. In countless cases he gets to be a millionaire—and that is *his* proof.

His commercial techniques derive largely from old English trading methods which, like English common law, have never been re-examined in the light of new psychological data, and so grow less and less relevant to known reality. Before the Americans started, English businessmen had already pirated half the earth in a most unscrupulous way, largely by trade, however, rather than by the sword, which is a somewhat more enlightened instrument at that. And English businessmen had produced several rather astonishing market collapses in their time even before Americans went into operation. The India Bubble was one such.

With this tradition, the American man of affairs started to work on his empire beyond the Mississippi and did a bang-up job. When he had finished there was more gear on the landscape than ever before in any nation's history—and there were more rococo palaces of millionaires per capita than ever before. New highs were established in every sort of large-scale piracy. The businessman even enjoyed a brief, baronial period of his own before his sources of wealth production were given a different direction by women. When that happened, he swiftly adjusted his activities to the new markets, but he kept to his old ideas of low wages and usurious prices (more and more by employing lawyers to conceal his processes in corporational mumbo-jumbo). To the extent that he reformed, it was not because women objected to scouring profits, but because the workers did.

Nothing he had carried over from British trading practice and nothing he had picked up in the western bulldoze had taught him to take any care or thought for the ultimate responsibility of his enterprises. If his method benefited the public good in any way, it was due to pressure from labor, or from a public conscience that had certain broad but occasionally reached limits, or to the pressure of his own vanity, which caused him to endow universities, build foundations, and use his advertising space for simple texts and lessons. And while he did his best, by duress, purchase, rapine, concealment, cartel, and other means, to wipe out competition, he insisted, at the same time, that because of the competitive nature of his business he could never be expected to co-operate with men in lines similar to his.

Out of this sort of flummery grew the triumphant catastrophe that is the mind of the American businessman. Bred from more dunderheads and bandits than moral idealists, nurtured by traditions of grab-and-suborn, dedicated to the woman's angle, and endowed overnight with the machine, it undertook to manage the world by improvised juggling, without discard or addition.

So powerful an organ of repression is the brain that all the businessmen were able, by misdirecting their noggins, to hold down the bulk of the bursting evidence of blunder, not to say impossibility, and keep millions convinced that a status quo could be maintained, though there is no such thing in nature as a status quo. This act went on for so long, and so intensely, that even now, when there is no actual "business" anywhere in the earth, the businessmen do not realize it and are still worrying about status quo.

Hypocrisy is a condition of the ego brought about by the use of the brain for the subjective repression of truth instead of its recognition. A hypocrite is a caught liar. He maintains his hypocrisy by denying, through his behavior, the lie of which he has been convicted. Hypocrisy is the most vicious mechanism of which the brain is capable, and the one against which Christ brought the full and continuing pressure of his arguments. Hypocrisy is, indeed, the *only vice* man is capable of. The chief hypocrites of A.D. 30 were the businessmen and they are still tops.

Businessmen act from sets of motives, principles, instincts, and traditions which cannot possibly be *logically* contained in any man's head. Elaborate self-deceit is required for the individual; equally elaborate public deception is the other, inevitable, prerequisite. Where the doctor was given magic, and mom was deified, the businessman was made socially sacrosanct. All elements of community life were avowed to impinge upon his immunity. He convinced himself, and everybody else, that anything which interfered with his managerial domain hurt the home, the church, the arts, the sciences, the nations, and what not, and partly because mere conviction is, itself, a powerful quality, the various accidents which befell these tottering asses *did* do harm to other categories of human living.

Starting with the thesis that competition is the essence of democracy, of which, indeed, it is an essence, the businessman undertook two main lines of bastardization of that truth. First, as recorded above, was the elimination of competition wherever possible and by all means imaginable. Second, was the establishment of the notion that business competed only with *itself* and never with any other requirement of mankind. By means of the latter absurdity, business was able to kick around and decimate the people and their needs with virtually no punishment, whatever the result. Under this code, the courts might transfer from you to somebody else a hundred thousand dollars because you had called the somebody a larruping Judas in public and hurt his business, but the courts could not get back one nickel for trainloads of widows and orphans rendered financially hors de combat to what was called honest corporate competition.

Any procedure that was technically legal, or could be made so to seem, became the businessman's definition of ethics and, thus, the public definition of morality. Rich robbers were admired and envied by the people from which they had stolen what they had. Standards of personal honesty in trade fell so low that, by 1941, according to actual field test, you could barely trust a grocer or a garage mechanic more than you could a footpad. Nearly two-thirds of them were proven crooks in their own trades. Swindle had apparently become the unnamed but accepted route to security. That is like saying suicide is the best life insurance, but it is the current American way of business, for the majority.

One can expect, of course, that some sort of compensation would appear in the objective world to conceal this vast, iniquitous, shameful, and disastrous corruption of inner mankind. The Romans traded bread and circuses for their tentative tyrannical powers. The businessmen—which is to say, most men—certainly owed a lot in return for their brief accession to the right of dishonesty and thievery. A good deal of what I have been anathematizing represents that quid pro quo, the hiring price of hypocrisy: the brass junk manufactured to promulgate domestic luxury, and the transfer of homage to the matriarchy—for which, of course, the mothers will also have to pay, because they demanded and accepted the present. Another deal of what I have discussed represents in part the effort of people to rationalize the predicament in which their indecencies have got them: the attempt, for example, to create of the true Cinderella a figure congruent with the business definition of human living. Still more of the matters I have cursed are forms of appeasement, such as false charity; and forms of escape, such as the public's self-abuse via radio. But the main pay-off is still in the future—albeit staring us in the face.

Around the inner core of business, around the irresponsible thievery, the declension of public morality, the stupidity, the uncriticized traditions, and the pronounced fealty to ideals the very violation of which kept business going grew up the outer world of shiny materials we are adjured to be proud of and warned not to criticize. The skyscrapers and clover-leaf intersections, the towering foundations and hospitals, the museums and the concert halls, the moderne houses and the gadgets, are all that business, so far, has put on the line in payment of blackmail to integrity. Without them, the people would have toppled the system and the businessmen. With them, they had the illusion that they were living in a world advancing at a terrific rate through the acumen and vision of businessmen. Each person, in fact, got hold of a private sample of the flashy glitter of the era. Possession of it won him wholly to the decayed principles of his times. The American moral rout is best of all exemplified by the automobile and what business did with it. It might reward us to consider the automobile at some length —and this is an excellent moment for discussing it, because a scarcity of rubber and the rationing of gasoline have brought it into the pained forefront of the American mind.

The low-priced car made it possible for almost all the people to go places sitting down—no more, no less. Compared to anything which

the common cluck had thitherto possessed, it was immensely compli-
cated. It has lately been made as "foolproof" as possible, which is the
engineer's assent to the proposition that most people are fools. The
driving of a car is still, however, an undertaking more demanding, in
a way, than the driving of a locomotive, since a car does not follow
tracks. It can travel wherever there are roads, and that in America today is just about everywhere.

The frantic desire of people to go places, which arose instantly upon
the invention of the car and was fanned to its outermost last mile by
the manufacturers, can and should be at least partially construed as
evidence that Americans do not like the places they are in. But mere
transit represents no kind of progress, in itself. The act of going has
value only in relation to the object of the motion. However, a people
already conditioned psychologically to identify material construction
with spiritual progress became, automatically, suckers for the illusion
that movement connoted advancement.

Cities were clumsily and unimaginatively arranged and rearranged
for the convenience of the increasing numbers of cars. The surrounding country was paved and repaved, and additionally garnished with
cement wherever one road crossed another, or encountered an impassa-
ble obstacle, or traversed some less flexible form of transportation,
such as a railroad or a canal. Places for people to go sprang up by
thousands along the thoroughfares—resorts and roadhouses—showing again that the Americans did not desire to visit new realities,
but only new juke joint counterparts of what was already around
the corner from their homes. That is another manifestation of the importance of the transit rather than the goal.

A certain amount of decentralization was made possible by the
cars, though residential suburbs showed a marked tendency to ape cities in appearance. A suburban apartment house is a city flat moved
into the country. A row of identical or similar houses is a city street—
even if it lies at the end of an hour's drive through fields, from the
place of city business to the place of city-like country residence. The

regions between suburbs, moreover, filled up solid with city. Even re-mote rural objectives were soon made as urban as possible; the jaded glare of neon was the automobile's gift to the wilderness.

Man drove. He drove to the corner for cigarettes. He drove to his club and to his office. He drove around for the hell of it. Whenever his inner self knocked on the thick walls of his ego for admission, he piled into his car and drove, as he rightly said, "to get away from himself." He gave up walking, even for his soul. When a hard and long tramp in the rain was indicated, he ripped off a hundred miles in his sedan. Not only that, but in this primary mover of the escapist he emplaced man's second great device for the maintenance of everlasting una-wareness of himself, or living death: the radio. This further distracted him from his true problems—and often, of course, from his driving.

The car made it possible for man to do more things by enabling him to go in a shorter time to more places where something was cooking. It also made it virtually impossible for man to think any longer. It mechanized the last chink of his time. Its operation—or even its mo-tion—demanded too much attention for introspection. With the radio going, it became a sort of cheapskate traveling circus: two rings and a continual performance. Sitting in his car, man decerebrated his spe-cies.

A sinister array of ideas was being thought up by people in nations without universal transportation—and more and more of the thoughts were being executed—but the American didn't notice. He rode around. Rode in his sheet-iron womb, carried by the matriarchy, lulled with the wayside show which swirled past as analgesically and as blindingly as amniotic fluid; and he listened to the radio which told an everlasting fairy story about people who did more, even, in the world of irresponsible folly than he dared to do. It is not surprising that one rare gent became so exasperated with his car that he drew a pistol and shot it five times, shooting himself with the last remaining bullet.

Other drivers, of course, found in their automobiles the same source of insatiety, falseness, betrayal, and corruption, but they were so firmly tied to them by a psychological umbilicus that they did not have enough sense of personal identity left to shoot their cars before they shot themselves. Instead, they drove them over cliffs and against trees and walls, and often—with that flash of horrid insight into the disproportionateness of their lives which is widely misconstrued as momentary insanity—they drove smack into the cars of other floating fetuses.

The tendency of man to mutilate himself in revenge for not doing what he knows he should, or for doing what he knows he shouldn't, is demonstrated clearly in the wreck records of those among us who, at last, get up outrage enough to smash ourselves to death—and, of course, our cars. They reveal that some of us do hate ourselves in our cars intensely in these perceptive if dire moments. That is demonstrated again, at least in a good part, by the fact that *smashing the car* is an integral part of the destructive compulsion. People who kill themselves because of automobile mania never park carefully and stick their necks under trolleys. They always get the car when they get themselves.

I have alluded to the car as a means of transporting a small house out of the range of parental scrutiny and its subsequent employment as a bedroom. That aspect of automobiles needs no further comment here, except the related one that the car is now regarded by nearly everybody as a part of the house, and by millions as the most important part. A poor man, consequently, will often own a good car, but live in a bad house, which makes of his two temporal abodes a fairly complete facsimile of the hard times his spirit has fallen on.

The fact that a good bit of our material civilization is, at the moment, dependent upon the automobile in no essential way justifies the automobile or the uses to which we have put it. A rubber famine has endangered the war effort to a very considerable extent, by hindering the mobility of civilians and stalling civilian supply. But, even though one grants the necessity of work-producing mobility and of every so-called "vital" service of supply, up to and including such luxuries as the collection and delivery of laundry, one can measure in the panicky reactions of most of the people to the prospect of a further curtailment of the car the exact degree in which their emotions and escapist complexes are bound up in the car. It seldom occurs to them, for instance, that if they had to they could carry their clothes on foot, or even wash them at home.

The line along which the average motorist draws his necessity begins at a point so far removed from any real necessity that it paints a stupendous panorama of his confusions. The picture of the average eastern American, in June, in 1942, should not ever be forgotten again, if society is to go on being mechanized. He screamed to assure himself of enough gasoline for a minimum of fifty weekly miles of mobility for which he would not have to be held accountable at all. Some two-thirds of the car owners of America solemnly swore that fifty miles a week was not mobility enough for their private cars under any circumstances and that they must have fluid for seventy-five, or a hundred, or unlimited miles. About a fifth of these deluded boobies decided that no urgency of the war could be permitted to reduce their measureless mileage at all! This occurred at a time when the nation was stripping rubber from its tanks and substituting iron, at the cost of speed and practicability—and when tank quality was having much to do with the fate of all future American motorists unto the thirtieth generation. It took place at a point in man's history when motordom had been in existence for less than four decades. In all the millennia of his history before then, man had got along without even one automobile.

A raging public seized every quibble that arose in Washington as a proof that the threat to its car was fraudulent, though the truths were clear to all but the willfully blind. Every conceivable effort was made, not to uncover the exact status of the gasoline and rubber famine, but to becloud and discredit all statements of the existence of any famine. As they applied for their rationing cards, the ravening motorists thought up enough lies and infantile excuses for their need of gasoline to shame the incumbent hordes of hell. There was nothing for their lips too snide, too cheap, too sneaky, too dishonest, too petty, too sniveling, too fanciful, too transparent, or too infantile. It did not matter that they were risking a sellout of everything mankind had stood for since his start, including even the American automobile. They had been self-cozened into the horrible obsequiousness of having to lie to keep the iron womb carrying them about, safe from all unpleasant dreams.

Such are the methods by which man is abolishing himself. His ultimate demise in a bombed house or a fired airplane is a mere finale of the process—one means in hundreds by which he settles his overdue account.

This infernal identification of Americans with their cars has paralyzed still another set of sensibilities and so has augmented the national precipitation into chaos in still another way. It has deprived most of us of our normal sense of shock at the sight (or even the thought) of mutilation and violent death. Some people have wits enough to perceive that the automobile, having produced more fatalities in a few years than all our wars, and far more mutilation, is ipso facto a more lethal entity than war has so far been. Of these, a few are made uneasy by the monstrous statistic. But even they, if they express their malaise, are comforted by commercial arguments which seem to circumvent the judgment of nearly every man alive, these days, bringing them back to the opinion that, even if cars are worse killers than kaisers, kaisers are all bad and cars are all good.

It is the people in the cars who do the killing, always, of course, because they start the motors and not the cars themselves, which respond only to human hands and feet. There has to be a point of blame and that point falls upon man. Half, or maybe three-quarters, of the people who operate cars are plainly unfit to drive, from an actuarial standpoint, and should in all humanity be ruled off the road. And that is exactly what the commercial arguments wish to conceal. That, again, is another blistering comment upon man's investiture of his passions rather than his reason in his car. The investiture has, in final consequence, compelled him to harden himself against ever-present death and mutilation.

Americans have accomplished this to a horrid degree, in the short space of a quarter of a century. If everybody was going to drive—and everybody was—some forty thousand people were going to get killed publicly every year, and a million torn open. Ergo, everybody had to get used to the idea of legs and arms lying around in the gutter, screams, blood puddles, and rolling heads—and damned quick. So everybody did.

The gangster assassinations, which came out of another of man's quandaries over his compulsions versus his taboos, furnished many a sanguinary photograph which helped steel the wife and kiddies for motordom. But the pictures of people in wrecks, and the actual sight of the people in the wrecks, really did the job. Nowadays, a woman who still screams at a mouse can drive right up to, or through, or past, intertwined masses of glass and steel among which are the red fractions of what had been, a moment ago, a half dozen of her fellow creatures. She can do it without a tremor, because a mouse is a creepy little creature but sudden evisceration on Maple Street is only a car smash.

The attitude is abnormal and man has had to pay in equivalent coin for the power which makes him able to stomach the horror aspects of automobility. The law of action and reaction works immutably in the psyche. This extravagant new callousness was won by man to protect his selfish purpose of having his ease in his own car—at least till it crippled him; therefore the payment had to be made by some other exposure of that same self—as, in bitter truth, it has been.

Man's normal recoil at the sight of a mutilated fellow tribesman comes from a projection of himself into the situation of the other person. The mechanism was designed to reveal the undesirability of said mutilation and to cause the beholder either to avenge the spectacle or to avoid whatever caused it. In the matter of automobiles, the American gadfly has no intention either of revenge or, most certainly, of future avoidance. So, when he hardened his wits up to the point at which this bone-shattering business was tolerable to him, he lost his sensitivity to bone shattering in general. He immunized himself to the whole threatening subject. No flesh-ripping was, any longer, an audible warning to him. Bruno Mussolini could make flowers out of Ethiopians with bombs, and the American could not perceive a danger to all men in the act. Nanking could be burnt alive, and the American would not care—because burning alive is also one of the accepted amenities of happy motoring. The Nazi concentration camps were far less appalling than they would once have been, because you could see babies with their jaws torn off on Fourteenth and Purdue almost any old time. In cooling down his reflex toward the crimson consequences of universal motoring, he froze the entire ganglion, pretty much, and thus was able with no alarm, to view crimson consequences of every sort.

Now, when they are rolling red and wild across his threshold, he is still blind to the relationship. Indeed, so immense is his thirst for gasoline and so dull his conscience that, when he hears men are frying in a tankerful of gas off his beach, he will burn some to get over and watch the charnel end of an effort at gas supply that failed. Death does not mean much to him, any more, because, it has to follow, alas— life doesn't mean much either.*

Until America went into the production of arms, the manufacture of automobiles was one of its largest businesses. Automobiles were made, distributed, wholesaled, retailed, financed, and advertised by businessmen. Big brains of every sort were engaged in the enterprise of turning out and selling these vehicles which bear so many elaborate relationships to our inner selves and to the psychological destiny of our nation.

---

* No revision is needed here: only the piquant addendum that during the Korean war (which we found so abhorrent and made such a fuss about and finally ignominiously quit—under the combined pressure of moms and mom-oriented businessmen) we killed and injured more people at home with cars than soldier boys were killed or wounded in Korea.

Who now fights for human freedom?

Who *doesn't* fight for automobiles?

But no *businessman* regards himself, or other businessmen, or business, as *in any way* responsible for a single one of the effects upon human attitudes and behavior which have resulted from the system of making, selling, and using either cars or any other objects manufactured by him. At most, his sense of moral responsibility extends to the matter of expediency. His bureaus for bettering businesses regulate business only when its conduct is so specious as to endanger people or property directly. The idea that man has any sort of moral nature, or even that (on the more fashionable and allegedly realistic plane) business procedure could dangerously miscondition a mass reflex, has hardly entered his mind.

He complains incessantly that "society" is raising hell with him, his rights, and his privileges. But any evidence that he is raising hell with society sends him into a convulsion. Such a suggestion is labeled communistic and press agents are hired to make an alarmed to-do over it; the nation is shown that its foundations are being threatened. By such tricks, and the use of already established indoctrinations of the people, business restores its control of its prerogatives without further question or examination. The heavy men behind the mahogany desks will perish bravely enough, if it comes to that, foundering gamely in a society they stupidly shot full of holes. But they won't stop shooting till they drop.

Their sales technique is so loaded and lopsided that the public endurance of it measures the public loss of conscience and judgment. A car, for instance, is sold under dozens of absolutist implications, not one of which is wholly true, and some of which are absurd: it is, the businessmen say, a necessity—but that statement is a highly limited proposition; it is a guarantor of the happy home—but that claim is rubbish because the car is also the main bone of contention in half the car-owning homes; it saves money—an appeal, in ninety-nine per cent of cases, to the nitwitted; it is good for the inferiority complex— a general implication that is subject to grave qualification in each individual case. There are a thousand more "reasons."

If the businessmen merely made cars, and devoted their advertisements to true claims about the mechanical advantages of the cars, their appearance, and so on, no one could argue with them about what they were doing. Cars are, after all, mechanical objects, and nothing else. The rest of the qualities that are attributed to them in the ads—say, roughly, ninety per cent of the sense of the pictures and the copy— belong to *people*. Purchase and possession of an object does not, in itself, do *anything* to an individual. To the extent that he thinks it does he has merely projected himself into a thing and so lost as much control and consciousness of himself as the amount projected.

Here is the fundamental immorality of modern sales procedure. It is not to be found in all advertisements, but in a sickeningly large number. The glib, continual assurance that a car, or an electrical mixing machine, or a new style of mouthwash will produce subjective benefits inevitably causes people to believe that they are dependent upon goods-fads and gadgets for their hourly contentment, adjustment, integration, "happiness," and social worth.

Communism, American salesmen might well meditate, falls for this same idiocy, in that it attributes all social ills to an improper or insufficient distribution of junk and expects by changing the economic rules, so that distribution is leveled and extended, to bring about a personality Valhalla among men. It is enlightening to note, as left-handed evidence of the foregoing, that the various consumers' societies, recently developed in America by socialist-minded persons, while they furnished critiques of an endless number of products on the market, never even dreamed of studying the dangerous subjective effects upon the public even of one single product. To the commies, as to capitalists, goods, if good, *must* be good for mankind. Both suffer the identical catastrophic blindness.

The total orientation of Americans toward the procurement and possession of goods was the ineluctable consequence, first, of the traditions of American business (i.e., those of the British, who had exploited their empire unintelligently for centuries, and those of the pioneers, who had ravaged the West); second, of the crummy heredity and folklore of American businessmen—whose ancestors had arrived on these shores, for the most part, to put one and take ten; third, of the demands of enshrined womanhood—who saw security in terms of the fancy house, the portable house, the loaded storage bin, and the domestic machines to save her work; fourth, of a business-reflected attempt to emulate the only remaining ideal in our society: that of science, which has to do with materials alone.

All the canned flapdoodle of commerce produces another effect worthy of a tome in itself and one to which I give a paragraph here as a marker in the unwritten work. While we have alternately scorned and dreaded the physical regimentation of the totalitarian societies around us, we have proceeded with the regimentation of our attitudes, prejudices, feelings, and values in a parallel manner, if not to an equal degree. To read the same stories, to see the same movies, to purchase from the same advertisements, and above all, to listen to the same radio programs, fifty million oafs at a time, is to accept unwittingly a stringent regimentation. Moreover, mass production, the very keystone of our society, is the author of these follower-principles; it not only regiments the millions at the lathes, but the consumers also. What the office and factory hours compel physically, the sales pressures apply subjectively. The advantages of intricate, cheap possessions are balanced by their cost in tedious production and by a national overspread of staleness, repetitiveness and sameness—footprints of the stamping mill. The car is the handiest example, but there is hardly an American who cannot find a hundred psychic cousins of cars in his head and touch a dozen in the room where he sits. Individuation, the obvious purpose of consciousness, is thus struck a fearful blow by the one apparent boon man has contrived for himself in three centuries of materialism. And if completely automatic machinery, the Nirvana of technocrats, merely gives total leisure for network programs, the blowups to come will make the present one a trifling preliminary. So regimentation—baneful word!—merely stands for foreign efforts to machine man for the machine. We have more than our share, without calling it by name.

How far we are off base is to be discerned, once again, in the distance between the promises we make in radio commercials, advertisements, and public boasts and our actual status now. It is ironic, in a way, that our society, like all the others of all the nations who tried to ape our production under one or another sort of economic system, has gone into its unstayable opposite. We (and they) have reached the impasse of war. The meaning of economics has been utterly frustrated. Shortages in consumers' goods are being followed by famines; there is rationing and restriction, priority and scarcity; everything for which we made ourselves work has been sacrificed, overnight, to another purpose. Each few weeks our "standard of living" dribbles backward some five or more years. But businessmen still are anxious about how the self-condemned process of irresponsible trade will be resumed after the war; more so, in the case of millions, than they are about the problem of the war itself.

It is childish, of course, to be worrying over the number of percolators we may be able to distribute in 1950 when it is apparent that any particular worrier may never live to see 1950, or that there may be no factories left standing, or we may have lost the war and the percolator distribution will be beyond our control, or that in 1950 we may still be making airplane instrument panels instead of percolators, or that there may be no coffee available, and so on. But we have so attached ourselves to goods that it is very hard for us to think of life in terms of anything else.

Our war aims remain nebulous, we are told, because nobody has yet hit upon a plan for the postwar world which satisfies the majority of the people on this all-consuming problem of goods. That is, of course, the last collective ditch of infantilism. Any individual ought to be willing to fight for his life, on the premise that he can decide what to do with it after he has saved himself. Many, however, are so thoroughly confused in their minds as to what is themselves and what is merely property that they actually throw away their lives when only some portion of their property is in peril. That is hysteria—the hysteria of a man who rushes back into his burning house to save a watermelon and is killed by a falling wall. A nation of people should have

a strong and clear instinct of self-preservation, and, also, if it finds allies for the attack of an enemy a family of nations should have the instinct. Ours is all too clearly bereft of a lucid concept of self-preservation and addled with a goods-identification; thus, to many, it hardly
seems worth while fighting to live until they can be assured that their
percolators will live, along with their cars, synthetic roofing, and dis-
posable diapers.

The economists have told us they are scientists and, as such, have
assured us that the causes of war are entirely economic, which explains
why even the "intellectuals" want economic doctrine as number one
war aim! But the economists have never bothered to go into the
causes of economics. According to them, the basic law is the law of
supply and demand. That the subjective and instinctual processes of
men may change the demands in a day, or alter the needed supplies, or
substitute the technique of theft for the technique of trade, the economists have not pointed out—ever. When a war arises, they and the
"thoughtful" businessmen take a rain check until it is over. They are
able to maintain the sophistry that war—stated by them to be an economically inspired activity—is itself not an economic procedure.
To the extent that American defensive psychology sprang out of a desire to defend such trade ethics as we still had it represented a fairly decent impulse: the impulse to go on doing business rather than to steal.
But, as soon as it became clear that war was a problem in attack (the
removal of the enemy and his goods by moving in upon him with destruction) and hence, in so far as the physical condition of the enemy
was concerned, a process to him analogous with theft, such small
standards of economic decency as we had subscribed to went by the
boards. The economists folded up on the present and began to debate the utterly inscrutable future.

This is not a way of saying that we should forbid anybody to consider a possible postwar future. Somebody should. But it is an attempt
to say that any consideration of that future wholly in the light of
trade-and-goods-according-to-ante-bellum-gospel is damned already,
both before and after the fact.

The businessmen are afraid they will lose their control and their profits because of socialization of government. They are afraid of what labor may do—and rightly, to the degree that labor continues to prosecute its goods demands by secret organizations and racketeering. In addition to the raw fear, there is a small fad going the rounds of businessmen and economists which asserts that neither labor nor capital will either control or divide control of the material destinies of men in the future, but managers. Perhaps they will, but there is no more necessity for taking that position per se than for taking the position I did about doctors: namely, that by organization and strikes *they* could come into the temporal power. Those who wish to ponder the picture of the future must do so without the use of special frames.

Few people have bothered to consider economics, or war, or the future from the standpoint of man as other than a goods consumer. One of the shrewdest contemplations to date (and this should dumfound liberals) is the work of Herbert Hoover.

But no business statisticians that I have heard of are making a graph of, say, the demands of moms as compared with the point at which their ability to absorb goods starts to work more social evil than contentment. And yet, that is a fearfully important graph.

Again, nobody is making boredom tables, to show to what degree how many men were willing to go to war, or even eager, merely as an escape from, or a rebellion against, the whole matter of having to live in Western industrial societies. In spite of the dangers evident in modern forms of war, a revolt from boredom has had much to do with the fact that it is possible to launch these wars. Man was designed by nature to hunt, to struggle, to endure, and to achieve on a personal physical plane; all his glands and hormones are integrated for such dangerous and exciting affairs. It is not normal for the creature to immolate himself for eight or ten hours a day, five or six days a week, in the acrid din of factories, where he is fairly secure but where he does the same one thing forever. It is not germane to his constitution, either, to stick it to a store counter or a desk for such periods. But our industrial society compels the procedure upon him willy-nilly, and gives him, for his leisure, the command of advertising to get busy using up in masses the stuff he has mass-produced. That he is often bored beyond endurance by the whole business cannot be doubted. That the operation of a tank or a trench mortar is, by comparison, an attractive alternative is testified by the unconscious looks and statements of millions. But there are no charts of *that,* either.

There are no jagged lines, anywhere, to show what pleasures people derive from escaping the monotonous lifelessness of running an engine lathe by taking up dive-bombing—which is highly alive because it rides on death and with death. And where are the figures on how much sordidness a bombardier feels he is avenging in his own background when he wipes out the sordid city of somebody else? Do the exuberant statements of our fliers, made after the shattering of Jap ships, reflect a psychopathic state of mind? Is it insane to talk about the act as "More fun than a World Series game"; "The swellest moment in my life"; "Cold turkey"; "A dream"; "A picnic"; "Shooting fish in a rain barrel," and the like? Have our boys gone mad? Or are they telling the truth, by chance? *Is* it fun? Ask anybody who has done it. . . .

It is more than fun—it is, often, the purest elation. But where we the economists' tables on such demand and supply?

Have the businessmen considered that, maybe, the price of unplanned and unrestricted mass production is too high for man to pay incessantly? The price, I mean, in the hideousness of cities, in the unfathomable dullness of repetitive operation, and in the standardization of spare-time activities brought about so largely by the subjective appeals of advertising? Would the idea frighten them? Would they say that wages will buy the workers, no matter what unnatural durance accompanies the pay? Or that if the ungrateful louts cannot be slaked with pay envelopes alone—plus a little frosted bread here and a circus there—then the state will take them over and a socialistic economy will keep their noses on the machines? Or that the skill of management will defeat the massed forces of greedy labor together with hopeful labor, and the capitalists as well, and society will be directed by the shop foremen? Will the short but already bloody history of industrial expansion support any such ideas?

A few businessmen have made a few generalized studies of another anomaly—the crazy irrelevance of living standards on the whole planet. They have thought that we cannot forever maintain a high wage in Wisconsin and a pittance in the Punjab, any more than we can maintain democracy in this nation alongside the fascism of an expanding Germany. They have gone that far, some of them, and now they are earnestly considering how to raise the wage of the Punjabi so that he can buy a percolator. They have not yet contemplated, however, all the possible effects upon Hindus of coffee nerves.

Freedom, obviously, consists in more than freedom to buy gadgets. But businessmen forever ignore or deny the otherness of freedom, whenever and wherever it tends to interfere with a market. That is how they ruin themselves and all of us. Their unconscious but absolute definition of liberty—and that of all the theoretical communists —is this: Liberty is the right to compel people to produce and purchase stuff.

Whenever man goes to war he makes his possessions into junk, indeed. This beating back and forth of spears and plowshares, tanks and jalopies, can be measured in terms of many demands besides those expressed in jalopy market quotations. It can be measured, as just one other example, in terms of all the individual fears of men. But the minute societies set out to guarantee each other freedom of trade they are inviting new sets of fears, even while they abolish old ones, and the minute they try to guarantee freedom from want they are putting everybody in peril of police. The minute they subscribe to the idea of freedom of individual belief they are either identifying the word "belief" with the proposition that men are created wholly to produce goods and consume them or they are inadvertently holding the clock hands so that all manner of men will be permitted to go on believing all sorts of superstitious crap which has no relation to the high degree of our scientific enlightenment and therefore will menace all other freedoms at every turn.

The businessmen have corrupted liberty by trying to propose it as a material quality. So have the economists of all schools. But material "progress" has to do with liberty only secondarily. Liberty is subjective. It is entirely personal and individual. A mob has no liberties—or a herd—or a nation, but a person only. Liberty is that degree of freedom of choice which a group grants to a person in it, but liberty can exist only in the precise degree to which each person and therefore all persons take full responsibility for their choices. The maintenance of liberty depends wholly on individual integrity of every sort—on insight, foresight, and on hindsight also. It depends upon wisdom—not, even, upon universal education as such, but only upon that part of education which teaches honesty. Where individuals make erroneous or stupid or avaricious choices—as they do in this nation almost universally—liberty dies that much. In its place comes slavery—slavery to instinct, to bosses, to lathes, to generals, to a state, which is then the repository of instincts instead of the church. But neither church nor state can do more than describe principles. So long as their descriptions present to each man eternally his problem, rather than dogmatic rules for the solution of it, they serve to maintain the freedom of men. When they become didactic they restrain freedom. If they are to prevent revolution they must contain as their fundamental premise the means of evolution. Creeds can be no more fixed than constitutions. Government and the church and business must become expressions of the right to change.

To an individual, positive subjective change, increase of wisdom—of awareness, mental and moral growth, is the be-all. In him, a spiritual status quo is stagnation, and stagnation is death even if his body continues to eat, sleep, fornicate, fear, and fight. To science also, because it uses only that same principle of integrity, increases of awareness and the resultant changes in knowledge constitute the be-all and the end-all. But to business, and to all the apologists for man as a consumer only, their one-track definition implies a single aim: the establishment of some mythical status quo, the freezing of some perfect system, the institution of some sort of technic by which man can live happily forever through the eternal speed-up of his mills. That is the most sullen enslavement of all, and billions have already perished in a hopeless effort to make it work by one method or another.

And yet, any more truthful attitude toward society is anathema to the businessman and to the social planner. Realism would compel the businessman to admit that, where his license to operate creates demands that are out of proportion to the value of the license, he must be curbed. Realism means that his duplications and overlaps must be intercepted. It means that he must not advertise and sell specious goods alongside sound products and that he must not be allowed to attribute to his wares qualities that are the property of human beings, and not goods. It means that he must be ready, at all times, to be superseded—but that hard law of nature is the one he fears and will not face.

What profiteth it a society of men if they are kept consuming an inferior article in order only that the maker may keep his bank accounts piling up? What good is it to let firms and corporations hide patents, obscure improvements, purchase progress and destroy it? The stock excuse of technological unemployment and the disturbance of capital structure is heady nonsense. There is genuine enough need in humanity to keep all the mills making mills for centuries, and all the workers working for as many hours a day as they have the stomach for without rebellion, if only the true requirements of men are considered, and not just his vanities and fripperies.

The same realism makes it evident that the perfectionist wish of the economist for a fixed system is piffle. We can no more delineate the rules of trade for the year 2000 than could Caesar have made an accurate assay of the 1940 automobile demand. We do not know what proportion of goods and services people will want in relation to what other material and subjective benefits. A logical economist would ask for this: (1) an opening of the books so that all may see who has what; (2) an exact physical appraisal of all goods; (3) an abandonment of subjective claims concerning goods; (4) an educational system which taught subjective integrity along with the scientific principle; (5) a social tenet which provided opportunity according to merit alone; (6) public protection from minorities bent on enforcing religious and other dogma inconsistent with current knowledge; (7) such planning for the future as science makes seem reasonable (but with the full knowledge that these plans may be proved wrong); and perhaps above all else (8) a system of reward based solely upon service rendered by work done.

Our economists, quite apart from our businessmen, are one hell of a long way from thinking about production and distribution in any such terms. Most of them have not even got around to considering the last-noted idea. Only socialists and communists have attempted to deal with it and their suggestion has been to wipe out ownership altogether—a notion as incongruent with man's nature as the American dogma cited below which does not distinguish in any way between kinds of richness.

And yet, there are two kinds of wealth and each of these is susceptible of limitless subdivision. There is earned money—and there is lucky money. There is the money which comes for services—for waiting on tables and running compressed-air drills and managing plants and writing books—and some men will always make more of that than the rest. The other kind is the sort that accrues to individuals through no efforts of their own whatever, or through efforts incommensurate with the amount received—inheritances, returns on gambling and speculation, vast sums plucked by persons who put themselves in the way of a flow of goods and take a toll out of proportion to any value they add to the goods, the millions of dollars that may accrue to a farmer upon whose cheap patch of ground oil is discovered, and so on. This unearned money is at present regarded as a substance as valuable, desirable, noble, and altogether enviable as money earned. Most people, indeed, covet it more—because of the social prestige that has been attached to it due to the fact that a majority of the very rich got it that way. Only recently have government officials begun to wonder about it. And, because they have taken a few steps in relation to it, business is already screaming that the nation is done for. Business cannot let go, without a monstrous, emotional fight, its perquisites of swag, won bets, tribute, lucky dough, family endowment, and so on. This is the gravy.

(To a psychologist, of course, the behavior of businessmen in such instances is revealing. As the matriarchy has become masculine, so has the businessman become womanish. As the adultness of the scientific principle [which creates so much of what the businessman sells] has, year by year, emphasized the infantilism of the businessman's refusal to cope with the subjective aspects of selling, he has behaved more and more like a spoiled infant. No longer a man, a creature in trousers, a reasoning and logical entity, he is an exponent of emotions and hysteria. His hurtability is an index of his childish tenderness, and the number of things that a businessman will tell you can hurt business is beyond counting. His press agents and his lobbies appeal to emotions and not to fact. If he disagrees with his government, he no longer sets out calmly to prove the administration is wrong. He merely hates it. He sulks, weeps, and curses—mad at the president or at a bureaucrat—but making no rational countermove against whatever it is he fears. A part of the press is busy being the sob sister for this stricken nonman. Business has engaged, lately, in a disgusting amount of the kind of irrational pseudo argument barraged up by angry dames—argument ad hominem, post hoc sed non propter hoc, non sequitur, and so on—as well as in fishwifery, viragoism, and every other kind of shrill, meaningless contention. Loudest and fiercest of the lot have been, perhaps, the congressmen, put in the government by the business-prejudiced people to be their soprano voice.)

We have got ourselves into a world of such interdependence that the injustice to all men of one man's lucky money is becoming very evident. Moreover, the contraction of planetary space to near zero by rapid transportation and the contraction of time to absolute zero by electrical communication have dissolved the curtains and the cushions which previously made the significance of the possession of lucky money fairly inscrutable to the ordinary, highly local individual. We can retain the profit motive (nobody ever gave it a higher name—such as the "profit ideal"—but maybe somebody should) and qualified remuneration according to the value of services, and a wide range in individual purchase-choices, and a flexibility of wage and price, and also a considerable amount of private control, competition, and ownership, but we are not going to be able to maintain the principle of lucky money much longer. The spectacle of who gets it, and how, and what they do with it has been made far too evident both by the shrinkage of space and time which puts all men in one spot and by our ever-growing interdependence; the public is not, indeed, tolerating as much of it now as it once did.

Since business evolves and mass-producing is evidently the direction of its evolution, owner-management will have to become responsible for much of the social (or mass) liability of man it has heretofore tried to avoid. The future big boys will have to have earned it—and they won't be allowed to hand it on to their children. All the sources of "lucky money" will have to be bought back by the people for their own collective use. "Little" businessmen will have to be specialists—or they will be swallowed up—and most men engaged in commerce will be agents of big businesses, as so many now are. The professional man will find a new level in public regard commensurate with his contributions and the twilight of the contemporary businessman, the determined freebooter, will be at hand. Momism would surely perish in any such rearrangement of power and energy according to the true inner nature of man.

I can detect a not-so-far-off sound from business tradition, the nature of businessmen, and the grotesque materialism of Western society in response to the above, and it is the sound of a great multitude crying, "Oh, yeah!" Perhaps I am a poor prophet. Maybe we will become communistic, or as near to it as we can bear. Or maybe we will have an age of managerial feudalism. Or maybe we will go on running our present system into the earth until we are so utterly confused that the third war with Germany, or someone, will make us henchmen. Maybe we *are* staring at the decline of the West. *You* decide—bearing in mind the fact that the U.S.A. can't stand any more votes for pork. To continue at all, we are going to have to put two and take one, for quite a while, after this war. The rosy color in the spectacles of business-men, lately, was blood.

CHAPTER XIII

Statesmen

I HAVE LET A DESCRIPTION OF DOCTORS STAND FOR ALL SCIEN-
tists and it is near enough as an analogy to show what I mean. The doctors practice on the people directly; the scientists practice the same preposterous sets of magic indirectly. The businessmen *are* the people, for the most part. But we cannot quite finish even this cursory inspection of some of the unidentified opposites and overlooked positives in ourselves and our society until we have glanced, at least briefly, at three other major classes of contemporary poops: the statesmen, the professors, and the soldiers.

Statesmen, at least the elective ones, are constantly inviting attention to their "record." Let us look at their records. The soddenest spot on the terrible road of man is the place where statesmen passed. The international achievements of the greatest of them in history have been mere territorial expansion, sly spadework for the businessmen, and the signing of treaties favorable to particular groups. Their activity has been so to distort and pervert human morality as to make seemingly just and profound all manner of national deeds which, if performed by persons instead of states, would get the persons hanged. They have been the verbose and tricky front of commercial exploiters. Whenever they have failed to effect their monstrous bargains they have called in the soldiers to do by the sword what could not be accomplished with scratching diplomatic pens.

246

We are all likely to tender statecraft the same lightheaded optimism and credulity that other men have accorded it before and, thereby, to permit the making of international bargains upon the seals of which man's rattiness or even his real hunger will begin to gnaw before the wax is cool. Versailles and Locarno stood for several years. It is noteworthy that in this era of speedy doing, Munich, a more modern document, became a scrap of paper in six months. We invest in statesmen's documents the same unwarranted trust of symbols that we ascribe to hats. All articles, treaties, confederations, and so on are scraps of paper, as are all deeds and contracts, when the goodwill underlying them runs out, and man had better begin to make treaties in the awareness that he is a creature of almost as much ill will as good, or each signing of a peace will soon be coincident with the outburst of war, which it very nearly is already.

There are men today, in Washington, who are busily trying to figure out a balance of power which will create some new sort of temporary impasse between nations, and thereby an illusion of stability and security. These pinheads mostly derive from the diplomatic school we set up after we learned, in 1918 and the other years that preceded it, that our louts and rustics, businessmen and politicians, were not as slick or ritzy as the London, Berlin, and Paris bandits. We Americans, in Washington, hastily developed a class of stoopnagels with Oxford accents and glib French who learned to make the gambits of power counterposed to power just as the French, English, Japs, and Germans had long and bloodily been doing. Their record, over the past ten years, has been about the same as Chamberlain's.

They learned a game that the Nazis wouldn't play—but they went ahead with it anyhow, observing all the old rules and protocols; some of them still convinced that Mussolini isn't such a bad chap and that Vichy was worth appeasing. These high altitudes of Victorian statecraft just mastered by our American boys have given rise to an incredible amount of misapprehension and dizziness in our government. The Germany in which they believe passed away with Bismarck. They fear and distrust Bolshevism, which has the best record for honesty in statecraft of any.* They concern themselves with the value of some millions of impotent South Americans more than with the value of some hundreds of millions of Chinese who are killing Japs all day long. They have made such ghastly errors so often that they are now wholly involved in the fantastic enterprise of proving that at least one —any one—of their past misconstructions was sound. Only by that proof, these statesmen feel, can they save face—and they will drag our nation through needless seas of blood and asininity in order to save their prides in their own estimates.†

High school graduates know more and can outthink them. But they have a franchise, and they are using it to raise hell with the prosecution of the war. Most of them are sissies—another product of momism into which I did not bother to go because I thought you knew about it already—and in American statecraft, where you need desperately a man of iron, you often get a nance.‡ They are fake Englishmen, without a knowledge or an understanding of the positive qualities of Britons—jizzling imitations of some of the most extensive

---

* I referred here to the forthright and unsubtle way in which the Russians have always said what they would do—and done it; I was not, at the moment, thinking of ultimate Soviet goals, such as the destruction of U.S.A., about which they have always been as candid as about other intentions. That might well have caused fear in our State Department, though never mistrust. We can trust the Communists absolutely to try for their final aim.

† This implies a currently overlooked truth: we "lost" China long before World War II began and Acheson had nothing to do with it. For we never had China to lose: the people of America and their State Departments were eternally apathetic about the Chinese save where two items were concerned: trade, and the welfare of missionaries.

‡ It was not McCarthy who made, ten years after this was noted down, the findings about homosexuality in the State Department.

malefactors who ever did wrongs by casual intent. They do not have the good of man at heart, or even a hope in man, because they were trained, alas, by the most decayed end products of a European diplomacy who cared nothing for man's future, really, but only for embassy kudos, and who had no faith in man, being professional cynics. Cynicism is the cheapest elegant posture man has invented so far.

The public never sees or knows these statesmen—by and large—but only suffers from their grotesqueries when it finds itself drowning in their results. It is no wonder that the Russians found a capitalist more to their liking than any standard diplomat and it is not surprising that we have got our best advocates out of the hills of New England, unpolished but sincere, rather than out of the covey of career boys who have been taught to toy with international affairs but not to direct them in any way.

A sense of inferiority to the vestigial pomposities of nineteenth century Europe got us started in the training of these contemptible clowns; our post-last-war isolationism made it possible for them to stay in the government because it prevented us from paying any attention to them; if the war cleans them out, it will be one of the rare purifying acts for which we can thank the Nazis. And the businessmen should be memorialized, en passant, to the effect that they, not Roosevelt, are basically responsible for the sisterhood in our State Department, which preceded F.D.R. by something more than a decade.*

Of course, a large part of the mistake we made in the case of the anointed prickamice mentioned above has been to believe that state-

---

* The "businessmen" have, by now, utterly obscured and concealed the simple truth stated here. They feverishly blame Roosevelt and his associates for several matters that began before Buchanan or Grant—and many more they instituted themselves. After all, the sissies and dopes in State here noted were, nearly all, Ivy League graduates, West Pointers, Annapolis men, or the Roman Catholic sons of Georgetown: Tories, all, sons of businessmen, themselves monkey-businessmen.

craft was a subject, like geometry, and that the best teachers lived abroad, as in savate, which statecraft more closely resembles than math. The illusion from which we suffered after the time of Wilson was that we had been outfoxed, and maybe that was not altogether an illusion. So we bred some little foxes of our own. The illusion from which *they* are suffering is that they can do anything as representatives of a democracy which has either significance or validity.

They cannot, because the electorate will speedily put in office some man or men who will undo, or contradict, or ignore, their pernicious notes and manifestoes. The only possible face which we Americans can show the world is one that is also recognizable to the electorate, and hence will stand a chance of being supported by the electorate. Because the electorate has the I.Q., instincts, values, emotions, feelings, and judgment of a child of twelve, no diplomatic maneuver beyond that range is sensible for us. In addition, most of the Americans whose intelligence runs a peg or two higher profess themselves to be liberal idealists of one sort or another, which further precludes forever from American statesmanship the hope of doing anything slick in the field of international affairs.

We are, as a people, the wonder and the hate of the world, its envy and its despair. We are in the midst of a time when we had better stick to a few extremely simple premises, such as that we will try to guarantee more freedom for more people after the war than we did before and that, having found every world balance of power a screwy device, we will now maintain enough power of our own to knock flat any nation or bunch of nations that sticks its head up against us, picking no fights, but taking no chances. Such a program is not diplomatic. It would throw the sissies of our State Department into a nervous sweat. The godly would not like it and the mothers of America would scream against it. It is not "idealistic" in the sense in which we have had an international idealism—which is, after all, the sense of sending missionaries over the earth, together with tourists and traders —to tell the rest of man it did not know its razzmatazz from a hole in the ground, while our diplomats, on the other hand, have been going around apologizing for not being Portuguese nobles, and bowing obsequiously to Japanese kumquats.*

But such a program as the one above, implemented with a few more very simple hopes (not grandiose pledges), is about all our statesmen can sensibly offer. It is conceivable that a few nations or dominions may someday want to join us and, if so, we might take them in, as there is no reason why we should not enlarge the nation by the same method by which it has grown for a hundred and fifty years. There is even a vogue at the moment for a union of our nation and the British Empire, and this is the sort of notion that pops into the minds of all men who are in great difficulty; it is also the sort that they are apt to marvel over, if they remember it at all, when they get out of their trouble.† It is, so to speak, like promising to tithe, or join the church, when your dory is sinking in a storm. The thing has great impact in the hour of distress—but it has brought little money and few converts to the church.

I, personally, would feel honored to belong to a nation composed of the British and ourselves, or the British, Chinese, Greeks, Russians, Poles, Arabs, Finns and ourselves if they and we would all give up our names and adopt a common language, give up our flags and design a new one, institute measures for proportional cross-breeding, and take other, similarly cogent steps to erase nationalism (save for a fealty to the new nation) along realistic, absolute, and instantaneous lines. But I am such an ornery and dissident bastard that I suspect this war will end in some doubts among the Allies, and that the most progress we can expect toward the brotherhood of man will be a new confederation of nations which will work fairly well, perhaps even for centuries, and might eventually lead to union, which is the conscious slaying of all nationalism, including our own.

---

* This still seems an appropriate thought but it is one State ignored. Of course, I did little here to ingratiate myself with the State Department.

† Remember, "Union now"?

The previous League of Nations did not necessarily fail because we stayed out of it. It did fail. And we were not in it. But I can think of hundreds of ways in which it might still have failed even though our American statesman had sat around its table. Indeed, the presence of our representatives, in the state of mind they have exhibited for the last quarter century, suggests that the League might have failed sooner if we had been participants. For we were absorbed in ourselves in a manner extremely hard for others to bear. Whatever future federation or league we get into, if we do get a chance to make one, should not cause us again, ever, to put our trust in treaties, wholly, just because it is a convenience for the businessmen and the taxpayers.

It is my distinct impression, and I have been very accurate for many years in predicting these matters, that under no circumstances will this great and contaminating orgy of war wind up in a welter of brotherly love and nothing else. Those other, decent, and earnest statesmen in Washington who are planning the world with this hope in mind may be deceived at the peace conference in a different way from the one in which Wilson was deceived, but a way just as heartless. It is much more likely, however, that they will be considerably undeceived before they even reach the peace conference stage, granting that they do so. For the last phases of the war may not consist of a fraternal march-in of the legions of honest men who have come to forgive and liberate the Germans and the Japs.

Here, again, is another of the endless bungles which Western man permits himself to make by refusing to recognize instinctual nature. A child, reading our current history, might guess that these were the days of the greatest hate-brewing on earth; but a grown man, conditioned by Western thinking, reads the same document and petitions against hatred while he plans brother love. What wishful, witless, nonsensical, and calamitous "statesmanship" that is! The Greeks are going to loathe and abhor the Germans for generations. Nothing is more certain, regardless of what happens. The Italians are going to despise the Germans, too, for letting them down and for treating them cavalierly, not to say with butchery. How, also, will the French feel about the

Germans, when they get back their autonomy? The Czechs? The Poles? And will a Russian sit down at a peace conference table, full of goodwill toward his enemies? Or a Norwegian? And how will the Chinese feel about the Japs? How will we feel, before *we* are done with them?

It is likely that the armies of the United Nations will rage into Germany when she collapses and that there will be no holding them because they will be crazed from having suffered too much, wantonly, under the talons of their tormentors. Two wrongs, as Americans prissily say (meanwhile committing six or seven), do not make a right. But the greatest wrong is the one which betrays the integrity of the doer—and we are not showing guts enough to be worthy of our human existence, when we pretend that we can work out a happy end— a Cinderella end—to this war on a piece of paper. It will take centuries of hard work, of giving, of lease-lend, of contributed money from American taxpayers, of unselfish labor abroad in countries we do not especially enjoy, of sacrifice and sweat, tears, penance, turmoil and even blood, to undo what *we have let* Hitler and the Japs do—for what now proves to have been the boon of ten short years of shaky, domestic sanctimoniousness. When Hitler called us weak, he was right; his very existence was a sign in the heavens of our infinite moral debility.

Statesmen forget these matters. Leather stationery, colonnaded offices, and historical fountain pens go to their heads. They need one quality which our successive administrations seem never to have, any more: humility.

Our domestic statesmen are of two sorts: those we elect and those who are appointed by our elected representatives. Among the latter group, too, are many men with plans, many economists, many city boys who have laid out schemes for farmers but never seen a farm, many rabid bureaucrats who seem to think that because they are flyspecks on the lever of government they can wrench around the whole population by an utterance. These micropoops are in various departments and they have got to go, too; otherwise the paper on which their plans are written will clog the Potomac, as if it were a drain, and it will back up and flush every sensible man out of the Capitol.

These are the issue of the professors—these, and the educated moms who decorate our political bureaucracy. They are extremely well-meaning people, so long as the ship of state is looping along in the precise course of their own meaning, whether it is pensions for the aged, tree planting for the young, high excess profit taxes, a garden behind every home or a bathtub in it, or a rose in every buttonhole. But, should the national constituency, or a senator, or a businessman, undertake to divert the ship from the exact proposition to which these bantambrains are dedicated, they build up caucuses, whisper in big ears, lie, threaten, cajole, write letters, get thousands to telegraph the Congress, and otherwise stir up what, in the myopic eye of Washington, appears to be a public uproar. The result is that upon the person of this nation all manner of sinister and silly experiments are forever being tried, and every sort of obsolete organ and fizzle is perpetuated with a bureau of its own, employees, and a treadmill to make it look active.

The imbecilic behavior of the elected representatives of the people has made many ordinary mortals wish that there were at least educational standards for the candidates. To have in Congress men who almost never know what they are talking about is unfortunate, not to say suicidal. But the experience we have had, knowingly or not, with many of the products of Harvard, Yale, Annapolis and Princeton* leads to the conviction that perhaps, beyond high school, education is not so important an asset as common sense, intelligence, integrity, and a self-sacrificing spirit.

---

* John Foster Dulles, current Secretary of State, attended Princeton. But, then, so did I.

CHAPTER XIV

Professors

THE BLAME FOR THIS LIES UPON THE PROFESSORS. THESE TOUSLED wearers of the flat hat, supererogated by the medieval magic of the cloister, and made additionally colossal by a little knowledge of some external or measurable facet of the universe, have failed wretchedly in their assignment of educating post-school Americans. They have so departmentalized knowledge that a quadrennium is not long enough to make a sciolist, and they have let the teaching of wisdom disappear altogether from the curriculum, because, doubtless, they no longer have any to teach.

Remembering my own years in college, and listening to the postulates of those who have attended colleges twenty years later, I cannot but come to the conclusion that our universities would be better abolished, so as to be turned into something fresh and vital, than to be allowed to carry on in the revolting enterprise of stowing into every brain a few slices of science, a tenth of a language, a one-semester course of pedantic gibberish concerning obsolete philosophy, and the brittle prejudices of some young upstart in the nonexistent sciences of sociology and economics and, after that, of informing the container of this uncongealed morass, via diploma, that he is "educated."

Our universities are hard at the chore of sending out into the world a tasseled rabble of reformers who either skid so hard and fast upon their pink* profundaments that they pick themselves up, get a job, and try to forget all about the college years, or else hie themselves to Washington and persuade some desk cowboy to try Professor Pusspocket's theory of negative money on a test area in the Middle West. Human nature has not changed so much that Pusspockets in every college in America can hope to help by indoctrinating all their pupils with new and starry versions of it. They should be thrown out or, if necessary, dragged out.

Let this light shine into the mausoleums where we send our children

---

* While the "pink" aspect of many professors was plainly to be noticed in 1941 (and not a Great New Finding of Congress made a decade later) it was seldom a true communism or even faith in Marxist theory; usually it was a vague trust in "economics" as the basis of human motivation, a belief also commonly held by capitalists.

The way those same professors were treated in 1952 and 1953 for what they maunderingly believed in 1935 or 1940 was far more scandalous and un-American—far closer to that emergence of raw instinct I deplore everywhere in these pages—than was ever any theory of those academicians a peril to America.

To remain Americans we must remain free to think and to say anything we see fit in good conscience to set forth. There is a vast—unrecognized—difference between slack or witless uses of liberty and the Russian Communist necessity of overthrowing America or going out of business.

Many professors somewhat abused freedom to express witless ideas: true freedom can bear all abuse; a few professors actually were Communists; free men used to be able to tolerate even that blunder. But more than a billion persons now, outside America, are voluntarily engaged, or engaged by persuasion, or compelled to engage in an absolute cabal (that includes war) to destroy freedom and its main support, our country. This goes unnoticed or evaded by American millions; and millions more are ready to forget it at the drop of a "peace" proposal.

for higher learning: a college graduate *ought* to be of more immediate usefulness and more enduring value, to the existing society, than a person who has not gone to college. A college graduate certainly serves no purpose by being fitted for a post in the Roman senate. A college graduate who has been nowhere, like the majority, but has only belonged to a commercialized athletic club in which it was necessary to do a little required miscellaneous reading to maintain the membership, should never have gone to college in the first place, and there should have been no such clubs open to him at so impressionable an age, for he is bound to go on trying to re-create the atmosphere all his life. He does so by the hundreds of thousands, and it is not an atmosphere that has anything whatever to do with being alive in these years of grisliness.

Football, indeed, has harmed college education next most to academic feudalism, or flat-hat fascismo, the American university way. When I indict football I include, naturally, its accompanying aura. I say this although I am a football fan, and went to such a college as I describe here. But I will trade a professional team for my fun, in return to football-less colleges any day. Siwash, the corny, did not vanish in the golden nineties, it overspread the educational scene; and now no Siwash can be discovered, simply because every university is Siwash.

The professors got their emphasis balled up so badly that, finally, professors were de-emphasized in colleges.

What the colleges need is, first, undergraduate bodies who are there for hard study only—all others being tweedy morons and a waste of human effort; second, courses not in economics, but in Sin. The only reason for the existence of learning is the maintenance and increase of some kind of morals—the more realistic, or homogeneous with natural law, the better. Thus, a college earnestly seeking to abet mankind would have, along with its science, its arts, and history, such courses as:

How To Tell Your Mother from a Wolf
The Life and Times of Frank Hague—a Study in Americanism

The Culture of Corporations
Horst Wessel and Some Union Leaders—a Review of Pimps
Rabble-rousing and Wrapping Yourself in the Flag—
Public Speaking for Future Leaders
Middletown—What's in Its Bureau Drawers?
Is the Bok Tower the End of the American Dream?
Adventures in Mother's Four-doored Womb
Domestic Failures of Prominent American Women
The Double-Cross of Protestantism
Virtue: a Field Course in Juking
Clean Cities and How To Have Fun in Them
100,000,000 Peeping Toms—a Survey of American Advertising

Students trained in the nature and reality of Sin by such courses as the above, and hundreds of others which I would be glad to list free of charge for any interested university, would go into the world, which is to say, back to their home towns, prepared to meet life squarely. Fore-armed with great learning, they would be hard to fool. The notion that their town was an incorruptible fountain of veracity and valor would not only fail to become their dominant idea for the rest of their days, but they would laugh heartily at the populace for believing in it and quote statistics which would bring blushes of anger of the type that leads to suicide on the cheek of every Rotarian and city commis-sioner. But, in the end, this brand of knowledge would prevail. A new spirit of civic skepticism might be born which would foster the aboli-tion of quacks and trumpeters and an institution of a government highly tolerant of individual penchants in the matter of private mores but determined upon the eradication of all forms of crookedness. Happy children would laugh and play in the streets and the professors would have brought it all about. Only, so far, they haven't even heard of these things.

They never seem to think of what, in their lofty and trusted spot as mentors of the young, they have not contributed to America. They drip with glib statistics on the number of kids who have been given diplomas in the past twenty years. The army has found that about four times as many soldiers per capita have been through high schools and entered colleges as in the days of their dads. But nobody points out that this extraordinary multiplication of higher education for common man has run parallel, like woman suffrage, to a series of public shames and disasters, blindnesses and idiocies, without precedent in our history. Nobody is daring enough to suggest that the two facts be set side by side: an increase of general "education" and a decrease of general wisdom to that point at which municipal and state governments are mental pigsties, the appointed national statesmen are social and economic faddists, the elective representatives are such incalculable fools that the entire land has taken to ridiculing them, the schism between labor and capital grows deeper every day and their methods of attack on each other become always more brutal and corrupt, there is not enough foresight and detachment in the whole land to get ready for the advertised onslaught of the conquerors in time to meet them on even terms—and the educators themselves are too dumb to see in the tall pyres of burning books the terrible threat raging toward such small stocks of information and faith as they have accumulated and protected up to now.

All the education of our yesterdays, or nearly all, has merely helped us miss the boat. The "lux" of its yesterdays is even now conveying myriad fools to dusty death. Its "veritas" is about things outside itself. There's not a drop of honest introspection in a barrel of learned critique of learning.

The intellectual position of American educators is threefold: (1) a devotion to tradition, that is, to an extension in time of the rites and flummeries of universities in the earlier Middle Ages, typified by the hooded dean pronouncing the baccalaureate in Latin; (2) scientific classicism, to which material truth is the be-all and which not only scorns but denies subjectivity, making it possible by the default for a physicist to try to insist upon defining cosmic radiation in terms of Congregationalism—a mighty departure even from the classical principle—and turning out, as another example, medical doctors who demand the right to treat the soul and maintain nevertheless that the soul must be cured with sulfonamides; and (3) the new identification of learning with economics, which is another sellout of subjectivity; another attempt to deal with all humanity in terms of temporal values, another ecclesiasticism—the ecclesiasticism of cash, which is responsible for the panaceas of the popeyed wights in Washington and for the horrid bilge uttered against honest work by the homecoming graduate till he is silenced by reality, or by force, or driven from his hearth into the bosom of some dogeared youth association or liver-colored periodical, there forever to keep changing his title, creed, purpose, fealties, values, and battlecries, without knowing he has lost his mind.

Of the three, the scientific allegiance to truth is, at least, half of an integrity, and the brightest, most honorable youths adopt it, becoming wise about matter, even if they remain absurdly befuddled about people. The monastic tradition is perishing of its own mordant nature, but there is no asceticism, no discipline, to replace it yet. The social and economic bents of modern teaching, which from school to school and classroom to classroom pile up frantic ideoglossaries and a structure of synthetic contradictions, furnish those students whose instincts are oriented toward theological quibble with a new theology of supply and demand and class revolution, which seems vaguely allied to science inasmuch as the terms of it are largely materialistic and only its meaning, which nobody studies, is metaphysical.

But these three intellectual positions never see man as a person or as a whole. Whole man is not just physics and chemistry, nor altogether the creature of his muddy past, nor yet entirely a producer and consumer of goods, but all three, and the creature of the future besides, unless he destroys the future by carrying to its ultimate end his preoccupation with the material aspect of now, alongside his denials of other kinds of time. That is Sin, and Aldous Huxley has written about it. It is their own sins which the universities will have to confess and for which all of us will have to do penance if education is, ever again, to educate. That, of course, is why a few pages back, I listed certain courses in Sin for colleges of the future. The kingdom of heaven is within—but hell is all around, without. It needs scientific investigation, which is to say, investigation made without a priori conclusion.

(One notes here, as an aside, that in setting down even the terms of logic, one must forever use Latin—and this, too, is a sample of the folly I am engaged in rebuking: we have no English for the formulae by which common sense is employed—only the words of a people who vanished hundreds and hundreds of years ago because of their unreasonableness. Here the educators, like the doctors, retain the prerogatives of their obsolete unctions and demand either that you join the club to become knowing or that you do without knowledge all your days. Educated businessmen, like women in what they call their thinking, together with all manner of other educated scientists, statesmen, and soldiers, cannot hold intelligent discussions any more, but rave like gibbons, because the technique of sensibleness has been hidden from them in words like "a priori," "ad hominum," "de facto," "post hoc sed non propter hoc," and "reductio ad absurdum." We have hidden away logic—common sense, that is—in Latin, because, no doubt, we are afraid to teach it in English.)

The professors, deans, instructors, college presidents, teachers, and lecturers would, were they not lost in folly, tear down most of the schoolhouses and college buildings in which they have labored, as a reproach to themselves and the world for the fruit of their methods. They are too stupid and too full of moral cowardice, however, to investigate more than the surface of this blot they have helped put upon man by convincing him he is wise when he has been given, instead of wisdom, a little knowledge only. But the students, still young and still with some instinctual sense of proportion because of their youth, are tearing down the structure themselves, for it is the august want in education that has converted the campus into an athletic club—not the innate perversity of youth and the times. The proliferation of great stadia, crushing the discipline out of the libraries and laboratories, and the attendant parties, proms, minor sports, social events, sartorial activities, fraternities, sororities, packed parking yards, and predilections for courses that are piddling fun—all these manifestations are youth's mighty rebuke to age, a testament of youth's discovery that the leaders cannot lead, that doctrine is for dopes, that the professor is a poop, and that education, because it is little help to a man or woman in these parlous times, might better be converted into trivial amusements, lest the years spent at it be altogether lost in starving. The time is at hand for the tetrarchs of our academies to rend their black gowns and pour ashes on their heads, which, if they cannot come by in modern edifices that burn oil, will be found in ample quantities on the cinder tracks around the playing fields.

CHAPTER XV

Congressmen—with a Footnote
on Mecca

THE COLLEGES SEND TO WASHINGTON LITTLE THAT HAS MEAN-
ing to help govern the land.

The people send even less.

It is a waste of words here to berate Congress. The people are doing the job. In doing it, the people are indicting themselves, of course,
for the men in our Senate and the men in our House of Representatives are, indeed, the representatives of the people. Each ribald hoot at
the selfishness, the arrogance, the stupidity of our elected statesmen
does not ricochet into nowhere, but bounces straight back, burning
and sharp with inescapable consequence, into the bodies of the hoot-
ers: the citizens themselves, the voting public. The withered emasculation of our democratic statesmanship is the withered emasculation of
America. The witch-hunting savagery of pompous male sluts in our
national halls is that quality of all the people. The petty greed and
relentless solicitation of these quasi males is our own. The sacrifice of
power, of dignity, of responsibility, of national security and interest to
a little patronage or the achievement of a trivial local profit is the
measure of our universal loss of aim, purpose, moral worth, view, vision, integrity, and common cause.

The appalling stupidity of these men, highlighted by the ferocious
peril of these hours, is the exact measure of the stupidity of the people in our states, cities, towns, and villages. When we condemn them,
which we rightly do with nearly every dispatch concerning their mul-

tifarious and nonsensical agenda, we condemn ourselves. When we say these men have abandoned their strength to the administration, because of pressure, we state how great has been our own eagerness to lay down the chore of civic duty and let an administration—or nobody —pick up and exploit our united strength. When we perceive that they are talking without knowing what they are talking about and doing without being able to guess the results of their acts, ignorantly busy giving unearned pensions and collecting unjust taxes, digging canals and having to fill them in, we are saying how little we, also, know or care about these matters. When we describe their pompous vanity and take exquisite pleasure in putting calipers on the immense littleness of their avarice, we are making records of our own littleness and avariciousness. When we see them knuckle to lobbies, abandon sense to the demand of minority blocs, weasel, quibble, and fail, we are watching the progress of a disease in ourselves, a democratic sickness, metastatic, and so far advanced that democracy may yet die of it —not because democracy was a mistaken plan for living together, but because the people have eschewed it out of their own greed and attached themselves to a bloc, to labor, to farms, to capital, to legionnaires, to pensioneers, to states, to congressional districts, to any of a thousand gangs within our democracy—but only rarely to democracy.

By putting this small mob fealty ahead of allegiance to all of ourselves, we have steadily moved closer toward the place when mobs will fight openly to rule us, and one of them, or a group of them, may win the foray. Then they will take to fighting among each other until it becomes necessary to appoint a dictator. If that is done, the wheel will have come a full turn and democratic man will again have lost his liberty, having spat upon it, abused it, laughed at it, neglected it, and so given it up because each individual man of him was not yet good enough for liberty.

Last winter, in the first precious weeks of war, our Senate used three of them to argue the moral turpitude of one member. That is as sad a sight as this democracy has seen in a century.

Many men in Washington know these things and are trying to lead the people out of them. But the people will have to be instructed out of them, if this is to remain a free state and a world where any freedom can exist. Otherwise there will come a benevolent despotism of bureaucracy and, since benevolence cannot be maintained by bureaucracy, but only by the will and vigilance of all the people, that, too, will fade away. Whoever uses power unwisely will be shorn of power. If we cannot elect men with sufficient education and honor even to try to be wise, we can number in a few score the years in which the elective power will remain ours. Liberty lives by morality alone—scientific morality, if you will. A country without complete candor is already enslaved.

As a start, we might raise the pay of senators and representatives high enough so that competition for the posts will be entered into by men who understand one of our symbols: money, and who are at the least able enough to get their share of money from this society, which, God knows, is not necessarily very able. Certainly the men who make our laws should be paid as much as the men who run our banks— since income is our first standard of excellence and since low-paid representatives lose such small values of prestige and respect as accrue to good pay, and more especially since our bankers can only break us, but our legislators can abolish the nation. We might also postulate minimal standards of factual education for our candidates so that a government of ignoramuses would be impossible. Colleges being what they are, it would be asking precious little to require that a senator or a representative must have a college education, or its provable equivalent. But the educators still permit the display of maps in high schools; we might ask that much schooling.

As it is, problems involving every science and every industry are being decided by men who cannot recite the multiplication tables. Small wonder our government has evolved into administration by appointed bureaucrats and away from government by the people's choices, since they have often shown themselves to be unable to attempt the task. The bureaucrats were necessary because government had to go on. But the only way by which the people can avoid a final passage of their powers and their rights into the hands of a person or a group of persons, now discernible only as inevitabilities and not in terms of names or titles, will be to elect representatives of their various political units who have the will, the knowledge, and the skill to govern all the people. There is, at present, no sign that any such fundamental premise exists in the heads of the electorate. Recent primaries for seats in the House and Senate have been neglected by as much as two-thirds of the registered voters in some states. It is asinine to presume that we can offer freedom of any sort to the world outside America, when we are steadily abdicating the basis of all freedom in our own communities. This, again, is a fact which has not been made apparent, evidently, to the Washington sachems, who continue to design great and statesmenlike plans for liberty and, at the same time, to usurp American liberty at every turn, not by any will of their own but because of public default.

Washington itself, indeed, might be abolished where it is, and transferred to a new place. Sensible men everywhere in this land might well hope—and earnestly pray—that an enemy bomber flight would reduce it to sudden rubble and compel the move. The mere necessity of a physical regeneration of the government plant would so illuminate the present multiboggles and sophisma of our central government that changes for the better might be expected on a new site. The people who have been crying that government should be given back to them would thereby have one more chance to *take* back the government, for the powers of government are always seized—either by the people for their own purposes or by tyrants, whether malevolent or delightful.

The loss of the physical city of Washington would be a benefit not only to government, but to aesthetics, because it is unquestionably the ugliest city of any pretensions that a human civilization has yet raised up to scar and blemish the countenance of the planet. Here is a city without a plan that has reference to modern life, a city filled with every classical incubus of architecture, with a hundred brown boxes of buildings that grow like fungus in the midst of its proudest and most highly marbleized environs, a city without proportion or color or quality, a city from which lurch dingy thoroughfares strewn with staggering edifices that present every sullen, rococo, snarling, sick, noxious, and absurd form of vainglorious house and apartment architecture designed in the long decades of Victorian false front and the subsequent age of atrabilious brick to assuage the cheap passions of the middle class and the Middle West.

Washington is in this, also, the stone symbol of rapacity converted to smugness, of tawdry imitation which is a condemnation of America as unoriginal and servile, as well as a revelation of the ghastly turn of our subconscious minds. This orgiastic claptrap has no honest meaning or no open purpose, and it is not livable. It is, rather, a smothering of the soul or a gallows boast, perfervid and florid—an unwitting confession of peewee excesses, of niggling lavishnesses, and of misapprehensions of the phony for the real and the swinish for the good. To abide in it composedly is to be either a lama beyond reach of all earthly things or perilously mistaken in the acceptance of slack composure as inviting, when it is hell's latchstring.

All the topographical and physical dreadfulness of America is lumped here, with only the relief of a few façades, a dome or two, and the sterile square obelisk dedicated to the founder. It is a forever dug-up city on a dirty river, unrelated in position to other cities, detached from trade and science, and ridden with the most dank and melancholy climate on the continent. As cities must, it expresses the approach to life of most of those who stay in it, and sensitive men who get there are consumed with a will to find excuses for getting away. Only the center of this sepulcher is whited; the necrosis of the rest shows forth shamelessly all the yellows, greens, browns, putrid reds, and indecipherable purples which are the colors of decay. Without refinement, dignity, or a sense of itself either as an entity or a necessary expression of other than America's worst, it is a painted bone-yard.*

---

* This portrait of our capital does seem a shade roguish, in retro-spect. The reader will reflect that I had just left off working for the government and *living* in Washington.

The portrait of *congressmen* given in this chapter, on the other hand, may seem to the reader extraordinarily accurate, timely, even prophetic—or as if written only yesterday. Let him consider then, that there's no miracle about it: the same words would have been appro-priate to Congress in the administration of Lincoln, of Van Buren, of George Washington; and they must be the approximate substance of Eisenhower's last thought before he drops off to sleep each night.

CHAPTER XVI

Military Men

WHEN, IN A REPUBLIC, THE STATESMEN FAIL, AND THE STUDENTS and their professors, and the representatives, soldiers are called upon as a last resort. These, in our society, like all other professional men, are pawns of the business satraps. In war, soldiers obtain a larger or smaller degree of authority. In peace, they have practically none. Their peacetime maintenance and their preparations for the next war are directed by the congressmen, who in turn are directed by businessmen, both local and international. These persons take the course of telling soldiers the next war has been outlawed. They do that because it is cheap.

The act of going to war is an admission that reason has failed; hence war is a demonstration of infantilism in man. It is a reduction of all his efforts, schemes, ideals, aims, hopes, faiths, purposes, plots, and possessions to the nursery level. It is an abandonment of sanity, a falling back to barbarism, an employment of national fisticuffing to settle dispute or to defend itself.

There is no other way to look at war than as the final proof of the infantilism of man—the revelation of his inherent lack of civilization, his serfdom to his instincts, and, therefore, his failure to achieve adulthood. War proves how wholly dependent we are upon the instinctual plane for our motives and what a thin tissue our repressive brain— our reason—has stretched between us and other animals. Yet, wars are as inevitable to us as the drawing of our breath, and will continue to

269

be so long as there are men on the earth in sufficient numbers to bring force against us and not dedicated first and above all to the moral nature of humanity, and only second or perhaps tenth to man's nature as a trader.

The people who decried war for twenty years after the last one were correct in all they said. But they uttered their protest (as always!) against *war*—as if war were a person itself or a race of people —and they did not cry out against men (*e.g.,* against themselves) without whom war would not exist on this earth. They focused the public attention upon the objective spectacle of war, and a public, conditioned always toward objective entities, readily agreed that war was shocking and must be done away with. The peacemakers contented themselves with their manifesto against military engines. They accounted war such an abomination that few so-called decent Americans could look at their advertisements and still pluck up the courage to insist that, for all the peacemakers said against war, its causes were highly alive—even in their own breasts. To the decent American, scandalous posters made even the tools of war—the protective armament and the vigilance that is the price of liberty in a barbaric world —seem so odious and disgusting that he scrapped his bulwarks, threw away his sword, and called the watchman off the tower. It was a great piece of mischief, and the peacemakers did it innocently—or, rather, ignorantly—and now we are being killed for it.

To stop war will take exactly as much money, effort, unity, determination, planning, and sacrifice as war takes—exercised continually in peace, rather than all at once in battles. These prices must be paid, and sacrifices made, ceaselessly, by individuals and by nations who must be aware of what they are about.

War is an objective balancing of the many and varied individual subjective imbalances in the warring groups. Because the subjective balances in truces and armistices are unrealistic, they accomplish nothing permanent for peace. To think, as most Americans have been thinking for twenty years, that by hullabaloo and advertising war could be put out of existence was the maddest nonsense. Nothing people say about war will alter the fact of war by a jot; but only what people do about themselves, and that only when it recognizes people as the perpetrators of war and not war as some sort of extrahuman affliction or disease.

The identification of weapons with the causes of war which led us to a reduction of weapons in the very hour when new causes for a new war were boiling up on every hand allowed us to make the error of going into this one nearly naked. It represented another perfect syllogism on the relation of inner and outer man: the outer man was appeased at the cost of the inner, and now both are engaged again in the occupation man sought to be rid of. Our disarmament, however noble in conception, exerted no effect on any cause, and so led us to our isolationism, which was a conscious choice of nonhostility on the material level, but not a guarantee of our motives on any other level. It was also an unconscious choice of vulnerability. To maintain our low degree of vigilance we had to adopt the airy notion either that nobody was preparing for war or else (since almost everybody was) that the coming war could not touch us. We necessarily chose the latter self-deception.

If any of the peacemakers thought that man's mere recoil from the bestiality of his past behavior would serve to keep him from a repetition of it, then those persons should have their heads cut off for being dangerous lunatics. The evidence of their wrongness was always so overwhelming that every definition of paranoid delusion elevates them to the top of the list. Dangerous lunatics, however, infest our society at all times, so the hope of beheading that particular sort is a mere literary figure. The fact remains that the more bitterly we assailed the act of war without reference to its causes in individual man, and without detached contemplation of what our neighbors were doing, the more certainly we were headed into war. Pacifism, as it was preached in the past twenty years, was not mere Phariseeism, it was a blinding of the eyes of the good Samaritan, so that not only the priest and the Levite walked past the stricken peoples, but the Samaritan too, because he could not look. Charity vanished and the helpless were eaten by their enemies, who finally became the enemies of the priest, the Levite, and the no-good Samaritan also.

If the peacemakers had used their ballyhoo and their advertising space to point out the piling tide of the sins of individual Americans, individual Germans, and all other individuals, in their relations toward themselves, their own states, and toward other men, the campaign might have had a powerful effect upon humanity. Even that is unlikely, however, for man is still so far from considering himself as the author of war that he would hardly tolerate a vast paid, public propaganda designed to point out the infinite measure of his private dastardliness and he would still rather fight it out in blood than limit the profitable and vain activities of peace in order to study his personal conscience.

To do so would hurt his profits, above all else, and he has not learned anything yet, to speak of, concerning the whole nature of profit. Demands for every manner of low-durability goods, for instance, could not be "created" in a society which was as busy with its soul as with its body. People would be content with less of many things and eager for more of many ideas, and those machines that wasted their lives, as a great many machines do, would be idle.

But, until man is willing to pay the cost of peace he will pay the price of war, and, since they must be precisely equal, I ask you to consider for how many more ages you think man will be striking balances with battles? In making your estimate, bear in mind that there will be no reason outside himself that will force man to go on fighting, after he has stopped the beast raging across the contemporary earth; bear in mind that only a failure to reason and to act reasonably will bring men to grips again; but recollect that, to have peace, congresses will be compelled to appropriate for others as generously as they do now for our armies, and the taxpayers will have to pay as willingly, and as many heroes will have to dedicate their lives to the maintenance of tranquillity as are now risking them to restore it.

Think of the American voters who will, in the end, decide about this, either by voting or by defaulting from voting. Think, also, about the defeated Germans and Japs, who will have to be reckoned in every thought of a future war. And think about the conquered nations and what kinds of tribute and revenge they will exact, and by so doing, what burdens of hate, suspicion, arrogance, fury, and woe they will lay upon generations as yet unborn. The task of pacifism is one of such magnitudes. The cheap service it got in America in the last two decades was illegitimate spawn of the old dragon.

The soldier has the job of rationalizing the infantilism which starts a war and reducing it, again, to an adult level of efficient co-operation and intelligent action which will bring about the defeat of the enemy and the restoration of peace: in his glossary, a state of nonwar during which the next war is fomented in human hearts. His profession, though it contains the highest possible ideal of personal sacrifice and is the final barricade of even a peaceful nation against the aggression of the apes, from without and within, has fallen into disrepute, more than ever in the last century or so. That is because of the Christian and Scientific Biphase Giant Combination Ticket to Perfection which has made every good American think he is both Christian and scientific, thereby setting up a spurious squeamishness in his person whenever he stands in the presence of that comparatively honest figure, a bombardier. This attitude is juicy hypocrisy, of course, and we are all engaged now in trying to undo it. It is difficult to go into war when many citizens have a hangover of faith from a recent gilded age of pacifism. And it is difficult to put young men in the mood for war when they come to arms fresh from reviling arms, and in the pantywaist, besides, which their moms had put upon them.

These soldiers of this generation, so often sullen, bored with parade, regarding war as a dirty job to be got over with (though, for what valuable task afterward they seldom guess or will not say), are a great astonishment to the old soldiers of our land. They take war as a cesspool meanly put in their path, out of which they must swim. They fight audaciously enough, but not for the old shibboleths. Their patriotism responds to few of the threadbare cries about liberty; they are skeptical of their government; their voices lack conviction when they sing of fighting and have it only when they sing of mom. They are insolent enough to win a fight—but insolence, the greater in victory, is not the substance out of which to build a world brotherhood. One might look at them, surprised a little, because they stepped forward from a debilitated society and drilled until they had learned to fight, as an ominous augury of any armistice. Many are doing this for themselves, because they had to, and they are thinking about the future in terms of goods and further sentimentality. They have wakened at last to the fact that mom is being attacked and they have ringed her in bayonets. It is possible that their mood will change in the slaughter to come and that mom may lose her potency; it is also possible that they may decide further to fortify her shrine by force and to hold it by force. Then, rue the day. For our fallacies of the years before we got into the war are ingrained in the new soldiers, and even the security of victory, if we gain it, will still leave us in the potential jeopardy of those fallacies.

About all this, the generals and admirals can do no more than their best. They are not professors, to teach morals. They are not statesmen, to conduct the secret treacheries of state, and, indeed, the soldiers must sweat at the disadvantage, in democracy, of having to be told whom to fight, and when; often at the last instant possible for any defense, and sometimes—as in the case of Pearl Harbor—of hardly being told at all.

Moreover, soldiers, of all kinds of men, are the most hidebound by tradition—in spite of being that group to which history has most frequently revealed the hopelessness of obsolete measures. More than the church, more than the university, the military has set up a hierarchy founded upon precedent and maintained it unexamined through the ages. Armies march today under a load of subjective ideology that is stamped into the men because it worked in the time of Alexander. And only today are other armies showing the effectiveness of ideologies in keeping with modern equipment. The machine has restored the individual soldier to such independence of action as he has not had since the days of cave fighting. But the military still deploys machines and boats in the geometrical patterns of phalanxes. "Right dress" cost us our planes, on the ground, in the Philippines, as Hervey Allen has said. "Right dress" makes a convoy duck soup for the "Browning shot." "Right dress" was the command that lost Singapore, when it should have been some still undevised command for counterinfiltration.

This is not a layman's argument against drill. Drill, as, again, Hervey Allen points out, is a Pyrrhic dance that has a profound subjective value. But this can be construed as a petition to the army and navy to try to breed, against future onslaught, a new type of military mind—a new type, even, of human mind—which seeks the new, studies the objective side and the subjective also, and takes the attitude that, if there is to be more war, let it be fought with every imaginable resource of death and destruction, and not as a stylized exercise or as a special game. The laboratory has undone every tactic but that which wins. It will again. Each new tool, each fresh formation, has lost and won a battle, often a war—sometimes a nation. But military tradition is to train men not to think. It is past time to reverse that. Past time— when no soldier yet has realized (for instance) that the airplane is not a new weapon but a new kind of *transportation* as revolutionary as the wheel was in its time.

Rarely have militarists been ready for improvements. Their tradition springs out of the levy and training of masses of men. They have always regarded fire power as the number of hands on javelins, the number of fingers on triggers, the number of grenade pins in sets of human teeth, while time without number a handful of men have turned the tide of battle with a new tool. England was saved, recently, by fewer men than would fill Radio City Music Hall. And, in some not distant future, a hundred men with a hundred new bombs might, quite literally, fight the whole of a war against a great nation in half an hour.* It is that weapon we should anticipate—that style of mind

---

* Writing of this sort used to throw people into paroxysms of laughter—or annoyance. Reviewers and correspondents spoke of it as, "reckless," "irresponsible," "nearly insane if not actually so," and "The very kind of 'thinking' military men must avoid at all costs."

we need even now for victory. George Washington, with one machine gun, would have achieved our independence in a few weeks.

To train masses in the battle-dance of individual fingers plucking triggers in unison demanded rigid discipline and standards of action reducible to the ability of the dumbest private in the rearmost rank. It demanded officers stamped in an exact pattern, with no imagination left in them, no private resource, no trace of the analytical method—which fathers invention but which, in soldiers of masses, would lead to departures, insubordinations, disagreements, criticisms—better methods maybe, but a less efficient administration of the old. The first step in making a soldier has always been to stamp the individuality out of him. But the concept of a single individual (usually a civilian and not a soldier, naturally enough) has turned the tide of many of the major wars on the earth.

Armies became a thing apart—a historical entity which lived without continually consulting where the rest of men were going, what they had learned, or what they were devising. The thought of newness and change was made difficult in armies by the concentration of effort upon squeezing out every innate tendency to novelty. This was, also, a great convenience to the inertia of old men who, through seniority rather than ability, always were in charge of armies and navies. Taught at the start not to take initiative in military behavior, they readily abandoned taking it in military science. A caste composed largely of dolts bled millions to death for thousands of years because it refused to learn by any way but defeat and, indeed, protected its bland although lethal leisure by convincing civilians there was no other way to learn.

The military mind is, therefore, not a mind but a habit—a custom —a tradition—a mental stasis—which common people accept as unthinkingly as do the exponents of the rigid attitude. The English might have won the last war with tanks—if they had made enough of them, used them all at once, and so set in motion fronts immobilized by the machine gun, which both sides happened to have at the start. The French generals built their Maginot Line, but not clear to the sea, which is as fabulous a sample of military rationalization as there is.

The Germans, starting from scratch, were slightly less hamstrung by tradition; with only new and unforeseen adaptations of already known arms they very nearly enslaved the whole world in eighteen months. We still have our battleship admirals. Even the appalling score against them has not moved them all and their printed rationalizations are historic comedy in the making. That, in itself, is evidence enough to bring about a complete overhaul of every military idea and principle we hold to.

But these men, bound toward they marvel not what, were trained to be incapable of reason, in the main. That is why Billy Mitchell, who tried to unseat a foolishness many years ago, found that logic got him nowhere and at long last tackled his brass-headed detractors with insult, violence, scurrilous statement, anathema, threat, imprecation, and dire warning—for only emotion could make the unthinking listen, as always. The coldness of the admirals hid the terrible emotion of intolerant stupidity. Those words of Mitchell's today sound more like the words of Isaiah than of a soldier, which is fitting, because he was a prophet—and prophets come by their prophecies through reason but must express them emotionally to make themselves heard at all.

After this war—and, indeed, immediately—West Point and Annapolis and the other sources of our military tradition should be recast. Those historical gesticulations which are taught for their instinctual value should be explained as necessary ritual, and not identified as all of war. A new tradition—the tradition that has grown in Germany and elsewhere out of a recognition of the true nature of war—should be made the dominant note of the future in our soldier caste: war is the use of all means to defeat the enemy. A soldier will have to be as avid, in the future, to learn new scientific fact and adapt it to new means of war as he has been reluctant to do so these last thousands of years. If we do not achieve this at Annapolis and at West Point, in the third world war, we will go down like wheat in a cyclone.* We still

---

* To risk a further prediction, I shall say that I do not feel West Point and Annapolis have achieved the recommended point of view. Of course, the Point has produced out of the Atomic Age an atomic

may, in this one. For this, again, is the continual price of scientific materialism: the more we proselytize the earth with it and the further we let go of inner integrity, the more we must dread repayment in kind—scientific formidabilities from foreign workshops, massacring millions.

These are hard things to think about, perhaps. But I am sure (and so will you be, if you consider the nature of men and of our present enemies) that, this very day, there are Germans cogitating the third war—Russians too, Japs and maybe Englishmen and Chinese. We would fail in the whole use of our intelligence if we did not bear the fact in mind and act upon it. When we make peace, we will hope to keep it forever. But we are not the custodians of forever—and we cannot impose our terms endlessly upon the future.

This is, at least, a more honest war than any we have recently engaged in. It was "total" from the start; others merely grew to be. Nobody is spared, to be deceived later in the making of peace. It attacks the mind as rapidly as the body—and that, too, is war. Future soldiers will have to give that element much thought. For, when our immediate ancestors drew up international humanitarian laws they bespoke their foolishness by the mere imagining that war was legal; from now on, soldiers must keep reminding the juicier administrations of Schrecklichkeit.

---

cannon and the Navy an atomic submarine. However, I suspect such achievement represents no new "thinking" but, rather, an unconscious determination to bend new findings to obsolete employment. We do have other weapons and conveyors, to be sure. One wonders, even so, if military reasoning is truly abreast of the times.

Supposing, for example, the Soviets finally do agree to a *bona fide* program for the control and inspection of all things related to the atom. Will it occur to our military men that their concession might be owing to the discovery, manufacture and secret storing of weapons far superior to, but different from A- and H-bombs? I tend to doubt it. Yet the gift-horse of a Soviet atomic truce would likely have a mouthful of just such teeth, some of them just possibly *psychological*.

We only recently reviled our generals and our admirals and advertised them in our periodicals as the stooges of businessmen who grew fat on munitions making. That was partly a fact; but even so, irrelevant. It is no fact now. We printed pictures of a doughboy and, underneath, the caption: "Hello, sucker!" We showed columns of uniformed American ghosts marching into space and wrote that it was for nothing. We despised war and we broke our weapons. Now, suddenly, we are bidding our soldiers to save us, for the love of God, quickly, and with little sacrifice. The generals are doing their best— the poor best of a race of men who denied to themselves such little enlightenment as lay about them because of their tradition, not because of the cupidity of munitions makers, and because of our great American prairie and skyscraper mentality which cut off their funds.

Shall we not, then, study ourselves, awhile, after this bloodletting passes, to see from whence it comes?

Shall we not indict the businessmen and limit their desecrated powers, get us better statesmen, throw out the flabby professors for moral ones, and choose soldiers who are, at least, capable of protecting that which we have without costing all of it, until such time as we can learn the true ways of peace?

Or shall we return after this fight to a more soul-enslaving merry-go-round of goods and gadgets, nuttier congressmen, viler unions, obscener corporations, stupider soldiers, womanlier men, more manlike women, moms who suck marrow as well as blood, doctors who cure nothing, sappier preachers who belong, with undertakers, portrait photographers, and window dressers, to a legion of the clammy-handed that merely wait upon fleshly vanity? Shall we have this one last post-war boom for which the men of Wall Street hoped until they had lost hope? One last dance macabre—with the machine, man, and man a prostitute of the embracing steel?

We may never get a chance to make even that choice. But it is utterly futile to think we will lose the war except only in so far as the thought spurs us toward winning. If we lose, none of us will ever again have the power to make a choice; men of honor will have already chosen to die; millions of the rest will perish anyway.

But the contest itself—unless our allies win it—rests on choices we have either made, or defaulted, recently or long ago. The issue is in the hands of the administration and of the high command. Our Congress controlled the education of our high command, and we elected Congress. The President we elected directly. Those elements are not altogether felicitous for total war.

The idea of total war was so anathematical to Americans that it was not taught to the officers of our armies and navies—although a people that produced Sherman should feel hypocritical at the oversight. We lacked conscious experience with regimentation, a necessary part of total war, excepting for certain New Deal activities which resembled part-pay charity as it might be administered by a corporate state. Such activities scarcely prepared us for the current burning exigencies of order. Rather, they imply in the government an altruistical purpose which has no place in the list of prerequisites for meeting the current exacting problem. The president has always been "navy-minded." If he had been a devotee of air travel, an interest in airplanes (instead of his interest in ships) might have made any war impossible and would certainly have shortened this one. He is, however, a man of brilliance, courage, and versatility, able to unlearn and to learn with a speed and an intuition rare in the history of heads of nations. Because of that presidential capacity the American people are fabulously fortunate.

An understanding of civilian psychology has not been, in previous wars, an integral element of military command. In total war, it is. We Americans will probably have to fight the length of this war without that advantage. Its absence might conceivably cost us the war. To fight without it is like fighting without artillery, or submarines. We are going to have to fight the Germans without another equally effective military weapon: the weapon of psychological attack—because we did not have foresight enough to learn about it; not knowing, we could not compel a study of it upon our military authorities either by pressure of public opinion or by administrative order.

Because our army has no real department of psychological warfare, American foreign propaganda, until recently, has been conducted by civilians. Domestic relations between the people, the high command, and the government have been without directive, aim, cohesion, or even sanity. I do not believe that there are many men in the army who can do as well with foreign propaganda as the civilians who operated under Colonel Donovan. And I do not believe Elmer Davis will make effective order out of war information, because the army and navy departments will not give him that information. They lack the training and experience to perceive what he could do with it, and are hostile, by and large, toward all civilians. The president will not care to make an issue of this vital point because it would become, at once, a prestige struggle which the generals and admirals would make into a cause célèbre so that either the president would have to fire them by dozens or he would have to bow to the tradition of military omniscience and silence. He would rather avoid any such disruptive internal fight, in the midst of world war, than bring it to a head—no matter how badly off public psychology might be and no matter how deficient our brain war against the enemy.

Generals and admirals are hostile to civilians because the civilians have scant confidence in them and have said so in ways calculated to intimidate any personages who hold their authority through political indulgence. Civilians have excellent reasons for their lack of confidence in the majority of their generals and their admirals and in those political leaders who have power over commanding officers. They have made too many mistakes. With rare and inspired exceptions— such as the prewar creation of the British fighter planes—the generals, admirals, and statesmen of the democracies have made nothing *but* mistakes, so far. Consider, for a moment, a sampling of their cosmic incapacity.

The French generals convinced us, for two decades, that the

French army was the finest on earth. It was the rottenest. They convinced us that the Maginot Line was a dam against Germany. Most of us didn't even know that the Maginot Line was only half a wall. Most of us did not know—though some did—that the Germans could fly over it anyhow. The American admirals called their western fleet the "watchdog of the Pacific" and led the British as well as their own folks to believe that the Pacific was our ocean and we could hold it; the British expected us to contribute naval power to the defense of Singapore. One minor air action pulled the teeth from the watchdog of the Pacific. The British colonial command was suffering from a degree of rottenness almost equal to that of the French army, though it was of a slightly different species. Hong Kong, Malaya, Burma are some of the proofs. The British high command is still so patently loaded with brass heads that the American man in the street cannot but know it. Our navy is still busy building great ships at fantastic cost. Anybody not wedded to the thrall of battle-wagons and cruisers bursting into smoky broadsides knows that is a horrible waste of materials needed right now for better equipment. Churchill's statement that the *Repulse* and the *Prince of Wales* were an essential part of the Empire plan to protect Singapore revealed that he, as late as last winter, was still purblind. Our generals kept profanely protesting that our original medium tanks in Africa and our early P-40 planes were as good as any, but the men on the field and in the air reported truthfully that they were far from adequate for the task demanded of them. The public, which is furnishing the men to do the dying, is frantically worried about our designs and furiously skeptical of the professional soldiers who do not yet seem to have envisaged even the notion of design superiority.

The foregoing are exhibits of blunders in actual mental process which have disenchanted the American people. The entire list of such blunders will crowd histories. Added to it is another list—the blunders that have been made in the handling of domestic policy, instruction, and information. The noxious roar of contradiction, and the sweaty back-and-fill of the administration in Washington since Pearl Harbor, has already put the citizen in such a chaos that, on one or more matters, the average man has abandoned all effort. The handling of gasoline and oil rationing, not so much where there was rationing as where there had not yet been any, has been so deleterious from the standpoint of morale that Goebbels could not have done it better by designing the whole affair for his own purposes. The failure to gear the flow of supplies to an imaginative assessment of military futures has been another debacle. The Office of Civilian Defense, after more than a year, had accomplished less of sensible and standardized organization, rule, and supply than any bureau of its size ever set up in America. The failure of the Selective Service System to arrange laws which would make it reasonably possible for men to anticipate their likelihood of being called up has added another prodigal confusion to the multitude, of which the above half dozen are, again, only samples.

These fumbles create endless psychological punctures and blowouts. The people of the United States are resilient. But they, like all human beings, have a limit of absorption and a point of absolute shock. Since they have for years been ceaselessly disappointed by the absence of tactical vision and military wisdom in the leaders of their allies, with very few exceptions, and since their own military and civil leaders in many cases have proved to be utterly mistaken (witness the long and boastful series of articles on sea power produced by Knox a few weeks before several dozen bombs and torpedoes canceled out all his premises), the people of the United States would be fools not to lack confidence in "generals, admirals, and politicians." If they had entered the war with any residual assurance, events on the domestic front would have further eroded it.

A supercommand, sitting above the army, navy, and air forces of the United States and of the other United Nations—one that included an all-powerful branch of psychological warfare—might not have erased many of the military defeats, but it could have braced the peoples against the results of those defeats and it could have taken control of the babble of civil authorities which has made many Americans as resigned to come-what-will as the citizens of a dictatorship. Such a command might, also, undertake a global strategy that was realistic, instead of lecturing about it. The supercommand, if there were one, would be appointed from men who, at the very least, made such distinctions as that mentioned earlier in this chapter anent airplanes, namely, that they are the beginning of a wholly new and different military age.

Nothing of the sort is likely—ever. We may expect a major part of the boggle and the confusion to last to the end of the war. Fortunately, we can doubtless win anyway. We can do it because of the brains and imagination of a few commanders and a few civilians who will provide enough of the proper materials and techniques to beat Germany —over and above the vast army being levied for no purpose yet shown and the vast navy being built for battles that cannot even be hypothesized any longer. We can do it, too, because of democracy. Every poll shows that, in willingness to fight and to sacrifice, the people are ahead of the politicians and in an understanding demand for new weapons they are ahead of the professional soldiers and sailors. The people, that is to say, are steadily in the lead even when they call for leadership and that (to violate my own rule) must make Jefferson and Washington and Lincoln sleep proudly—because that *is* democracy!

We can win, also, because the Axis is not very hard to beat. That is a revolutionary statement, I know, but I think it will prove to be a sound one. Our multiple harassments by obsolete methods are expensive, but they will keep the Axis from consolidating and exploiting its great gains. Meanwhile, we will build the comparatively cheap tools that can wreck the Axis. By that I mean bombers. For ten years and more I have been talking bombers and writing about bombers and advocating their construction on a scale still regarded as outrageous by generals and admirals. I can see no reason to change my long-held opinion now, and I believe that future facts will substantiate it—in a year, or maybe in three years, depending on how fast we get those bombers over Germany, how imaginatively, and how effectively. I cannot see, and I could never see, why a nation, with the *proper* air equipment, ever needed or ever will need any other sort, any more than I can see why our navy, while it was good transportation, might have needed sailboats when it had engines, or why our army might have needed muskets when it had Garands.

Perhaps if we told the generals and the admirals the secret—that the airplane wasn't a new kind of power to compete with or a new kind of weapon they could hope to find a defense against—but just the simple old revolutionary thing they have effectively seized before —a new means of transport for men and weapons—we could get both sorts of those very valorous gentlemen out of their foxholes and off the sea bottom.

All the dilemmas noted in the last few pages, you may observe, stem from one blind spot and it is—like every sin against which I have been preaching—a subjective evil, a spiritual (or mental) error, a flaw, not of the outer world, but of the inner world of people. We cannot attribute any of it—or any of the suffering we have yet to endure—to any other cause than our own vanity.

CHAPTER XVII

The Man on the Cross

THE REPRESENTATIVES OF SIXTEEN MILLION AMERICANS IN FOUR religious denominations—Episcopalian, Baptist, Methodist, and Presbyterian—have now gone on record for a return of Prohibition. Prohibition marked a new speed-up in the decline of American morality. Nobody who remembers the standards and attitudes of common American men and women before Prohibition can doubt that they deteriorated afterward, or doubt that the main milestone of the change was the Volstead Act. The law, itself, like disarmament, innocently undertook to reform all men by fiat instead of by education.

The effect of success in such campaigns, upon reformers, is to make them smug. It invariably appears to them that they have given a reality to their hypocrisies—that, by forcing others to wash their hands, they have cleaned the souls of others and displayed the spotless condition of their own. That is witchcraft. It may be assumed that the sixteen millions who want Prohibition again do not drink. Thus they are making no choice whatever for themselves. The process is entirely meddlesome. But if by political conniving, chicanery, and the rest of the techniques of the former prohibitionists they achieve their goal (it is politically impossible by any other means), we may expect to have Prohibition again.

The Volstead Act was the greatest of our modern catastrophes. With a stroke, it undid the liberty of the land by fettering a major individual choice. It bred nasty offspring, the first of which was hate, the second, irresponsibility, and the third, angry nonco-operation. It introduced the gangster era. It hardened all men against murder—both those who supported the bootleg business and those who supported the impossible law. In principle, it was precisely as degenerate as a law restricting love to universal public perversion.

No man can say whether it is good or evil for another particular man to imbibe alcohol. But for a man to drink too much alcohol is psychopathological, and not directly a moral problem; hence the Volstead Act was, in effect, a statute against lunacy, with penalties and fines imposed upon one group (bootleggers) because certain individuals in another (drunks) were insane, or, at least, deeply neurotic. Nobody believes for a moment that the law prevented a single human being from drinking. On the contrary, it is known that more people drank after the act than before—and they drank worse liquor. Sixteen million church members now propose to create new drunks by millions.

Half or more of the homes in America became party to the violation of federal law, under Prohibition. Otherwise honorable people—professors, doctors, lawyers, bishops even—turned lawless. Because of one amendment, the Constitution of the land was made preposterous. No old evil was inhibited—and all kinds of new evils flourished where there had been no previous tolerance for them. The Prohibition agents became America's first Gestapo. But the people went on drinking. And, since it is difficult for most human beings to keep one set of precepts while violating another, easy consciences were led by breaking the Volstead Act into unguessable millions of other illegal deeds. When a revolted nation finally overthrew this filthy tyranny, the gangsters did not turn to honest pursuits, but mingled with other men, took hold upon other decent aspects of our life, and corrupted them to the core. Without the "noble experiment," it is safe to say, we would not know the fearful peril of thug-dominated unions.

All this came to us in Jesus' name and through virtue—the hypocritical projection of a denial by a certain group of piddle-brained citizens whereof the church members were storm troops who had denied themselves nothing by their act. The experience of man should have taught them that all efforts to compel upon the people outward evidences of nonexistent private virtue backfire upon the authors of the compulsion and everybody else. That, again, is the Law. Moral choices can be made only through understanding. To try to force them is to tamper with God Almighty and to make yourself prey of the devil.

The Christian soldiers, marching as to war, came close to undoing all the morals there were left in the land and their original handiwork is not yet finished. At the doorstep of these lovers of Jesus, who for generations have monkeyed with everybody but themselves, lie all the young who died in Prohibition smashups, the poisoned, the bodies of the gangsters, and, now, the victims of gangster-run unions. Invisible in the pews of these associations of the self-described worshipers of Christ sit goons and gunmen, pimps without number, harlots more numerous than the congregations, and corpses of law enforcement officers. The cackle of many a lunatic is a sound underneath the organ music, as is the shuddering curse of every sane American who experienced the great viciousness. It was, perhaps, the *most* vicious act man has ever tried on his person. All so-called vice, compared to it, is mere erotic play.

Now, sixteen millions of Americans apparently want to do it again.

I know a great deal more about drink than most of the sixteen millions who are ready to drive it, and us, and themselves into the gutter by legislating against drink. And I would as soon shoot at another man as vote away his right to make his own choice in the matter of what he drinks. The Christians have gone crazy. They do not know about man, or life, or their Lord, any more.

So this next-to-last chapter is an essay on Jesus Christ for sixteen million Christians who belong to churches and to hell:

Jesus Christ was not trying to teach what the churches say he tried to teach. He would be shocked at the use of his own life as a perfect pattern for other men, and he warned against the practice, urgently, according to his biographers. The pagan cast which the church has given to the doctrine of atonement would throw him into convulsions. His own deficiencies were apparent to him and to many people around him. He had one message—one only—and it *was* fundamental. But the message has escaped the church.

Christ had powerful flashes of insight into the deep nature of man's consciousness and he used every device he could invent to try to reveal the process of that insight to those who would listen. He failed. The real meaning of his gospel was largely lost even to his disciples. Such of it as they salvaged, they set down badly, and they showed their incomprehensions in the way they wrote about their master.

The one, great positive idea which Christ repeatedly tried to express was the thought that no individual human being could know himself unless his inner honesty was complete. The peace he talked of was an inner peace, and he said so, always. The way to it was through truth and through the abandonment of preoccupation with temporal matters—with worldly goods and with trade and gain. He did not overlook the necessity of objective living, but he admonished against considering a life oriented wholly out toward matter as a satisfying life. The light to which he so often made reference was the light of truth— inner truth—and his use of the idea of repentance was identical with the modern psychological technique of integration, which teaches the individual to go back over his life and discover in it his real motives, real fantasies, real purposes, urges, instincts, escapes, lies, cheatings, and vanity. No man, according to Christ, could know himself unless he knew all the negative and inferior aspects of himself—which is a thoroughly reasonable and scientific principle. A man, Christ also said, who did not know himself could not in any way trust what he thought about other men or the world. Which also is a logical—indeed, an inevitable—conclusion.

It was Christ's theory—taught to him, doubtless, out of Oriental wisdom, by the teachers with whom he came in contact in the synagogue—that this first, obviously essential step of self-knowledge led to further developments of wisdom and understanding which could be followed to the outermost capacity of each individual and which, in the cases of the most deeply reasoning, honest, and imaginative individuals, would lead to a transcendental experience. Christ made a point of showing that no such experience was possible without first taking all degrees and steps toward private integrity. That is also logical, because it follows the same logic which states that no correct mathematical conclusion can be made if there is an error somewhere in the process of approach.

His premise was, therefore, that an individual man is able, through integrity alone, to follow the elements of his subjective nature to their outermost boundary. He concluded that any man who did so would find the boundary infinite and immortal. The subjective discipline which he tried to explain was precisely analogous to the scientific method toward objective fact now used in the modern world. If it be granted that man has instincts and that he can readily identify their existence in many forms, such as his legends, then it may be further postulated that, by a scientific examination of his past record and present behavior in the light of what he learns about his instincts, he will have access—logical, alive, real, and within himself—to the whole history and meaning of the origin of nature, of which he is manifestly a living part. The realization of that would not be, necessarily, an experience that could be neatly put into words, because words are the most recent of nature's methods of communication; but, since man's psyche operates in various other ways than those described in words, realization might involve one of the other operative means for its expression.

I am not trying here to set up arguments with boobies about transcendental experience or the ultimate effect of subjective integrity as an introspective tool. I have my own ideas about those matters from my own mediocre efforts and they are not in this book, which has been written about human behavior on the much simpler plane of morals. I merely point out that inner integrity is obviously essential, if you are to do a whole job of thinking about anything, and add that modern science has bashed inner integrity to bits and gone to work on the half-problem of objective integrity. I have said and shown this

halfness of the scientific method many times. Nobody can deny it, because it is an exceedingly plain fact. Who the thinker *is* is as much a
a part of *what* he is thinking about as the thought itself; just as, in relativistic math, the nature and position of an observer is as much a part
of his conclusion as his measurements of the observation.

Christ, then, took the very solid position that unless you know who
you are you don't know what you're thinking about, and you can only
find out who you are by a difficult job of detached self-appraisal. He
stated as a corollary that, if you don't really know what you're thinking about, what you do will be cockeyed, probably, and at any rate it
won't matter, because it isn't real, being phony by definition. You may
not have permitted yourself to know who you are, though you may
think you know what is going on in your mind (possibly because
other people think as you seem to) and if you haven't worked down
into yourself from every imaginable critical angle you can't trust
your estimate of yourself—or, in consequence, your estimate of the
ideas of others. Because of this, nearly all men may be—and, indeed,
are—grossly mistaken in their appraisal of their thoughts and deeds.
Only a very few have the scientific courage and honor to get to know
themselves well enough so that they can trust themselves and thereby
judge which parts of the behavior of others they will join in with, and
which they will repudiate.

If you understand yourself, you have got hold of the root of understanding, because an enlightened self becomes conscious and is able to
face all situations, since, through instinct, it has learned about all of
them. It also becomes the chooser of what you do and are. You are
identified with this new and ever more understanding self; thereby you
disenfranchise the various habits and deceits which have victimized
you in the person of your less honest ego—the escapism and fugue,
the pleasure hunting and the dread of pain, the hypocrisy, and so on.
All such choiceless business, according to Christ, sloughs itself as
you develop a more integrated personality—which is precisely what
Freud, Adler, Jung, and others have rediscovered by modern scientific
methods and stated in a great variety of ways.

Unfortunately for the fate of this simple theory about man's personality, mind, ego, soul, psyche, awareness, or whatever you will call it, Christ lived in an era when there was no Western terminology. He was compelled to try to define the principle in value-analogies and in pictures. He used pictures, largely, from the industry and agriculture around him and also from the books of prophecy and rabbinical law in which he, as a rabbi, had been educated. This attempt to express the subjective approach to life and to describe its fruits—an abstraction exactly like that expressed by the phrase "scientific principle"—bogged down heavily.

Furthermore, Christ's own obviously complex and perturbable disposition interfered with his detachment. His tendency (common in so many men who have hit upon some aspect of this same great principle) to identify himself with God, the prophets, and the decalogue of his own church, increased the muddle. Thus his flashes of enlightened counsel about conduct and attitude conflict with his repetitions of church dogma so that we find, for example—on the one hand, traces of his great tolerance for people and, on the other, a vilification of people that is scarcely surpassed by the barbarities of the prophets in the Old Testament. His inadequate study of his own nature led him to say that he had come to save sinners and not the virtuous; but when people offended him by not recognizing his works or his person, it caused him to stand and curse them to worse oblivion than Sodom's. For that offense against his egotistical identification of his philosophy with himself, he blasphemed whole citiesful of people.

He exhibited a degree of personal violence, private fear, and childishness to be expected in a human being enthralled by the magnitude of a profound discovery, voluntarily dedicated to its promulgation, and frustrated at every turn by incomprehension, disinterest, ecclesiastical quibble, and widespread ridicule. The accounts of his behavior in those categories furnish an extraordinary body of internal evidence that the gospels represent real and rather appalled memories of a real person closely observed. Bible students and theologians have created a mammoth literature anent Christ and the evidences of his

existence. It has no more occurred to them to adduce information
from the implications of the text, however, than it has to check the
psychological principle expounded by Christ through self-examina-
tion—the only technique by which Christ said it could be demonstrated.

When a fig tree did not provide figs to satisfy Christ's hunger, he
bade it wither, with the infantile fury of a child kicking the stone upon
which it has stubbed its toe. Persecuted, threatened with violence, forced
often to dissemble and to run in order to save his life, Christ exhibited
an overdetermined dread of the police and the courts. But his prem-
onition of execution at the hands of the courts, when it grew strong
enough, turned that anxiety into resignation of the most bitter and
hopeless sort. Save for one or two furious retorts, he made no effort to
save himself when he was offered a hearing by the church and when
he was on trial before Pilate. Another man, whose fear had not become resignation, might conceivably have used both opportunities for
the dramatic promulgation of his theory, aware that he had only one
life to lose and chancing it on a positive and creative effort rather than
on a personal and negativistic reluctance. There, again, his psychology
was defeatist and infantile. His identification of himself with the
foredoomed Messiah of the prophets certainly implemented that behavior, but it is surprising that his own inner symbol of truth and courage became so seriously bound up in the frustration of the tradition
that a black death wish flowered above all of it, making his final silent and sullen pride like suicide.

As a rabbi, he had been heavily indoctrinated with the laws of
Moses. His strictures of those laws infuriated the other priests. To
Christ, all good deeds done publicly were without merit—or, rather,
contained their own reward in their publicity—and only the good
deeds done anonymously reflected enduring values upon the doer.
Thus the vain rituals of the Pharisees, scribes, priests, and other self-
important persons nauseated him, and he said so violently—as he
would say of the charities of the modern church. The importance of a
gift or a good deed, also, was measured by Christ in terms of sub-

jectivity, and not of external value, so that the widow who had put two small coins on the plate put more than all the rest of the money there. That aspect of inner values has dropped altogether out of sight in most churches; the current standards of our society keep it invisible by force.

When the old rabbinical law conflicted with the understanding arrived at by his insight, Christ was often in a quandary and not always as lucid as he was in the matter of the hypocrisy of the scribes and Pharisees. That murder, stealing, envy, and so on were despicable was evident. The old law held still. That the literal keeping of the Sabbath laws was foolish, on the other hand, he made plain. But his ratiocinations and reactions concerning sex morality were very confused. He found attractiveness in women appealing; he liked attention; he let Magdalene busy herself with the administration to him of creature luxuries while Martha worked for him like a servant, and when Martha complained he bawled her out. He flatly demanded adherence to the commands against adultery and yet adulteresses fascinated him. He recognized the ubiquity of fornication, forgave it readily, and recommended spending time with those who were openly guilty of that sin rather than with those who were outwardly perfect but inwardly licentious and arrogant. He hated the successful businessman of his day with a passion that often became a vituperative torrent when he encountered them—and found only a few such men to accept as friends. He dwelt with publicans whenever possible because they were not hypocritical. His ultimate observation about sex morality was that the choice of celibacy, or chastity, was possible only to a few who elected to discover the results of that particular kind of asceticism.

He does not seem to have become aware completely of the function of dogma. And no church before him, and no church afterward, has ever understood the reason for it.

Dogma is, superficially, an attempt to codify instinctual patterns and to set up value standards. On that level it supplies definitions which seem to be germane to archetypal concepts of good and evil, worth and worthlessness. But dogma, on its own instinctual level, represents an effort to set up a discipline, an asceticism, suitable to the low-grade disciplinary volitions of large numbers of people in a particular society, at a particular time. The organization of all nature, whether looked out at or regarded as a set of inner effects—whether seen, that is, by extroversion or by introversion—presents a pattern of order and of law, of cause and effect, of balance compelled by every imbalance, and so reveals its discipline to every kind of consciousness. There is no mistaking the premise, and science accepts it under the description of true or false, just as subjective man recognizes it as right or wrong, true or vain, and so on.

Out of that premise constantly arises the impulse, the irrevocably felt need, for a codification of subjective principle. If a religion is to have many followers, the codification must be acceptable to and understandable by many people. Since churches, at least, exist only to the degree of the manyness of their followers, the codes must be modified, simplified, banalized, and stultified to suit public taste. "Know thyself" is not clear enough advice for the average Methodist, because it involves too much effort. The golden rule, old in human-knowing long before the time of Christ, is, by the same token, too general and hard of constant application for the ordinary Presbyterian; it demands too many stoppings to count ten, too many self-searchings, too many painful projections upon other people, and the too frequent projection upon the one of the agony of the other. Didactic rulings have to be made instead, and hammered into the heads of the denominationalists.

Those rulings which evolve out of the postulate of doing as you would be done by, such as the manifesto against murder, stand as simple and reasonable precepts for personal conduct. There is no excuse for taking an ax and chopping down your next-door neighbor. But when even a basic tenet like that against murder is examined on the subjective plane, the reason for individual self-knowledge becomes vividly apparent: many murderers who do not know they have killed are living in good repute among us.

They killed not with an ax, but with psychical tools—cutting down their victims slowly by meanness, inconsideration, truculence, the willed but witless evil of their advice, and all other kinds of cruelty. These murderers, including myriad wives and husbands, follow their spouses to their graves weeping sorrowfully, thinking them to be dead of high blood pressure or a stomach ulcer, and not aware for one instant that they have murdered them through some spite or some wish for escape, as surely as if they had fed them arsenic. I have seen several notable examples of this kind of assassination in my day, and it is horrible. No doubt the reader can think of one or two.

Such murders, and the lesser villainies like them, pockmark the private lives of our civilization. We scarcely notice them. If, by chance, the wretched victim of a miserable wife hangs himself, we may say, "She drove him to death." But we never prosecute for driving people to death. And if the death is finally precipitated by what are called "natural causes" we are apt to sympathize with the widower or the widow and we would ragingly resent any statement that our sympathy was being tendered to a killer. To admit that is to let in doubts about all behavior which most of us have not got the nerve and the honesty to bear. And yet, the violation of so simple an edict as the one against murder, on the plane of subjective action, is very common and furnishes an exquisite reason for even modern scientific man to give some attention to the nature of himself. The great astronomer may be discovering facts about the red shift of island universes and slowly, at the same time, pushing his son or daughter into the grave, making himself not really a great man in the main, but the foulest kind of man that walks on the earth. A violation of the principle "Know thyself" will have undone him.

Thus, even on the individual level and in the most evident matter, dogma establishes one morality on the physical plane and another on the subjective. The wretches sitting in our electric chairs have one just and bitter complaint that they never make because they do not know about it: we don't ever try to stop nine-tenths of their breed from performing.

On any mass level, dogma suffers further degradation. This is be-

cause masses have no choices, but only instincts, and the true way
of nature is more bleak and violent than the way an individual man
can choose to live—as a rule, and in a sense. Thus the command
against murder does not relate to masses at war—or, at least, in war
it is condoned and altered. Still, the people who damn war as murder
and will have nothing to do with war for that definition—"conscien-
tious objectors"—follow the dogma and not any truth, for there are all
manners of wars and all manners of reasons for getting into war. Such
damning of all acts without reference to their true motives is, also, a
sin, because it is a stupidity, and therefore not truth. Christ taught
patience against aggression, and the turning of the other cheek, but he
was not a passive resister in any definition and, indeed, was often physically violent in his vindictiveness.

The dogma of "Thou shalt not kill" is not a possible dogma, even
on a physical plane, to the masses, on account of the essentially instinctual nature of their collective behavior; that particular dogma must be
set aside as pretentious and silly until the time when all men have
cleaned out their private urges to kill on a subjective plane. Contemporary pacifist churches, I might say in passing, are having a hell of a
time with this simple fact, and have got it so looped with bull, fiat,
interdiction, and metaphysics that they are going to violate a still
more fundamental dogmatic principle: they are going to lose more
millions of members soon by making themselves palpably absurd.

For masses of people, "Thou shalt not kill," considered on a subjective level, becomes so incomprehensible a command that it is not
even studied by the theologians. The ingrained vanity of one class,
grinding against another, murders millions just as the cruelty of a
wicked wife erodes the guts of her husband until he dies. Intolerance
of race and creed and nation, of rich for poor and the organized poor
for the embattled rich—all these and a myriad other social processes
collectively engaged in—make murder on the plane of subjective
crowd behavior an everyday affair and we are all parties to these
murders. In such ways we, who keep a million badly tended lunatics
in a living death out of our "tender nature" and "sentiment," when

euthanasia would be the mercy of God, destroy each other in shoals and packs and multitudes by our heedless devotion to the pursuit of money at any cost, the pursuit of power, the pursuit of fame, the insistence upon state and national superiority, and the universal acceptance as our "right" of prerogatives taken at a price to other men that drives them to poverty and despair. The black and white people perishing in Miami every day, which I have told about, are victims of these mass subjective vanities, and their skeletons hang, unseen, in the closets of their betters.

A church, compelled to have a dogma and selecting even the simplest arbitrary rule, soon finds that it has also tangled with the sinister and sordid instincts of man and that even a most decent goal, expressed in terms suitable for blanketing the many, must be forever modified, bastardized, honored in the breach, and turned into appalling hypocrisy. Here, again, the theory of introspection for the individual should reassert itself. In the face of reality, with every dogma confounded by every congregation, there remains only the one principle of individualism: the hard and scientific elicitation of a private truth from one's own self and a continuing, incessant effort to adhere to that realized truth. As in science, so in the spirit. Truth in, and for, crowds becomes impossible except in so far as it exists in the behavior, attitudes, and understanding of separate persons in the crowd. One would expect each churchman, then, to recoil from the monstrousness of pretending that any general dogma is being applied generally and revert to a study of himself and an admonition of his parishioners to do the same —which would amount, in effect, to a resumption of the teachings of Christ.

This would mean, of course, a great new awakening of persons to their responsibilities. But it would also mean the rise of as many material evaluations as there are people. The net effect of such new standards, derived by private integrity in the heart of each man as a new body of knowledge for his future guidance, would be to list endlessly and increasingly the behavior and morality of masses. Some such social process was what Christ had in mind. When he saw that he was not achieving it, his failure, as much as the prophecies, surely contributed to his bitter refusal to defend himself and to his assent by default to his crucifixion. He may also have thought that the enormity of their murderous error would stamp at last upon the minds of some an awareness of the breach between inner and outer living and that, thereby, his death would become the ultimate testament of the meaning of his faith in subjective life. It didn't, of course. It became, instead, to most, a vulgar hiring price: an atonement. If Christ ever really said his impending death was an "atonement" and meant by the word what the church now means, it was either the most masochistic violence of the many he worked upon himself, or else it was a statement of irony so formidable that, like Hitler's big lies, nobody caught onto it, as nobody did to so many other statements he made. Certainly, at the Last Supper, washing the feet of his disciples, he made a parallel gesture of humility, and his statements about his coming sacrifice could be construed most logically as passionate exaggerations of his mood of utter failure.

The church will forever inevitably discover the preposterousness of any lasting dogma for the many on any level. The one remaining logical possibility for the church—the abandonment of doctrine and the admonition to introspection—true Christianity, in short—would create for each man anew his own conscience, and therefore his own credo. Christ was fully aware of that. "In my house," he said, "are many mansions." The infinite numbers of the kinds of "kingdoms of heaven" were shown by him, and it was only the road to those kingdoms—the road of truth—that was not multiplied and diversified, in his definitions. But the church could not, and cannot, abide by this postulate. To do so would rob it of all authority and thus all temporal power. It could not command and it could not even collect, without criticism. Nobody would listen to a bishop because he was a bishop, but only because he was true to a mighty principle and gave no orders except such intimations of the processes of truth as he was intelligent and unselfish enough to apperceive. Every man, on such a plane as this, would feel as free to condemn the encyclical of a pope as he

would the speech of a politician. The spiritual enfranchisement of
the individual which would subject him only to the law of integrity
would, indeed, make him free, within himself, precisely where these
days most men are mordant serfs of every institution, tradition, organization, prejudice and vanity. Temporal law would be a law apart,
as it was with Christ, and man would not only obey it better because
he understood it better, but he would continually exert his private effort, and so a mass effort, to make temporal law more congruent
with man's whole nature and less a body of reflex to fear, superstition, and nonsense. This is the truth that sets men free, the only truth
there is in the subjective half of consciousness, the truth which, even
in portions, has served thousands of psychiatrists as a tool to integrate
the neurotic and cast out every sort of devil, and this is the one truth
that the church cannot afford to tell. Instead, it has developed the
desperate notion that truth is a road of many branches (dogmas) and
undertaken to solicit man for his journey toward the kingdom of
heaven by all the denominational side roads and theological blind
alleys the greedy and egregious churchmen could invent.

The church never thereafter could recommend realism; it never has;
it seems unlikely that it ever will. Two thousand years have gone
into the monkey business of creating dogma, departmentalization, de-
nominationalism, and theological rigmarole which serves the sole purpose of establishing authority and conceals the core and the heart of
Christianity. Every possible kaleidoscopic combination of the ritual,
tradition, and scattered dicta of religions before Christ, molded with
irrelevant material surrounding the life of Christ, has been made the
basis of every imaginable body of creed and so become a religion:
Covenanter or Catholic, Baptist or Buchmanite, Mormon or Methodist,
Quaker or Congregationalist, Greek Orthodox or Gallician, Holy
Rollers, Jehovah's Witnesses, Lutherans, Presbyterians, and God alone
knows what not, and every solitary one of them has a particular bill
of goods to sell that is recommended as the one and only true, divine,
inspired, fundamental, literal, real, one-dollar-the-bottle elixir of sweet-

and-bleeding Jesus Christ and none genuine without this signature.

Remembering how Christ tore into the dogma of the synagogue, one wonders what he would say about the dogma that has been derived from him today. By the mathematics of least squares, it might be possible to determine how many of these religions are how far off the target—but by the simpler expedient of looking at the goal as stated, and then at the aim of the churches, it is possible to observe unequivocally that none of them is even shooting at the mark, but, rather, in the opposite direction, as in the year A.D. 30.

When the nonchurched person realizes that the representatives of some sixteen millions of the members of these insectile sects, from the sheer inertia of dogma alone, are undertaking to try to bring back by allegedly democratic and decent methods the most profane blot ever smeared over the nation's escutcheon, he should logically decide that, before dogma does away with the principle of democracy itself, the principle had better be invoked for a full and just expression of opposition to this colossus of blind evil and folly. Not sixteen, but seventeen million people should be formed immediately into an even larger bloc. Its purpose should be to inhibit the urges of a hypocritical and self-righteous polyglot of interfering morons, and also to administer to them an evenhanded rebuke, by urging the people to vote onto the constitution of the nation an amendment forbidding these sixteen millions to enter their churches ever again, lest the nonsense and harm they brew there destroy the last honor, tolerance, decency, and understanding left among us. Such an amendment would not be in accordance with the teachings of Christ, on the face of it, or the principle of liberty, and I do not offer it seriously, but when the dogmatic, in the holy sense of self-righteousness which is their one and only real tenet, undertake to proliferate the work of hell itself, then it is high time to think about driving them out of their temples, as Christ did the money-changers. At the least, they should be instructed out.

A generation, in solemn truth, of vipers.

* * *

I am led sometimes to marvel—hypocritically on my own account, since I came by the understanding only recently—how it is possible for the average man to go through his life without discerning any innate differences in all that he calls his mental processes. As soon as a person has learned to count and to read it might be presumed that he would be taught something of the other functions of his mind. The instinctual ones, I have discussed at length; and the law of opposites; but the difference between feeling and thought, I have not.

We make our decisions—which is to say, our choice—very often, or perhaps almost always, in a flash of time. Whether to go to the movies or to stay at home and read a book, to take a job in California or to carry on in Denver, to break a habit or to conceal it, and so on, through the range of our doings. We say that we have decided these matters because of what we think. Some other decisions, of course, such as to run when frightened or to stand and fight, are made for us by instinct, but it is not such behavior that now concerns us.

Obviously, upon analysis, we make innumerable decisions without thinking at all, for thought is the exercise of the logical process and it demands an accumulation of all related data, an appraisal of that data in relation to each part of itself, a conscious application of the principles of logic, and the eventual arrival at a determination. Thought takes time. If you tried, by thought alone, to decide whether to go to a movie or to read a book, you might easily spend the whole night thinking, and so neither see the movie nor read the book. You might, imaginably, become so involved in the ever-deeper relationships of this one problem to the elements of your life, your consciousness, your past, and your future that you would spend the remainder of your days studying a decision. That is unlikely, but it is theoretically possible, just as it is theoretically possible, granted absoluteness of inner perception, to adduce the whole universe from any one fragment of it, such as, say, a peach pit.

You do not think out your choices, as a rule. Mathematical reasoning plays no active and conscious part in any but the most important or obtuse decisions of your life. You reserve thinking, if, indeed, you think at all, for special facets of your existence. Thus, if you are a crooked banker, you really do think out a scheme to swindle a depositor; if you are an honest doctor, you think to the uttermost of your ability about what the ailment of a patient is, and how to treat it.

However, in choosing between the book and the movie, if you do not need to consider what to do about the baby in the event that you decide to go out, your selection is instant. Each of such choices presents an immediate Gestalt. You have a feeling that you will read. You say so forthwith. You have a feeling that you would prefer to go to the movies. You close your book and rise.

You have not thought at all, in the real sense of the word, but you have made a decision, nonetheless, out of your feelings. Perhaps you never consider it, but this fact postulates that there must be at work within you a process like thought but not thought—a process that is like an adding-machine total of all your past thoughts, on tap, complete, for the purposes of appraisal. You refer to it as feeling, without much ado about it. You "felt" like the book or the movie. This process seems more personal to you than the process of thought—which is always impersonal—and so it is, since it derives from your private values, both conscious and unconscious. You decide, through conscious feeling, to read the book because you feel it will entertain you more or give you an enlightenment which you feel you need. Or, unconsciously, you may assent to the movie, say you wanted badly to see that particular picture and even believe you do—though you may have heard it is a poor movie—because, actually, inadmissible to yourself, is the feeling that you would rather sit through a rotten picture than sit around trying to read while your mother-in-law jabbered all night.

Your feelings are a composite, then, of your values and the values of other people in your society, which you may have accepted uncritically or from which you may have accepted only certain ones after exerting your private criticism upon them. Without bothering to analyze and contemplate their nature, you use those feelings as a continual guide to what you do. The objective world, also, projects feelings into you, to which you respond. The death of a friend makes you feel sadness, the need of a helpless person makes you feel compassionate, and so on. You are affected by outer phenomena in the realm of your feelings—and you act upon outer phenomena according to your feelings. Sadness represents a world of various values inside you; so does compassion. Events that make you sad or joyful or indignant or peaceful may not have the identical effect on other people. Your feelings belong only to *your* set of values.

You probably refer to your feelings as "emotions." Jung's distinction between emotions and feelings is, however, worth learning. A feeling, in his definition, is as abstract as a thought. It is a response to a value, and no more. An emotion—rage, envy, hysteria, panic, or any other—represents a conflict, as between thoughts and feelings, or feelings and instincts, or instincts and thoughts. An emotion is unintegrated, undigested, unassimilated, and therefore has autonomy; it seizes hold of you. If you can resolve the conflict that gave rise to it, you can restore yourself to a balance, rid yourself of the emotion, and return to pure values and pure concepts—to feelings and thoughts. If you are unable to resolve the emotional conflict which has made you frantic or hysterical or furious, you will try to lie it out of existence by rationalizing or to escape from it by getting your attention fixed on some other matter, or your friends will try to do it for you by kidding you or slapping you or changing the subject.

Your feelings, like your thoughts, will often lead you into emotions. But, because emotions are conflicts, they are unfinished business. You try to find for yourself a set of values which will prevent you from being turned over to rule by emotions. You select values according to whatever is the aim of your life as you see it in broad outline and also in immediate dimension. The more values you adopt which yield only immediate composures and balances, or pleasures and entertainments, the more likely you are, of course, to overlook the values which will give integration to the long trajectory of your years. You can, of course, recover past feelings by recollection and to some degree anticipate future feelings; thereby, in any moment of present time, you are at least able to adopt values that have a great range instead of an immediate pertinence—even if you never try to do so.

To simplify and illustrate that, consider the value attached by you to the care of your teeth. The thought of going to the dentist gives you a feeling of apprehension. If your long-range value of dental care outweighs the value of that apprehensive feeling, you will not have to think in order to get yourself to the dentist; you will go without *emotion,* in spite of your apprehensiveness. But if your immediate apprehension is as powerful a feeling within you as is your constant evaluation of dental care, you are headed for emotional conflict. To get yourself out of *that,* you may have to do a good deal of thinking or of re-evaluating. Meanwhile, you may spatter everybody in your vicinity with the emotion—becoming inexplicably grumpy, mean, irascible, "unreasonable," and otherwise infantile. If your apprehension is *greater* than your basic tooth value, you may have emotional conflict, but you'll put off going to the dentist till pain prompts an instinct: that of mere self-preservation.

Feeling is the automatic response to a subjective value, and, depending upon the integrity of your values in relation to yourself, to your society, to your inner nature, and to all outer nature, it is as reliable as a process of thought. A value that is real and honest both subjectively and in the objective world is as solid a route to a true decision or choice as the most mathematical of thoughts. Many people feel their way through life rather than think it through and they have, in the ability to *direct their feelings,* as useful a function of personality as they have in their ability to direct their thoughts—at least potentially. Besides, feelings have the advantage of operating swiftly. They are not necessarily swift—but ordinary value Gestalts are quick, and reactions to them reflect, approximately, the whole body of individual values which normally would be brought to bear upon a situation even in a long time of feeling about it, or a far longer time of thinking.

A "hunch" or an "impulse" is, very often, the product of a feeling.

We frequently wish we had obeyed an impulse which we disregarded after due thought—because we find, in the end, that the sudden feeling represented a greater accumulation of validities than the later doubts and questions which were permitted to inhibit it. On the other hand, our impulses cannot be wholly trusted, because they may come from mistaken values as readily as from real ones, or they may come not from any value at all, but from one of a pair of instincts—in which latter case the person who acts upon half an impulse, without being aware that another and opposite instinct belongs to his act, is bound to be overtaken by the unknown or unrecognized opposite. The kind of impulse which we most commonly regret not obeying is the honest feeling that rises in us urgently for a moment, only to be frustrated by social values which are false. We didn't give the old man a lift in our car because it would look funny when we drove down Maple Street; a decent value of pity and humankindness has risen in us— only to be choked back by a more pretentious value of social prestige.

Feelings, it thus begins to appear, demand the same honesty of approach and thoroughness of understanding as thoughts. Individual values must be felt out as individual ideas are thought out. Bad logic is, by comparison, easy to spot. But wrong feeling also is detectable; our own feelings palpitate the feelings of others—rather than our reason. "It shouldn't have made him so disappointed," we say, because we feel that his values are inferior and his disappointment was disproportionate to the feeling he ought to have had.

The schools and universities, churches and governments, do not unite with all other pontificating institutions to teach the value of values even to the extent that they do the meaning of meanings. That is another evidence of the circumambient flux of medievalism and another exhibit of the smallness of our discernment in relation to the mighty vanity of our smug undertakings. For, every social structure which has the perquisite of sounding off, or which is toady to a dogma, is busy night and day blindly *creating* unexplained values: true—false —modern—obsolete—crummy—vulgar—wise—ghastly—sensible— insane.

The church insists that people adopt its values—those, in the main, against which Christ broke himself trying to correct—rigid rules for what to do on Sunday, ostentatious giving, loud and repetitious praying, mass, ritual, atonement, Prohibition, and other hooey.

The little red schoolhouse proffers its little drab values, its lies, its false patriotism, its ridiculous heroes, its worship of the state, its reverence for government, and all the moppets sit in the benign goo, aware from the first grade on—through notice of other, more current and popular values—that most of this is stuff and rubbish, and so undoing through their incompetent skepticisms what slight good school might perform. The young brains wither and rot into what is called good American citizenship by the method, hating afterward most learning, work, discipline, fact, morality, common sense, honor, and dignity.

The university insists upon its great value—the scientific method—and, in the flash and sizzle of high-tension laboratories, proves the merit of inductive reasoning while it denies the existence of inner evaluations upon which the same method might fruitfully be applied. By this means scientists are produced—anti-everything-but-test-tube-contents—agnostic—atheistic—pragmatic—empirical—convulsed with passions of negation—brilliant legions of the half-conscious.

County government describes in cash values the quick benefits of political corruption; federal government pays lordly lip service to the original values of democracy as described by the founders and then evades every one of them to keep itself in office.

Business, mightier in the eyes of the vipers than knowledge, God, or government, sets upon all things mundane and spiritual, artistic and mechanical, all dreams and dreads, hopes and fears, pain and pleasure, thoughts and feelings, its supervalue: $$.

Out of such elements, with the dollar topping the lot, are values compounded in America. That is to say, American feelings reflect, and give re-rise to, that body of stuff. A fine pottage to try to live by! A fine and fecal puree to have to feel about, through a human life!

Nobody teaches the moppets (or the masters of art) that what goes on inside them is bound up in these values and that their joy and woe, satisfaction and despair, contentment and neurosis, ambition and frustration, will—all of it—ride witlessly upon these fundamental rails forever, unless they do some hard thinking or unless they do some hard feeling. That the power of evaluation—parallel to logic—exists of itself within them, they also never know. Thus they permit the atrophy of a giant organ of their personalities while they are children, because they never heard of it or learned how to use it; when they become of an adult age, they may have the logic of Einstein but they will usually have the values of children and all their feelings will be infantile. Technical nomenclature of the most abstruse sort will not cloak such puling childishness.

Their feelings will flicker and revolve around the focus of pain and pleasure both in the physical and in the subjective realms, where the feelings of children are oriented, and the feelings of primitive men, and the feelings of cats and dogs, who have few other values. The greatest anthropologist can thus be put out by a trifle, made ridiculous by a small cupidity, defeated by the length of the automobile of another anthropologist, thrown into a hell of infantile feeling by the rejection of his sexual attention at the hands of some fragment of female candy, and all the time sit marveling over the enigma of how so great a brain has been brought to disaster by such trivia.

This man—these men—these women—the moms and their slaves —all the people have not caught on to the truth of the relationship of temporal values to their feelings or the truth about changes in feelings, which can be brought to them only by an inner search for values with an ever greater profundity and an ever broader basis of reality. These, even unto the great professors, maddened by the infantilism of the world around them and haunted by their own, have not yet sifted out true evaluations of things both tangible and imaginable, and they do not recognize the silly fealties inside them which make them act like spoiled brats—they having spoiled themselves or been spoiled by mothers, ministers, and teachers. So, clinging to their spiritual putrescence, not willing to abdicate the most infantile premise of

all, namely, that a great integrity toward the cephalic index of pre-
historic men does not, ipso facto, connote integrity anywhere else in
the skull of the thinker, they never discover that a whole man can be
produced only by four-dimensional preciseness and exactitude.

It is this principle of feelings as the obverse side of values with
which Christ was largely concerned. He did not have a trained, intellectual audience. He did not, himself, have the education in logic that
some Western men have achieved and, when he tried to think about
or define his insight in terms of *thought,* he became confused and his
disciples were utterly confused. But, within the function of feeling
and values, he was neither restricted by language nor entangled in
seeming paradoxes which he lacked the intellectual means to unravel.
Values, in A.D. 30, were extraordinarily like values today—and much
of this book has been in token of that fact, in reminder to the reader
that material advances do not constitute any sort of improvement in
people whatsoever. Christ's method of expressing and re-expressing
values, as a means to true, moral, and scientific feeling, would be
found to cover almost as wide a range of perceptibilities two thousand
years ago as it covers now—if anybody bothered to analyze it.

It was, that is to say, twice as complete and effective a route to psychological and philosophical principles as the route followed by Kant,
Spinoza, Descartes, Leibnitz, and James—who were only thinkers.
Christ followed the route in a very antique and Eastern way, but with
a balanced attention to the subjective consciousness of the inner and
outer worlds, the nature of those worlds themselves, and their unconscious and hidden aspects. Placing the individual in the center of the
construction, where he unshakably finds himself to be anyhow, and
noting that only the individual can analyze these surrounding elements
for himself, Christ set man to the task of knowing himself—after
Christ had made some extraordinary private progress in the study of
his own evaluations.

His progress was not complete, final, or absolute in all directions.
He admitted it when he hotly protested being called good. He was
never able to put what he knew to be true into syllogisms or other

intellectual designs. That task, if it is ever done, will be done by men with the vocabulary of a new science and the strong attachment to logic, which are prerequisites of it.

Exactly what Christ discovered concerning himself, one would have to be Christ to find out. The modern parallel of it, whatever that may be, could be discovered only by a personality of similar sensitivity, energy, imagination, and integrity, which devoted itself to a disciplinary method of living, as ascetic, against this twentieth century background, as was the method of Christ. Such a person would have to begin by following the advice of Christ, and trying to abolish every currently accepted value, in order to have a clean slate for new values; he might find, as Christ did, that certain dogmatic values still stuck to him and interfered with the clarity of his perceptions and the power of his new feelings. I do not know. I advise anybody who dares, to try it, and I admonish everybody to try all of it that they dare. Certainly there isn't any mysticism in the method. It is as sensible as geometry, which, in fact, is identically like it—and relativity also, and all other mathematics, and music, too, in another way.

Christ undertook to describe the feeling-value road to truth, by setting forth examples. These are the parables. The many representations of the kingdom of heaven offered by Christ stand for the new inner state brought by faithfulness to his technique: *heaven is the kingdom within you.* The mustard seed and the leaven are illustrations of the pervasiveness of a small true principle acting upon a whole personality. The kingdom of heaven is like them. Divided against itself, it falls. The last shall be first in it, which is likely enough. A rich man, sorrowing over the mere thought of abandoning his goods values, will find it very hard to enter the kingdom of heaven. He will go away sad —a feeling that is a pure value response. Truth, the way to this heaven within, is like the sower who sowed on various kinds of ground, and some is assimilated, but most truth, sooner or later, dies out. Again, a person who contracts for so much of it and no more has no just complaint if other persons are given more for a lesser effort, for there is no statistical, individual quid pro quo in the kingdom of heaven, and none in all nature; each man is beholden only to himself in the matter and not to justice defined in terms of an equal division of value received; nor can he thus judge other men. The widow's two mites are of greater value than the whole pile of fives and tens on the plate, because of the feeling which prompted the gift of one farthing. The rejected stone becomes the cornerstone. Many are called but few are chosen. No tentative values are of any use in the achievement of this kingdom, for inadequate and brief values will leave you in the lurch, like the foolish virgins, just at the moment of opportunity. And the feeling function must be worked at—or you will be like the servant who hid his talent in the ground.

As analogues for the basic natural values, the parables are transparent. But ministers, priests, and all manner of pulpitatious pipsqueaks have whacked and hammered them into unrecognizability in an effort to fit them to temporal values, or dogmatic values, or any of a number of other sorts of values—a process necessary to rationalize personal falsities, or to hold audiences which would have fled from the truth and brought down the church to nothing, or to seem learned and knowing—a monstrous fatuity.

The attitude of clergymen to Christ is, indeed, next most deplorable to the dogmatic interpretations of Christianity elaborated by the church.

Religion, if it is anything, is a way to peace. If it is not a way to peace, then it had better be avoided, because, God knows, there is war enough that cannot be avoided. As a way to peace, religion should be approached peacefully. The approach should be desirable. The feelings of the inquirer into religion should be pure in essence and his intellectual attitude one of integrity. Any perturbations, emotions, and melancholias, or manias that are brought about by religion *should* come from the psychotic uproar of the individual, not from the truth itself. For the truth is always here in nature and in the earth and in man's consciousness—changeless, real, dispassionate toward past and future, good and evil, psychical and physical—and no reactions to it can be in *it,* but in man only. The way, the word, the life, the truth, the whole awareness of all that is, exists of itself just as the bend in a ray of light exists in the region of a sun, whether anybody notices it, or measures it, or understands it—or not. That very (and irrefutable) fact is enough to make men everlastingly interested in enlarging their consciousnesses as individuals in every possible direction, and it is, indeed, the manifest tendency of the two billion years of evolution on this planet which have shown consistently during all that time an undeviating tendency toward individuated consciousness, of which man is the current most-developed example.

But ministers do not have any such natural honesty of approach to the religions they rig up for in-line Sunday production. They are afraid of the Bible. They are afraid of Christ. They therefore fawn on, drip over, and butter up their Lord, like the detestable sycophants they are, or else they convert their apprehension into an exaggerated form of whistling in the dark, and yell and scowl from their pulpits to hide the fact that they, themselves, are terrified. Thus they engage in a foolish attempt to escape their fear by handing it on to their congregations and so making fear commonplace enough to be tolerable.

These simpering or clamorous windbags preach Christ the Redeemer, Christ the meek and mild, Christ who died for your sins, Christ who suffered agonies unparalleled, Christ the mystical, Christ the worker of miracles (who, since the invention of the steam engine, can work only spiritual and no physical miracles due to Ohm's law and the relation of hydrogen ions to acids), Christ the simple man, Christ the great academic philosopher, Christ the Torquemada of Jehovah, Christ the prince of peace, Christ the tolerator of adultery, Christ the bigot, the spigot, the wellspring of joy and man of sorrows, Christ the scourge of the temple, Christ the physician, Christ the know-it-all, Christ the Miss Fix-it, Christ the mineral spring, Christ the autocrat of the breakfast table, and bingo on Friday night. They never preach, teach, screech, or beseech the truth, come hell or holy water. If they knew how, they would get the scientists back into the pews.

The Bible has caught these infantile delinquents into such a morass of quandaries, from which Christ himself could not altogether extricate his mind and heart, that they preach the Bible in even more ways, and more fantastic ways, than Christ and all his whiskered contemporaries. The fact that the Bible is full of libidinous poetry, four-letter words, startling accounts of murder, violence, bestiality, infidelity, whoring, crime, revenge, contradictory precept, and old wives' nonsense is, indeed, reason enough for them to be alarmed. They know nothing about legend, and hence nothing about instinct. They have no training in the direction of their feelings and no true values of their own, hence the parables are lost on them. They cannot remotely hope to reconcile Biblical dogma with scientific fact. All the learned textbooks they have studied have provided them with no more than top-spin of technical verbiage, which further confounds them and their hearers. They have the moral sensibilities of dinosaurs and do not know they have even that much. Their utterance, for hundreds of millions and billions of people for two thousand years, has been about a man and a book and a moldy assortment of churches.

But in the book and in the man there is only this: a study of individual integration—a statement of a principle for the analysis and synthesis of inner man as old as the hills and as new as cryology. In the book and in the man there is only a science for the psyche identical with the science of physics for matter.

Nothing to fear, hate, love, avoid, doubt, abandon, rage over, despair over, canonize, apostrophize, codify, emotionalize, evangelize, interpret, enflame with, or have orgasms over—any more than Newton's laws or Archimedes' principle. But every bit as profound and valuable.

The Word is all, as John said.

But they preach the book, the man, and the church, because they do not know the Word—never did—never will.

They do not even try to live by the Word. To this I, personally, bear witness, having seen it in the behavior of thousands and thousands of prickamice in many churches, and rarely having found one among them who, even for a moment, acted in any way as if the values described by Christ had affected his consciousness.

I would like to be Daniel for a while and write, "Mene, mene, tekel, upharsin," on the walls of churches of the sixteen million Presbyterians, Methodists, Baptists, and Episcopalians, who are so numb to feeling, to reason, to experience, and to nature as to want to bring back the evils we have just now and only partly managed to put aside. Underneath the cabalistic inscription, in all these churches, just before the walls fell, I would write, in fire, another word, and the word would be: "Horsefeathers."

Christ reviled those who wanted to preach the goodness of himself. He often repudiated the old book: it is full of legend, history, scandal, and all manner of claptrap—a museum of a race, interesting, amazing, and at times illuminating. Christ, who had insight, eschewed all the symbolic forms of worship and recommended realism alone. But the hordes of squeaking pips who followed him, the apostles and the saints, the reformers and protesters, the popes and the prelates, snatching back the values of the Pharisees, took back also, willy-nilly, the dreadful creed of Jehovah, the aimless quidnuncery of the theologians, the rattling dither of dead swarms of barbarians and Dark Age bores, and made their denominations out of whole cloth, so far as anything Christ tried to say was concerned. Then, of course, they worshiped the cloth and the cloth worshiped itself. It is a pretty study of costumes designed to hide frustration.

People never seem to realize that, no matter what their mouths insist upon or what they back up with a willingness to die (which is often only a patent-leather brand of the death wish), neither their exhortation nor their sacrifice gives any validity to their motives. Mere say-so is substituted by them for considered reason. This is a mass business, and a terrible prophecy anent the radio, already revealed in part. People may be cooped up in hell and as busy raping the souls in propinquity to them as Japs, but if they yell together that they are saints they all believe it. This is the power of mob conviction. Its extent shows why each man ought to be at considerable pains to convince himself of truth, rather than of a dogma, or of half a truth, or of nothing. For those who subscribe to dogma or who hold half a truth to be all of the truth, or who say, "I know nothing," make a palsied spectacle of themselves and it is not only unpleasant to live with them, but God-damned dangerous in addition.

Down the shuffling ages have gone myriads of people calling to Mohammed, as Christians call to Christ, and revering Buddha or Confucius, as Christians say they revere Christ. All of them think of each other as heathen—and they are, all of them. Each of them, and many more, has a man and a book and some have a word, but none will listen to the word of the other to see if anything can be learned by it. Their cities rise and vanish. The stupefying multiplicity of their wars and arguments rust and are silent. They never think: I did this for nothing, or we died for nothing. But the pyramids were for nothing. All the holy dead in all the crusades died for nothing—though the economists, swallowing a caravan of camels, will tell you it was for trade routes. The fiefery of Jerusalem is in doubt at this very moment, and that of Mecca and Benares, and there may be, before nightfall, cannonading in Lhasa. Neither the Christians nor the heathen have yet established much lasting good and even the Christians have lost sight of what goodness means, though they still cling to the starveling hope of it.

Kingdom, power, and glory, forever accessible to man, are forever so meanly snatched at that they turn to clay in the hands of men. The dimout has extinguished even the frail lantern of Diogenes. Christ asked only that you set truth first ahead of all other fealties, and that you examine yourself, not your brother, with its light. Whenever the door of hell opens, the voice you hear is your own. Darkness congeals around us where we stand and it is too late to put a nickel on the drum.

CHAPTER XVIII

Conclusion

IT HAS BEEN FAIRLY FANCY OF ME, I KNOW, TO WRITE SO LONG
and noisy a book just to say that if we want a better world, we will
have to be better people.

That's all I've said, of course.

All the founding fathers said.

All Christ said.

All there is to say.

But it would not be fair if I failed to follow my own rule and reveal
in this miscellaneous Jeremiad a glimpse of *its* opposites.

That I shall do. Balancing the evil, the stupidity, the rapacity and
the foolishness of men is the goodness of men. All the goodness there
is reposes in them. But goods are incidental to goodness; they cannot
be identified with goodness; a dominant concern with goods always
blights goodness and leads the way back to despair.

I should like to review that theme before I turn over the coin on
which I have etched so much viperishness of the generation that now is
rolling toward limbo.

America began with the idea of giving to every man an equal
chance. The noble thesis that the majority of common men, properly
informed, will judge every problem rightly was the philosophy which
prompted that definition of liberty. It was another way of saying that
a knowledge of the truth would set men free: each man, and all
men. In action, it meant that individual human beings would strive

316

incessantly to become more conscious of reality and would put obligations to others ahead of their own ambitions.

That is democracy.

The idea is so fundamental to man's psychology that any compromise of it, or any deviation from it, is necessarily a backward step. A step, that is, toward less individuated men, less informed men, less civilized men, men less aware, men in bondage to whatever notion caused the backward step.

The apparent handicap of democracy is inefficiency. The inevitable accompaniment of democratic living is the struggle of every sort of minority against the majority to force particular judgments. But, according to the philosophy which I have just discussed, there can be no advantage without cost.

The uproar in our free press, the fumbling of our Washington bureaucracy, the conflict of our laws, and the disagreements of our leaders are results of democratic behavior. They can be regarded as handicaps, however, only by those men who have forgotten, or never knew, or willfully abandoned the concept of democracy. To relieve organized society of contradictions by fiat, as has been done in Germany, is to create genuine handicap: a society in which the *valid* feelings and ideas in minorities are driven into silent places. There they eventually become autonomous. They turn into worries—and then into fears. They establish such mechanisms as I have listed: the bully contains the potential coward; the conqueror is obliged to fight the inferior knowledge of his guilt as hard as he fights his physical enemy; the whole people, exulting first in the efficiency of their paranoid method, at last becomes lost in what was always mania.

Another way to regard social organization is to realize that the philosophy of the state is only a magnification of the philosophy of the person, and the philosophy of all states only a magnification of the philosophy of one. To the man and the woman who understand the philosophy of democracy and live by it, there is never any confusion about how to feel or what to do. Such people know that the confusions are superficial, that a thousand democracies could perish, but that democracy would prevail everywhere in the end. Such people are occupied in the spread of an understanding of democracy. Patriotism, therefore, is to be concerned about your country—not necessarily to adulate it.

Too many of us have lost sight of the single, simple truth by which we were first associated and by which alone we can continue in any lasting association. Too many learned men—and too many fools.

A new corollary of truth is never evident at once to the masses. That is why minorities must remain vocal. Only through freedom can they educate masses to enlargements of the fundamental concept. The danger opposing that is the chance it gives minorities to embrace lies —new and old—and to force them upon unwatchful masses or to put them in effect through the political default of masses.

That is why a person who does not vote is betraying himself.

That is why a person who does not do everything in his power to find out about both sides of a question, and all candidates, is digging the grave of his liberty.

That is why a person who does not consult his own decision rather than the political predetermination of a bloc is chaining himself link by link to the old mobism that has spawned, swarmed and sloughed since the Ice Ages.

We can have one categorical premise only: the democratic premise—leaving no room for any other—demanding the right to all information as the route to all understanding and judgment*—and tran-

---

* It is the steady loss of this right which, since 1945, has caused me to assert in every possible medium that liberty is perishing in U.S.A. Common man did not see, after Hiroshima, that to make any part of abstract science a *secret* was to deny to all mankind access to basic truth. Uncommon man, a very few physicists excepted, did not see that formidable point, either. And neither group perceived that a little start at making mere *knowledge* secret would inevitably spread, so that much knowledge would soon be hidden, much policy would in consequence be shaped in secret, and the people would no

scending in private, national and international existence all special
pleading. It is the only possible social ideal. It is also the ideal of
Christians and of scientists, of all little men and of all truly great men,
and it has been in all their history. It is not a road to imminent perfection. The squabbles of democracy—even its civil war—while they tes-

---

longer be "properly informed" wherefore able to make "appropriate
decisions"—indeed, any decisions.

In 1945, and every year since, I have published the view that a failure of the Soviets to enter into an open, free, inspected world community of scientific knowledge, including what is called "military
secrets" must be regarded by the American people as an intolerable
affront to American freedom and therefore an obligatory cause for
ultimatum. I have continuingly pointed out that the only alternative
—a secret America—a land where even the elected representatives no
longer can be "cleared" to learn all the facts, truths and data relevant
to good government—leads to what in effect amounts to dictatorship,
since it is not free and open government.

I have said that such a condition—recognized or not—would breed
increasing *fear* in a people thitherto accustomed to knowing (by their
constitutional rights) *all* the facts. I have said that their automatic
terror—conscious or *not*—would lead the people of this country into a
state of hysteria—a state of inappropriate response, a state in which
some would become apathetic to every peril, others would seek to
vent their unidentified terror by punishing "whipping boys," and still
others would try to escape by attitudes of "eat, drink and be merry,"
or by plunging into religious paroxysms—"trusting" God to accomplish duties they would not themselves even face, or embracing fugue
and fantasy—imagining that "it can't happen here" or that little men
from outer space would save us from the bombs.

As early as 1946, I named the years to come—these years—"The
Terror" (always providing we kept failing to see that a secret Russia,
by compelling secrecy on U.S.A., abrogated our basic freedom—
freedom to know). The hysterias I predicted are manifest in our na-

tify to the imperfections of men testify also to the completeness of
his idealism.

There are not four freedoms, but one only, and the other name of
it is truth. Turned about, it is equally real to say that there is not just
one freedom, but an infinite number of freedoms, or as many freedoms
as there are people willing to sacrifice themselves for the freedom of
others. We will always be engaged in political struggles "testing
whether this nation, or any other nation so conceived and so dedicated, can long endure." We who made thirteen inharmonious
colonies into one democracy and who preserved a democratic nation
even after its states had warred upon each other cannot repress a burning impulse to make the world safe for democracy—to give it what
our president has dramatized as four freedoms.

In the period that followed the War Between the States, the
South, staying in the nation gamely, made a measurelessly greater
spiritual contribution to democracy than the victorious North. It is
still making that contribution. And the light to be elicited from the
vanquished nations in this war of democracy for the world is that kind
of light. That is the light which went out in 1914. That is the light

---

tional life today. So far, we have failed to see that awful meaning of
our lost liberty; we have failed to take the formidable, self-evident
steps against Russia; we have failed even to realize that we are now a
kind of permissive "dictatorship" wherein the man in the street no
longer controls his government because he no longer knows what
"secrets" effect its policies, its plans, its expenditures, and so on.

It is not surprising, then, that we exhibit the classical forms of hysteria on a wide scale—or that we do not appreciate these symptoms
for what they are: such self-blindness is one symptom of the familiar
disease.

There is no such thing as a free and *un*informed people; there is
not even such a thing as a free press in a land of government by restriction and classification. Without all knowledge, liberty expires;
so all of us who think we are still free are bitterly deluded.

which is beginning to shine in all of Asia. That is the light for which our polygot democracy is an intended torchbearer. The discovery of America and the rise of the United States as a free land welcoming all peoples was a teleological anticipation of this age. The circumstance can be credited to God, to human instinct, or to chance—but it is manifest. The seeds of democracy ripened here in the breast of every sort of human being. Now, the winds of chaos are scattering them over the earth. When peace comes, we have only to tend the crop. And if some of the seeds haven fallen upon stony ground, we will have to enrich that place.

Man's blackest hour is this one. But it can be made the hour before dawn.

Such recollections of the democratic ideal—the ideal of ancient people and the ideal of ourselves in the past few generations—such exhortations as mine—will be repugnant to many wishful thinkers, impatient individuals who have surfeited our scene, these last laggard years, with economic panaceas and social nostrums. There is no true left or right, but only the middle way. The vendors of patent social medicines expect, to a man, that by deviating from the long, hard route they will uncover a short cut for everybody. The universality of the grisly battle joined on account of their error is not a lesson to them, for, having embarked upon their diagonals with great to-do, they would rather risk a millennium of doom than the exposure of their fallacies.

They are quacks. They claim that a dose of an ism will cure all human ills. They have been lost in the corrupt theory that goods and good are one. Each has half of the truth—like the doctors and the scientists described in this book. The complexity of our society has, by mystical transference, convinced them that the old, simple philosophy is not sufficiently intricate any more. So they have thought up numberless pseudo-spiritual ideologies which are based upon the physical elements of modern existence. Insisting that their ends are holy because they are superficially unselfish, they also insist that any means justifies those ends. Many of them are willing to compel liberalism or collectivism or toryism by machine guns and we are in as much peril from erudite boobs as from mere boobies. The day they can show how a machinegunning of the people, by the people, for the people will make the survivors nobler, I will recant.

The tendency of many of these ardent asses to point to fighting Russia as a "proof" will give us tragic trouble in the future unless we try to understand the Russians now. They are the products of twenty years of indoctrination by violence. Their gallant unity in the past year is cited as convincing evidence that a machine gun leveled at the masses is the new and sacred methodology of public virtue—if the gunners themselves are "idealists."

This is a horrible delusion.

The enemies of the Russians—the Nazis—were similarly indoctrinated by force, and they are as fanatically brave and as furiously united, which should ice the marrow of those who argue that force is humanitarian. There are many other reasons for the magnificence of the Russian stand.

The Nazis, deliberately embracing all that is hateful, are the most logical target for righteous anger mankind ever had. The Russians were unremittingly instructed to detest them. That we Americans failed to show the enemy our united fury from the first is a measure not of our understanding heart, but of the degree by which we had defaulted moral responsibility. Russia is fighting what it loathes. The Russian people have a tradition two thousand years old: a love of mother Russia which a mere quarter century of collectivism could not erase even if it had tried—and it did not. The Russian is an Asiatic; he does not hold all his sense of being alive in his ego and can die without the clamor of a midwestern isolationist bank president's wife. The people of Russia discovered, when the Nazis attacked them, that their years of terrible sacrifice had not been for nothing. It must have surprised and heartened them immeasurably to perceive when the battle was joined that the Soviet government had secretly created a mighty war machine to defend them. The starvation, the scarcity, the torture and the mass migrations in retrospect took on a new significance and the people became overwhelmingly proud of their tyrannical government. The revealed splendor of the Red army exalted and emotionally fused the Russians. Someday the revealed splendor of our own will give us a new, unifying pride in the achievements of our common sacrifice. Last of all, the Russians were aware that the world had been watching them through the years and was watching them as never before. That, too, builds morale.

The final judgment by the democratic people of the morality and idealism of the Russians both as human beings and as subjects of a collectivist state may change again, as it has before. I do not believe that the democracies will ever bring the guilty leaders of fascism to trial. Closer neighbors, among them the Russians, will get there first. I do not believe our propaganda of postwar trial and condemnation is adequate propaganda. It does not prepare Americans for what will almost surely happen when the Germans collapse. I do not believe we are facing, yet, the validity of hatreds born of valid fears. And I believe that, to whatever extent we can communicate with the enemy people, it would be more honorable and more effective to tell them that each hour they contribute to the Nazi cause will augment their suffering when the cause is lost, than it is to tell them we will close in upon them with kindness. That is not the strategy of truth, but a stratagem of deceit, unless we really expect to go through this war in the cheerful belief that nobody has been annoyed by the vandalized debauchment, the murder, the enslavement and the pitiless mutilation of millions upon millions of decent, helpless people. The wrath we should have, the Russians have—and others. They are justified in it; we are beginning to share it; it is the wrath to come.

Only when it has exhausted itself can we offer our democratic message and then only if we have clung to its meaning through holocaust. Then, the faces of two billions of exhausted people will turn toward America. Then, if we have sacrificed, worked, shared, understood, thought, talked, stripped off our luxuries, planned a world mission, prepared ourselves to give much and ask little, we can offer the world a new charter and new liberty.

The quack doctors must not prevail at home ever, or abroad again. If we analyze their remedies by the litmus of the simple philosophy of democracy, we can always discover the dross in each. There is, in consequence, no reason for us to be misled or confused or frightened except the selfish reasons in our heads.

The liberals believe in the pure principle: the justness of informed common man. But almost every liberal wants to define and restrict the nature of the information given to common man, and has some extra premise besides: a fiscal policy, for example, or pacifism, which is irrelevant to American democracy so long as there are undemocratic men or undemocratic nations.

No Communist can be democratic. His dogma comes before his belief in ethical humanity. It is obvious that we should learn not to exploit each other. It is obvious that we should seek ways by which the productiveness of machinery will enslave none and serve all according to their creature needs and, in addition, according to their individual abilities. But if every man were as rich as a king it would mean only that the wars were fought with more extravagant ammunition until every man became as wise as God and as humble. That day is far off.

The conservatives, like the liberals, are of every shade, while the Communists all have one dogma—though they switch it often enough. Conservatives, like Communists, put more trust in the materialism of common man than in his idealism; they believe that the profit motive is the foundation of morality. It might be arguable, at least, if the conservatives could throw into the argument their own motives for their own profits, but even to attempt that requires a higher symbol than materialism. In consequence, conservative philosophies also contain extrademocratic premises, of which the "sanctity" of private property is a sample.

There are in America from fifteen to twenty million religious fundamentalists who are dedicated to doctrines incompatible with democracy in that they insist upon their prerogatives as first principles. An even larger group feebly follows the trail of fire breathed by these fundamentalists. They are the most dangerous minority we have because they categorically eschew the reasoned judgments of the majority. Democracy properly allows them the right to worship as they choose. It should never have conceded them the right to establish schools. Education is not a function of any church—or even of a city —or a state; it is a function of all mankind.

Collective bargaining is an earned democratic right. It is not democratic to run unions by any but the democratic method. It is not democratic to allow them to become untaxable corporations. It is not democratic to let them keep their books secret. The wish of labor in society at any time can be expressed only by the free choices of the people who work—not by liberalism, conservatism, communism, or fundamentalism. Individual farmers belong to all the above groups. Through their organizations they have formed a political bloc in Washington which has artificially pitted them against several other groups, especially labor. Actually, the farmers are part of labor now. They depend upon the machine. Their land has become raw material for the factories. Attempts to distinguish them from labor are based on concepts of a past age. Their organization for collective bargaining should in the future parallel the increase of labor's voice in management.

Nobody with any sense can doubt that common man is tending toward a new schedule for the distribution of his profits. That will gradually shift part of the responsibility for agriculture and production management. But if the tendency brings an end to private ownership, democracy will have to start all over, after a later, greater catastrophe than ours. On the other hand, if an increase of sharing of profits with labor and with farmers is revolution—then there is a revolution on hand and let those who are frightened make the most of it. The years ahead will see many particular experiments in socialization. America has made them throughout its history. Some will fail, and the materials, industries or services involved will revert to private management. Some will succeed.

I do not believe, however, that Americans will find lasting satisfaction in the socialization of their industries. The sources of all raw material except land for farming may some day be bought by the people

and evenhandedly administered. But I doubt if creative enterprise will
be government-controlled for long, no matter what experiments are
made in that direction. The reason for my doubt is subjective—but it
should be a consolation to those terrified individualists who still are
rugged and honest. Americans are the foremost builders and producers
in the history of man. They always will be. As such, they will not tolerate the inefficiencies in their material activities that they tolerate in
the operation of their democratic institutions. The blast of rage which
followed revelations of governmental mismanagement after the last
war has not waited for peace, in this one, and each of the millions
upon millions of angry shouts now leveled at the blundering of bureaucracy is actually a note of exhilarating encouragement for those
who fear postwar collectivism in America.

The businessmen—good, bad and indifferent—are too myopic to
realize that. But it is true. The New Deal has compelled us to be basically responsible for each other—which we should always have been.
It is also performing the second, involuntary favor of proving that such
responsibility cannot be extended to absolute domain. When the war is
over and the story of the new bureaucrats is told, honest, decent, hard-
working Americans—whether rich or poor—will not wish to trust
their whole agricultural and industrial destinies to any "Washington."

At the moment we are living in a dictatorship. The government can
order any man to do its will. It can commandeer any plant or property
or invention. But we still vote and we still have our free press. I can
still write a book like this and you can say what you please about it.
Hitler, who never walked the streets of a republic or drew a breath in
a countryful of air impregnated with liberty, cannot understand this.
Those Germans who have always lived in Germany cannot understand
it. But you can and I can. It is our illustrious achievement: a country
wherein a man can still speak his mind *—even when war means that

---

* This "illustrious achievement" has been deprived of meaning, as
I indicated in the prior footnote. A man may still speak his mind
(though a great many have been made afraid to do so owing to our

he must do as he is ordered till peace returns. No government that is so fluid it can convert to dictatorship to meet a war emergency—or legislate partial socialization to meet a depression—and yet through both permit any man to say what he thinks—is a weak government or an unrepresentative government or an unsuccessful government. It is the mightiest government men have ever had. It is democracy.

What you and I possess today is worth all the sacrifice of our forebears and all the sacrifice we are capable of—to impoverishment and to death. It is worth all that we can give and all that we are—excepting only *itself*.

When the war is ended, we will have to rebuild the world. It would be useful if we were planning the job now, and telling the conquered people about our plans for them. Washington is still afraid to do that, owing to certain prejudices which are the vested mental property of the American Old School Tie appeasers in various government departments. But we know the building assignment will be America's: nobody else can undertake it. The world will be a wreck, just as Hitler promised, because it chose to be ruined rather than ruled by him. We cannot let our two billion fellow men revert to barbarism in those ruins, any more than we could allow Hitler to make slaves of them. Had we done that we would have been nothing more than the last band to be enslaved. If, with victory, we abandon our comrades in their rubble we will merely join them ultimately in poverty and pestilence.

We will have to lend them money—at low interest and for many years. We will have to give them much. Such extensions of trust will

---

hysterical condition and its exploitation by a few sinister fools) but the "mind" a man (or a magazine) speaks today is uninformed—and everybody knows it. Those few who *are* informed are not allowed to speak at all until what they are going to say has been "cleared" by administrative appointees.

We still *pretend* there is a "free world." All that's left is the wan, danger-drenched hope of the restoration of human liberty.

be America's price for her lack of trust in the past—her lack, even, of interest in other people. We will pay the price in taxes and probably, on occasion, in disappointments. Such a world contribution cannot be made by a collectivist bureaucracy. It would be unthinkable to totalitarians. Most of it will not be good business in the narrow sense of visible six per cent returns. It may mean that our national debt will increase for a time more fabulously than it already has; the very thought requires more democratic idealism than materialistic scheming. And yet, it is the only possible way to repay the debt in the end.

If we are idealistic enough—and I think we are—our giant enterprise will set in motion the material activities which will solve the vast problems of postwar conversion. Conversion for immediate domestic consumption would create a short-term boom—and little else, perhaps. Conversion for world reconstruction would open up the one everlasting frontier. We can win the war and re-establish man. Hitler did not foresee that capacity. He understood the fallacy of our Cinderella legend; he never knew about other American legends—about Paul Bunyan, or his modern cousins, Superman, Buck Rogers and Popeye. If we tackle the job in that spirit, all the lamps in all the earth will begin to burn again. But if we have not learned our lesson—if we ignore democracy and pursue some tempting ism—if we elect ignoramuses to the House and send loud local pleaders to the Senate—if we give up any more of our precious hold on democratic morality—if we restore mom and Cinderella and class cupidities—we are done for, just as I have said.

This war is a true crusade. It can be the last one.

Material gain is incidental to self-discipline and has always been.

It depends on you.

Your old institutions will be gone. Your church will be a new experience in subjective truth—or it will have vanished. Your schools will not be wringers for the unsorted mob, reduced in discipline and intellectual content to meet that low norm, but competitive societies, like life, offering advancement for working ability, and not because of family funds. Education will be a harder moral regimen, from kindergarten to the graduate college. But it will be more interesting. The opinionism of school boards will not jaundice it. The acids of the gelded moms will not scald it. A hundred Walt Disneys in a dozen nations will make of every course, moral and factual, a fascinating lesson, talked by the greatest professors and displayed in all the dimensions of sound, color, motion and transparent diagram.

Your children will think that you were an evil person—which you were. Their concepts of truth and purity will surely scandalize you as they do from generation to generation, wherever men are growing spiritually.

You will have a road to Tierra del Fuego and a road to Alaska. You will have ferries between the Diomedes and a road that goes to Moscow and on to Paris and from Suez into Africa. For a while, you will drive your light metal and plastic cars over those roads. Then you will use them to haul fuel for your private planes. Nothing is surer. You—not your children—will weekend in Paris or Rio. You will hunt in the Andes—a few hours from your office. You will fish in the waters off New Zealand—a long trip: twenty hours. In your living room, in a few years, will be a continual moving picture, with color and sound, of any place where something is going on. Your son will talk to his girl in Ceylon over a gadget that shows her moving picture.

All this—mind you—if you can keep your single ideal of democracy fixed on the point of giving and sharing. Endless riches of the human spirit. Endless physical attainments. The second, because of the first.

No distance. . . .

No time. . . .

No isolation. . . .

One world *—and you in it.

Your suburb will be several hundred miles from your city and you will commute. Your nation's debt may be a trillion dollars—but you

---

* This phrase was soon to be given wide, if futile distinction by the late Wendell Willkie.

will be unworried by it, because you and the rest of the Americans will have reduced it a half in two decades. You will not think about war because nobody is thinking about war or planning war. Everybody is too busy.

Solar power gatherers will cover the Sahara. Deserts below the level of the sea will have been filled with water made fresh by energy from those gatherers. Death Valley will be a sweet lake and a garden. You won't "catch" a disease—ever; there will be no bacterial infections. You will be rugged and alert until you are eighty. Your home will be as beautiful, as clean, as durable, as light, as strong—as the wing of an airplane. It will be cheap too. Your food will come from all the earth. Your streets will be bright and air-conditioned. Your wife will bear your children safely and painlessly. You will have a winter cottage in Madagascar, if you like. You may be the business partner of another human being who lives in China. You may be an American expert working for the Soviet. Or you may be the operator of an automatic machine with more power under your thumb than there was in all Caesar's legions.

You may be a musician, writing the unimaginable symphonies of tomorrow. You may be an artist, painting its pictures, or a writer, concerned with the residual hypocrisies and misunderstandings, urging your contemporaries to seek more truth. You can inherit the earth: the fellowship of crowds, the friendliness of people, and the solitude of polar mountains. *You.*

These things shall be.

The only question is, how soon? Twenty years? A thousand?

Its answer depends upon your fealty to truth, your willingness to give up prejudice, your everlasting readiness to die to maintain that world for others, your humility before the common weal, and an awareness of your littleness which keeps you fighting to add to surrounding greatness. Thus, the meek inherit—not because they try to purchase peace but because their only aggression is against the evil within themselves. Thus, to him that hath shall be given. And thus, from the person or the nation that has not truth everything shall be taken away.

Never was chaos so great.

Never was paradise so near to the reach of common folks—like you, and clowns*—like me.

---

*An unhappy term, since, coming at the book's end, it seems to have helped to persuade many persons that the author was not, and is not, "sincere." All I intended to imply by it was a kind of *humbleness:* the realization one has, on finishing the writing of a book, of the inadequacy of words to express even the simplest convictions or the most lucid passions.

PETROS ABATZOGLOU, *What Does Mrs. Freeman Want?*
MICHAL AJVAZ, *The Golden Age.*
The Other City.
PIERRE ALBERT-BIROT, *Grabinoulor.*
YUZ ALESHKOVSKY, *Kangaroo.*
FELIPE ALFAU, *Chromos.*
Locos.
JOÃO ALMINO, *The Book of Emotions.*
IVAN ÂNGELO, *The Celebration.*
The Tower of Glass.
DAVID ANTIN, *Talking.*
ANTÓNIO LOBO ANTUNES, *Knowledge of Hell.*
The Splendor of Portugal.
ALAIN ARIAS-MISSON, *Theatre of Incest.*
IFTIKHAR ARIF AND WAQAS KHWAJA, EDS., *Modern Poetry of Pakistan.*
JOHN ASHBERY AND JAMES SCHUYLER, *A Nest of Ninnies.*
ROBERT ASHLEY, *Perfect Lives.*
GABRIELA AVIGUR-ROTEM, *Heatwave and Crazy Birds.*
HEIMRAD BÄCKER, *transcript.*
DJUNA BARNES, *Ladies Almanack.*
Ryder.
JOHN BARTH, *LETTERS.*
Sabbatical.
DONALD BARTHELME, *The King.*
Paradise.
SVETISLAV BASARA, *Chinese Letter.*
MIQUEL BAUÇÀ, *The Siege in the Room.*
RENÉ BELLETTO, *Dying.*
MAREK BIEŃCZYK, *Transparency.*
MARK BINELLI, *Sacco and Vanzetti Must Die!*
ANDREI BITOV, *Pushkin House.*
ANDREJ BLATNIK, *You Do Understand.*
LOUIS PAUL BOON, *Chapel Road.*
My Little War.
Summer in Termuren.
ROGER BOYLAN, *Killoyle.*
IGNÁCIO DE LOYOLA BRANDÃO, *Anonymous Celebrity.*
The Good-Bye Angel.
Teeth under the Sun.
Zero.
BONNIE BREMSER, *Troia: Mexican Memoirs.*
CHRISTINE BROOKE-ROSE, *Amalgamemnon.*
BRIGID BROPHY, *In Transit.*
MEREDITH BROSNAN, *Mr. Dynamite.*
GERALD L. BRUNS, *Modern Poetry and the Idea of Language.*
EVGENY BUNIMOVICH AND J. KATES, EDS., *Contemporary Russian Poetry: An Anthology.*
GABRIELLE BURTON, *Heartbreak Hotel.*
MICHEL BUTOR, *Degrees.*
Mobile.
Portrait of the Artist as a Young Ape.
G. CABRERA INFANTE, *Infante's Inferno.*
Three Trapped Tigers.
JULIETA CAMPOS, *The Fear of Losing Eurydice.*
ANNE CARSON, *Eros the Bittersweet.*
ORLY CASTEL-BLOOM, *Dolly City.*
CAMILO JOSÉ CELA, *Christ versus Arizona.*
The Family of Pascual Duarte.
The Hive.
LOUIS-FERDINAND CÉLINE, *Castle to Castle.*
Conversations with Professor Y.
London Bridge.
Normance.
North.
Rigadoon.
MARIE CHAIX, *The Laurels of Lake Constance.*
HUGO CHARTERIS, *The Tide Is Right.*
JEROME CHARYN, *The Tar Baby.*
ERIC CHEVILLARD, *Demolishing Nisard.*
LUIS CHITARRONI, *The No Variations.*
MARC CHOLODENKO, *Mordechai Schamz.*
JOSHUA COHEN, *Witz.*
EMILY HOLMES COLEMAN, *The Shutter of Snow.*
ROBERT COOVER, *A Night at the Movies.*
STANLEY CRAWFORD, *Log of the S.S. The Mrs Unguentine.*
Some Instructions to My Wife.
ROBERT CREELEY, *Collected Prose.*
RENÉ CREVEL, *Putting My Foot in It.*
RALPH CUSACK, *Cadenza.*
SUSAN DAITCH, *L.C.*
Storytown.
NICHOLAS DELBANCO, *The Count of Concord.*
Sherbrookes.
NIGEL DENNIS, *Cards of Identity.*
PETER DIMOCK, *A Short Rhetoric for Leaving the Family.*
ARIEL DORFMAN, *Konfidenz.*
COLEMAN DOWELL, *The Houses of Children.*
Island People.
Too Much Flesh and Jabez.
ARKADII DRAGOMOSHCHENKO, *Dust.*
RIKKI DUCORNET, *The Complete Butcher's Tales.*
The Fountains of Neptune.
The Jade Cabinet.
The One Marvelous Thing.
Phosphor in Dreamland.
The Stain.
The Word "Desire."
WILLIAM EASTLAKE, *The Bamboo Bed.*
Castle Keep.
Lyric of the Circle Heart.
JEAN ECHENOZ, *Chopin's Move.*
STANLEY ELKIN, *A Bad Man.*
Boswell: A Modern Comedy.
Criers and Kibitzers, Kibitzers and Criers.
The Dick Gibson Show.
The Franchiser.
George Mills.
The Living End.
The MacGuffin.
The Magic Kingdom.
Mrs. Ted Bliss.
The Rabbi of Lud.
Van Gogh's Room at Arles.
FRANÇOIS EMMANUEL, *Invitation to a Voyage.*
ANNIE ERNAUX, *Cleaned Out.*
SALVADOR ESPRIU, *Ariadne in the Grotesque Labyrinth.*
LAUREN FAIRBANKS, *Muzzle Thyself.*
Sister Carrie.
LESLIE A. FIEDLER, *Love and Death in the American Novel.*
JUAN FILLOY, *Faction.*
Op Oloop.
ANDY FITCH, *Pop Poetics.*
GUSTAVE FLAUBERT, *Bouvard and Pécuchet.*
KASS FLEISHER, *Talking out of School.*

FORD MADOX FORD,
    The March of Literature.
JON FOSSE, *Aliss at the Fire.*
    Melancholy.
MAX FRISCH, *I'm Not Stiller.*
    Man in the Holocene.
CARLOS FUENTES, *Christopher Unborn.*
    Distant Relations.
    Terra Nostra.
    Vlad.
    Where the Air Is Clear.
TAKEHIKO FUKUNAGA, *Flowers of Grass.*
WILLIAM GADDIS, *J R.*
    The Recognitions.
JANICE GALLOWAY, *Foreign Parts.*
    The Trick Is to Keep Breathing.
WILLIAM H. GASS, *Cartesian Sonata*
    and Other Novellas.
    Finding a Form.
    A Temple of Texts.
    The Tunnel.
    Willie Masters' Lonesome Wife.
GÉRARD GAVARRY, *Hoppla! 1 2 3.*
    Making a Novel.
ETIENNE GILSON,
    The Arts of the Beautiful.
    Forms and Substances in the Arts.
C. S. GISCOMBE, *Giscome Road.*
    Here.
    Prairie Style.
DOUGLAS GLOVER, *Bad News of the Heart.*
    The Enamoured Knight.
WITOLD GOMBROWICZ,
    A Kind of Testament.
PAULO EMÍLIO SALES GOMES, *P's Three*
    Women.
KAREN ELIZABETH GORDON, *The Red Shoes.*
GEORGI GOSPODINOV, *Natural Novel.*
JUAN GOYTISOLO, *Count Julian.*
    Exiled from Almost Everywhere.
    Juan the Landless.
    Makbara.
    Marks of Identity.
PATRICK GRAINVILLE, *The Cave of Heaven.*
HENRY GREEN, *Back.*
    Blindness.
    Concluding.
    Doting.
    Nothing.
JACK GREEN, *Fire the Bastards!*
JIŘÍ GRUŠA, *The Questionnaire.*
GABRIEL GUDDING,
    Rhode Island Notebook.
MELA HARTWIG, *Am I a Redundant*
    Human Being?
JOHN HAWKES, *The Passion Artist.*
    Whistlejacket.
ELIZABETH HEIGHWAY, ED., *Contemporary*
    Georgian Fiction.
ALEKSANDAR HEMON, ED.,
    Best European Fiction.
AIDAN HIGGINS, *Balcony of Europe.*
    A Bestiary.
    Blind Man's Bluff
    Bornholm Night-Ferry.
    Darkling Plain: Texts for the Air.
    Flotsam and Jetsam.
    Langrishe, Go Down.
    Scenes from a Receding Past.
    Windy Arbours.
KEIZO HINO, *Isle of Dreams.*
KAZUSHI HOSAKA, *Plainsong.*

ALDOUS HUXLEY, *Antic Hay.*
    Crome Yellow.
    Point Counter Point.
    Those Barren Leaves.
    Time Must Have a Stop.
NAOYUKI II, *The Shadow of a Blue Cat.*
MIKHAIL IOSSEL AND JEFF PARKER, EDS.,
    Amerika: Russian Writers View the
    United States.
DRAGO JANČAR, *The Galley Slave.*
GERT JONKE, *The Distant Sound.*
    Geometric Regional Novel.
    Homage to Czerny.
    The System of Vienna.
JACQUES JOUET, *Mountain R.*
    Savage.
    Upstaged.
CHARLES JULIET, *Conversations with*
    Samuel Beckett and Bram van
    Velde.
MIEKO KANAI, *The Word Book.*
YORAM KANIUK, *Life on Sandpaper.*
HUGH KENNER, *The Counterfeiters.*
    Flaubert, Joyce and Beckett:
    The Stoic Comedians.
    Joyce's Voices.
DANILO KIŠ, *The Attic.*
    Garden, Ashes.
    The Lute and the Scars
    Psalm 44.
    A Tomb for Boris Davidovich.
ANITA KONKKA, *A Fool's Paradise.*
GEORGE KONRÁD, *The City Builder.*
TADEUSZ KONWICKI, *A Minor Apocalypse.*
    The Polish Complex.
MENIS KOUMANDAREAS, *Koula.*
ELAINE KRAF, *The Princess of 72nd Street.*
JIM KRUSOE, *Iceland.*
AYŞE KULIN, *Farewell: A Mansion in*
    Occupied Istanbul.
EWA KURYLUK, *Century 21.*
EMILIO LASCANO TEGUI, *On Elegance*
    While Sleeping.
ERIC LAURRENT, *Do Not Touch.*
HERVÉ LE TELLIER, *The Sextine Chapel.*
    A Thousand Pearls (for a Thousand
    Pennies)
VIOLETTE LEDUC, *La Bâtarde.*
EDOUARD LEVÉ, *Autoportrait.*
    Suicide.
MARIO LEVI, *Istanbul Was a Fairy Tale.*
SUZANNE JILL LEVINE, *The Subversive*
    Scribe: Translating Latin
    American Fiction.
DEBORAH LEVY, *Billy and Girl.*
    Pillow Talk in Europe and Other
    Places.
JOSÉ LEZAMA LIMA, *Paradiso.*
ROSA LIKSOM, *Dark Paradise.*
OSMAN LINS, *Avalovara.*
    The Queen of the Prisons of Greece.
ALF MAC LOCHLAINN,
    The Corpus in the Library.
    Out of Focus.
RON LOEWINSOHN, *Magnetic Field(s).*
MINA LOY, *Stories and Essays of Mina Loy.*
BRIAN LYNCH, *The Winner of Sorrow.*
D. KEITH MANO, *Take Five.*
MICHELINE AHARONIAN MARCOM,
    The Mirror in the Well.
BEN MARCUS,
    The Age of Wire and String.

WALLACE MARKFIELD,
  Teitlebaum's Window.
  To an Early Grave.
DAVID MARKSON, *Reader's Block.*
  Springer's Progress.
  Wittgenstein's Mistress.
CAROLE MASO, *AVA.*
LADISLAV MATEJKA AND KRYSTYNA
  POMORSKA, EDS.,
  Readings in Russian Poetics:
  Formalist and Structuralist Views.
HARRY MATHEWS,
  The Case of the Persevering Maltese:
  Collected Essays.
  Cigarettes.
  The Conversions.
  The Human Country: New and
  Collected Stories.
  The Journalist.
  My Life in CIA.
  Singular Pleasures.
  The Sinking of the Odradek
  Stadium.
  Tlooth.
  20 Lines a Day.
JOSEPH MCELROY,
  Night Soul and Other Stories.
THOMAS MCGONIGLE,
  Going to Patchogue.
ROBERT L. MCLAUGHLIN, ED., *Innovations:*
  An Anthology of Modern &
  Contemporary Fiction.
ABDELWAHAB MEDDEB, *Talismano.*
GERHARD MEIER, *Isle of the Dead.*
HERMAN MELVILLE, *The Confidence-Man.*
AMANDA MICHALOPOULOU, *I'd Like.*
STEVEN MILLHAUSER, *The Barnum Museum.*
  In the Penny Arcade.
RALPH J. MILLS, JR., *Essays on Poetry.*
MOMUS, *The Book of Jokes.*
CHRISTINE MONTALBETTI, *The Origin of Man.*
  Western.
OLIVE MOORE, *Spleen.*
NICHOLAS MOSLEY, *Accident.*
  Assassins.
  Catastrophe Practice.
  Children of Darkness and Light.
  Experience and Religion.
  A Garden of Trees.
  God's Hazard.
  The Hesperides Tree.
  Hopeful Monsters.
  Imago Bird.
  Impossible Object.
  Inventing God.
  Judith.
  Look at the Dark.
  Natalie Natalia.
  Paradoxes of Peace.
  Serpent.
  Time at War.
  The Uses of Slime Mould:
  Essays of Four Decades.
WARREN MOTTE,
  Fables of the Novel: French Fiction
  since 1990.
  Fiction Now: The French Novel in
  the 21st Century.
  Oulipo: A Primer of Potential
  Literature.
GERALD MURNANE, *Barley Patch.*
  Inland.

YVES NAVARRE, *Our Share of Time.*
  Sweet Tooth.
DOROTHY NELSON, *In Night's City.*
  Tar and Feathers.
ESHKOL NEVO, *Homesick.*
WILFRIDO D. NOLLEDO, *But for the Lovers.*
FLANN O'BRIEN, *At Swim-Two-Birds.*
  At War.
  The Best of Myles.
  The Dalkey Archive.
  Further Cuttings.
  The Hard Life.
  The Poor Mouth.
  The Third Policeman.
CLAUDE OLLIER, *The Mise-en-Scène.*
  Wert and the Life Without End.
GIOVANNI ORELLI, *Walaschek's Dream.*
PATRIK OUŘEDNÍK, *Europeana.*
  The Opportune Moment, 1855.
BORIS PAHOR, *Necropolis.*
FERNANDO DEL PASO, *News from the Empire.*
  Palinuro of Mexico.
ROBERT PINGET, *The Inquisitory.*
  Mahu or The Material.
  Trio.
A. G. PORTA, *The No World Concerto.*
MANUEL PUIG, *Betrayed by Rita Hayworth.*
  The Buenos Aires Affair.
  Heartbreak Tango.
RAYMOND QUENEAU, *The Last Days.*
  Odile.
  Pierrot Mon Ami.
  Saint Glinglin.
ANN QUIN, *Berg.*
  Passages.
  Three.
  Tripticks.
ISHMAEL REED, *The Free-Lance Pallbearers.*
  The Last Days of Louisiana Red.
  Ishmael Reed: The Plays.
  Juice!
  Reckless Eyeballing.
  The Terrible Threes.
  The Terrible Twos.
  Yellow Back Radio Broke-Down.
JASIA REICHARDT, *15 Journeys Warsaw*
  to London.
NOËLLE REVAZ, *With the Animals.*
JOÃO UBALDO RIBEIRO, *House of the*
  Fortunate Buddhas.
JEAN RICARDOU, *Place Names.*
RAINER MARIA RILKE, *The Notebooks of*
  Malte Laurids Brigge.
JULIÁN RÍOS, *The House of Ulysses.*
  Larva: A Midsummer Night's Babel.
  Poundemonium.
  Procession of Shadows.
AUGUSTO ROA BASTOS, *I the Supreme.*
DANIËL ROBBERECHTS, *Arriving in Avignon.*
JEAN ROLIN, *The Explosion of the*
  Radiator Hose.
OLIVIER ROLIN, *Hotel Crystal.*
ALIX CLEO ROUBAUD, *Alix's Journal.*
JACQUES ROUBAUD, *The Form of a*
  City Changes Faster, Alas, Than
  the Human Heart.
  The Great Fire of London.
  Hortense in Exile.
  Hortense Is Abducted.
  The Loop.
  Mathematics:
  The Plurality of Worlds of Lewis.

SELECTED DALKEY ARCHIVE TITLES

FOR A FULL LIST OF PUBLICATIONS, VISIT:
www.dalkeyarchive.com